To Ali,

Spiritual Being

A User's Guide

*With warmest
love —

Happy
4 Nov '14*

To Ali,

With warmest
love –

Happy
[illegible] it

Spiritual Being

A User's Guide

by

Happy Dobbs

GEORGE RONALD • OXFORD

GEORGE RONALD, *Publisher*
46 High Street, Kidlington, Oxford OX5 2DN

Reprinted 2005

British Library Cataloguing in Publication Data

A catalogue record for this book is available from the British Library

ISBN 0-85398-415-8

●

Typesetting and cover design by Leith Editorial Services, Abingdon, Oxon, UK

Printed and bound in Great Britain by Biddles Ltd, King's Lynn, Norfolk

Contents

Section IV
Meditation and Prayer

Section V
Detachment, Sacrifice, God's Will, Free Will

Section VI
The Word of God – Pass It On

To all my friends and relatives
for so effortlessly, consistently and generously
providing me with the lessons in loving
and 'opportunities for victory over self' —
God knows I need you!
And
to my children, Rob, Elizabeth and Jessica
and my grandson Justice
for being so very easy to love
And
to Nima – you asked for it!

Acknowledgements

My thanks to my mother and father for all the raw materials and the love to bind them into something; to Rason Dobbs: believer, teacher, inspirer, encourager, tour guide and partner – thank you for this incredible journey; to Lollie Johnson, sister of my heart, for the daily demonstration of love applied and for standing at the end of my tunnel shining the light; and to Alice Nightingale for showing me how to rise to the ultimate challenge and allowing me to come along with her.

Section I

Guidance

I

Did Anybody Bring the Compass?

INTRODUCTION

Guidance is expected and actively sought for every facet of our lives: new appliances, games, computers and tools all come with an instruction booklet. We go to school to develop our mental abilities; we have training in how to care for our bodies with nutrition and exercise; we use maps for trips to new places and recipes for learning to cook new foods. In every area of our lives instruction, education and training are available and necessary.

Without guidance, we could still make use of our minds, our bodies and the products, and we might still travel, but we would be severely limited, our efforts would be clumsy and our experiences probably wouldn't be as satisfactory, inspiring or fulfilling as they could be. We would be deprived of countless potential powers and possibilities.

Guidance – which, to be effective, requires Teachers, exemplars, instruction books and operating manuals – is also required for learning how to participate in and enjoy being human in a satisfactory, inspiring and fulfilling way. Without it how could you know:

• what you're created for?

> Why am I here? (Plants and animals are free of the nagging question that plagues humans.)

• what your purpose is?

> What should I *do*? (They don't spend much time on this one, either. For us, it seems to come with the territory and creates some fascinating expressions of creativity!

3

Kind of like giving a baby a calculator to work with; or like having eyes and no light.)

• how to use your life and 'humanness' to create happiness for yourself and others?

How can I *use* all this power and intelligence? (This one gets downright tricky, and can give rise to various horrors, depending on one's limit on the definition of 'others'; kind of like giving a baby a set of knives or a hand grenade; or like having eyes and only horror films to look at.)

This *User's Guide* will give you everything you need to set off on your quest: to become acquainted with infinite powers and possibilities. The only way you can go wrong on this adventure is by not beginning.

MEMORIZE

'Abdu'l-Bahá says:

. . . make a beginning, and all will come right.

'Abdu'l-Bahá quoted in Honnold, *Vignettes*, p. 122

2

Human Being!
What's Involved?

. . . in the world of nature conscious knowledge is absent. Nature is without knowing, whereas man is conscious. Nature is devoid of memory; man possesses memory. Nature is without perception and volition; man possesses both. It is evident that virtues are inherent in man which are not present in the world of nature. This is provable from every standpoint.

If it be claimed that the intellectual reality of man belongs to the world of nature – that it is a part of the whole – we ask is it possible for the part to contain virtues which the whole does not possess? For instance, is it possible for the drop to contain virtues of which the aggregate body of the sea is deprived? Is it possible for a leaf to be imbued with virtues which are lacking in the whole tree? Is it possible that the extraordinary faculty of reason in man is animal in character and quality? On the other hand, it is evident and true, though most astounding, that in man there is present this supernatural force or faculty which discovers the realities of things and which possesses the power of idealization or intellection. It is capable of discovering scientific laws, and science we know is not a tangible reality. Science exists in the mind of man as an ideal reality. The mind itself, reason itself, is an ideal reality and not tangible.

Notwithstanding this, some of the sagacious men declare: We have attained to the superlative degree of knowledge; we have penetrated the laboratory of nature, studying sciences and arts; we have attained the highest station of knowledge in the human world; we have investigated the facts as they

tangible may be touched, something perceived by touching; real, actual; evident

sagacious possessing or showing sound judgement and keen perception; wise

superlative of the highest order, quality or degree; surpassing or superior to all others

5

are and have arrived at the conclusion that nothing is rightly acceptable except the tangible, which alone is a reality worthy of credence; all that is not tangible is imagination and nonsense.☺

Strange indeed that after twenty years training in colleges and universities man should reach such a station wherein he will deny the existence of the ideal or that which is not perceptible to the senses. Have you ever stopped to think that the animal already has graduated from such a university? Have you ever realized that the cow is already a professor emeritus of that university? For the cow without hard labour and study is already a philosopher of the superlative degree in the school of nature. The cow denies everything that is not tangible, saying, 'I can see! I can eat! Therefore, I believe only in that which is tangible!'

Then why should we go to the colleges? Let us go to the cow.

'Abdu'l-Bahá, *Promulgation of Universal Peace*, pp. 360–1

credence acceptable as true or valid

☺ Well said, eh! Non-sense(s)! The word itself is an indication of how pervasive this outlook is. But, of course, it can't be *imagination*, since they wouldn't believe in that – it's not *tangible!*

'Mankind', 'man', 'he', 'him' and 'his' in the quotations from the Bahá'í writings denote all of humanity, not just males. 'Abdu'l-Bahá says, 'Man is a generic term applying to all humanity . . . In Persian and Arabic there are two distinct words translated into English as man: one meaning man and woman collectively, the other distinguishing man as male from woman the female. The first word and its pronoun are generic, collective; the other is restricted to the male' (*Some Answered Questions*, p. 76).

generic general; applicable to any member of a group or class

3

Education: Beyond the Cow

If there were no educator, there would be no such things as comforts, civilization or humanity. If a man be left alone in a wilderness where he sees none of his own kind, he will undoubtedly become a mere brute; it is then clear that an educator is needed.

But education is of three kinds: material, human and spiritual. Material education is concerned with the progress and development of the body, through gaining its sustenance, its material comfort and ease . . . Human education signifies civilization and progress . . . Divine education is that of the Kingdom of God: it consists in acquiring divine perfections, and this is true education . . .

'Abdu'l-Bahá, *Some Answered Questions*, pp. 7–8

POINTS TO PONDER

What is meant by mineral, vegetable and animal education? (For an answer, see 'In Need of an Educator', *Some Answered Questions*, pp. 7-11).

What are the three kinds of education?

According to 'Abdu'l-Bahá what is 'true' education?

'Abdu'l-Bahá, the son of Bahá'u'lláh, is, to Bahá'ís, the Exemplar: His life is our example of a perfect human being in loving action. He is often referred to as 'the Master' and was named by Bahá'u'lláh as the interpreter, the one we should all turn to for explanations of the Bahá'í teachings.

READING

'Abdu'l-Bahá asks us to consider:

What are the animals' propensities? To eat, drjnk, wander about and sleep. The thoughts, the minds of animals are confined to these. They are captives in the bonds of these desires. Man becomes a prisoner and slave to them when his ultimate desire is not higher than his welfare in this world of the senses.

'Abdu'l-Bahá, *Promulgation of Universal Peace*, p. 184

MEMORIZE

God created man perfect in powers and possibilities.

'Abdu'l-Bahá, quoted in *Ten Days in the Light of 'Akká*, p. 97

POINTS TO PONDER

Animals' propensities are never degrading to them, as they were never intended to rise above their physical needs and desires.

Is a person who never rises above these physical needs and desires degraded? (It might help to think of the word 'degraded' as 'taken down a grade).

Do the 'bonds of desires' that can enslave us always have an attractive side to them, looking like harmless fun or entertainment?

☺ The philosophical tenet: 'I think, therefore I am' . . . so true! Well, what are you? Miserable? sick? fearful?

What are some specific examples of a person being a prisoner and slave to material desires?

What powers and possibilities can you think of that human beings might have? Write down three examples.

VIEWPOINT

Being created perfect in powers and possibilities implies being limitlessly perfectible; this, suffice it to say, is a *whole* lot different than saying 'God created man perfect'! Obviously, humans have no need for additional specialized education in eating, drinking, wandering about and sleeping – most of us have reached a fair state of perfection in these already. We apply ourselves to the practice and enjoyment of them daily and don't require much outside guidance.

The material world is the world of limitation – which means that everything about it has a beginning and an end. It is an important classroom in the development of our souls because with our dual natures (material and spiritual) comes our opportunity to make choices. The state of our bodies is important, for they are filled with limited 'powers and possibilities', but if we live our lives for our bodies alone, when we have to leave them behind at death – which, whoever you are, is inevitable – we may find ourselves without essential assets.

So studying at the feet☺ of the cow is necessary – even delightful at times – but peripheral to our focus here, which includes the infinite (endless and undying) powers and possibilities of our intellect – our consciousness – thus making the entire universe accessible to us.

☺ Philosophers used to lecture outdoors and their students would sit at their feet.

4

Universe: Me & All Else Besides

INTRODUCTION

R. Buckminster Fuller, a great philosopher, scientist and inventor, said that when he set out to explore and discover realities, he wanted to be sure he didn't overlook anything: so he always started with 'universe', which he defined as 'me, and all else besides me'.

Since the concept symbolized by his definition of the word 'universe' is a semantic equivalent to the concept symbolized by the word 'God,' that's how we'll start too. Bahá'u'lláh tells us where to start looking. He poses the question:

semantic pertaining to meaning in language

> Dost thou reckon thyself a puny form,
> When within thee the universe is folded?
> Quoted by Bahá'u'lláh in The Seven Valleys, p. 34

puny small and weak; petty

POINTS TO PONDER

Is there *room* for a universe in your body? It really can't contain 'you and all else besides you', can it? (Although after a really *huge* meal, it can seem like it!)

Can an animal or any part of the material world other than a human even conceive of an idea like 'universe'?

What part of you can explore these ideas and find this 'universe' of powers and possibilities?

What do you suppose has to 'unfold' within you for the discovery of a universe?

Does 'unfold' imply a gradual process?

. . . the great divine philosophers have had the following epigram: All things are involved in all things.

'Abdu'l-Bahá, *Foundations of World Unity*, p. 52

The more you know of yourself and the universe within you, the more obvious this statement will become to you.

READING

Man is the supreme Talisman. Lack of a proper education hath, however, deprived him of that which he doth inherently possess . . . Regard man as a mine rich in gems of inestimable value. Education can, alone, cause it to reveal its treasures, and enable mankind to benefit therefrom.

Bahá'u'lláh, *Gleanings*, pp. 259–60

talisman something producing extraordinary effects or able to work wonders

☺ If 'ordinary' is the world of nature without intellect, what do you do daily that's 'extra' or 'more than' that?

POINT TO PONDER

Think of yourself as a talisman. What are some of the extraordinary effects you produce every day? Write down two examples.

READING

Intellect is, in truth, the most precious gift bestowed upon man . . . Man alone, among created beings, has this wonderful power.

All creation, preceding Man, is bound by the stern law of nature. The great sun, the multitudes of stars, the oceans and seas, the mountains, the rivers, the trees, and all animals, great or small – none is able to evade obedience to nature's law.

Man alone has freedom, and, by his understanding or intellect, has been able to gain control of and adapt some of those natural laws to his own needs . . . God gave this power to man that it might be used for the advancement of civilization, for the good of humanity, to increase love and concord and peace . . . Use your knowledge always for the benefit of others . . .

'Abdu'l-Bahá, *The Reality of Man*, pp. 11-12

When 'Abdu'l-Bahá visited Boston, Massachusetts, in 1912, William Randall was invited by a Bahá'í to hear the Master lecture. Mr Randall was interested in religion and had studied about it from many different angles. He felt he knew all there was to know about it.

Listening to Him ['Abdu'l-Bahá], he thought that this Man was certainly a very great Man, truly a Saint.

At the close of the lecture, as Mr Randall was leaving the hall, he heard one of 'Abdu'l-Bahá's secretaries ask, 'Is there anyone here who would be gracious enough to buy 'Abdu'l-Bahá some grape juice? He is very fond of it and would like some after His lecture.' Instinctively, Mr Randall replied, 'I would be very glad to get it.' At the corner drug store he bought six bottles of grape juice and took them to the hotel where the Master was staying. He could give them to someone who could take them to 'Abdu'l-Bahá, as he did not want to become involved. When he got off the elevator, he was drawn swiftly into conversation with friends who were standing near. Hardly realizing what he was doing, he handed his bottles to one of the Master's secretaries.

The next thing he knew the secretary returned with a glass of grape juice on a tray and said to Mr Randall, 'Since you have been so kind to bring this to 'Abdu'l-Bahá, won't you take it in yourself, Mr Randall?' Not liking the idea – yet not wishing to be ungracious – he consented, but planned to put it on the nearest table and make a speedy exit. He put aside the little curtain before the Master's door, saw just the right table and deposited his tray.

Just as he was backing out, pleased that he had not disturbed 'Abdu'l-Bahá, who was all alone at the far side of the room, seemingly asleep, the Master opened His eyes and looking at him, said, 'Be seated'. Feeling that he could not well refuse, Mr Randall seated himself on a couch in the centre of the room. 'Abdu'l-Bahá settled again into His chair and closed His eyes. William Randall sat still for a few moments and then began to get angry, thinking the Master did not know in whose presence He was sitting. He became more and more angry. He wondered, 'What does it mean that I have to sit in the presence of this old Man while He falls asleep?'

He thought about getting up and leaving the room, but decided against this approach to his predicament. 'Abdu'l-Bahá had told him to sit there and he must not be rude. Then his legs began to go to sleep and grow numb. His whole body began to get numb. Even his collar, starched and stiff – he prided himself that it was never wilted in public – drooped down. At the peak of his rage, a voice inside him said, 'You have studied all the great religions of the world and what good have they done you, for you cannot sit in the presence of an old man for twenty minutes with peace and composure?'

As the challenge of this thought struck Mr Randall, 'Abdu'l-Bahá opened His eyes and said, 'The intellect is good but until it has become the servant of the heart, it is of little avail.' Then the Master smiled at Mr Randall and dismissed him. He had not been asleep. Mr Randall never forgot the Master's words – they were a turning point in his life.

Honnold, Vignettes, pp. 136-8

MEMORIZE

The intellect is good, but until it has become the servant of the heart, it is of little avail.

'Abdu'l-Bahá

POINTS TO PONDER

What does having the intellect 'become the servant of the heart' mean?

What are some qualities of a person whose intellect is the servant of his or her heart?

Would having your intellect be the servant of your heart be humiliating or difficult to do?

Would you seem weak or a victim if your intellect were a servant of your heart?

Was 'Abdu'l-Bahá weak?

How to turn the intellect into a servant of the heart is not, at present, a subject that is being taught in the schools and universities. It's not shown on TV or in the movies or in the lives of the people around us. It is not being probed by scientists (although that's drawing nearer! Science now knows that it's *all* about attraction and relationships). For this education we will have to look elsewhere – somewhere inclusive of universe; somewhere that doesn't deny or exclude our bodies, our minds or our emotions. Somewhere, in fact, where 'me and all else besides me' has value, meaning and clarity.

MEMORIZE

'Abdu'l-Bahá tells us to be sure to develop both our physical and spiritual natures:

> Never deny the spiritual things to the material, rather both are incumbent upon thee.
>
> 'Abdu'l-Bahá, *Bahá'í World Faith*, p. 377

incumbent resting upon, as an obligation or duty

POINTS TO PONDER

Does this mean that it's necessary to deny the material part of our nature in order to develop our spiritual side?

What does '*both* are *incumbent* upon thee' mean?

If we have an obligation or a duty to affirm (which is the opposite of deny) both of our natures, who benefits when we fulfil that obligation?

. . . and He says that we'll *stack up* delights by doing this!

> . . . if material happiness and spiritual felicity be conjoined, it will be 'delight upon delight'.
>
> 'Abdu'l-Bahá, *Promulgation of Universal Peace*, p. 166

A Persian mystic poet says it this way:

'Abdu'l-Bahá describes gravity as the phenomenal expression of love; Buckminster Fuller describes love as the metaphysical expression of gravity. Either way, it's all about *love!*

phenomenal any occurrence or fact that is able to be perceived by the senses

metaphysical based on speculative or abstract reasoning

If of thy mortal goods thou art bereft
And from thy slender store two loaves
   alone to thee are left,
Sell one; and with the dole
Buy hyacinths to feed thy soul.

Bahá'u'lláh speaks of 'the hyacinths of divine wisdom' which 'spring from the heart and not from mire and clay'. (Bahá'u'lláh, *Hidden Words*, Persian no. 36). Why do you think that these lovely, fragrant flowers are used as symbols of spiritual wisdom?

Hyacinths are lovely, very fragrant flowers that bloom in the spring, frequently while there's still snow on the ground. Many small blossoms make up the main flower on a stalk. One hyacinth can perfume several rooms.

5

Freedom: Delight upon Delight

INTRODUCTION

Even though humans have outer freedom as described by 'Abdu'l-Bahá, in order to live and be civilized we must limit our personal freedom so that we don't damage ourselves and violate the rights of other people. For instance, we are not free to go into a person's home and take his possessions or to run red lights or to beat people up when we're angry at them. So our outer freedom is, naturally, limited for our own good. The laws that limit us also protect us, so we actually have more freedom by giving up some freedom.∞ We are, willingly, submissive to civil laws and we sacrifice our freedom to do certain things (such as run red lights or steal from others) in order to live in a civilized, safe, happy way together.

∞ This is called a *paradox*, a seeming contradiction that can appear absurd, but which nevertheless is true; all truth contains paradox because to be true, it must be all-inclusive, that is, it must include all sides and viewpoints. We will meet a lot of paradoxes in this *User's Guide*. Notice that they'll sometimes annoy your ego until your spiritual nature brings enlightenment – sort of like those 3-D paintings that you can only see by softening your focus.

POINTS TO PONDER

Our freedom is also, obviously, bound by physical laws, although we can, with education, get around them somewhat: for instance:

Even though we are bound by gravity, we have learned how to travel by air – but this doesn't mean that we aren't still bound by the law of gravity, does it?

If we walk off a roof and fall on the ground and break a bone, is gravity punishing us for not being obedient? If we choose to be obedient or submissive to physical laws, do we complain about how they've robbed us of our freedom? (Who does that gravity think it is, anyway, pushing me around?)

Do we take it for granted that physical and civil laws restrict our lives in order to protect and enhance them?

Do we actually get more freedom by giving up some freedom?

Is that why we don't complain and struggle against civil and physical laws: we don't focus on the restrictions part because we're aware that the benefits outweigh them?

What are some more examples of paradox? We'll run into plenty of them as we go along – try to spot them, then ponder the truth they contain in their seeming absurdity.

VIEWPOINT

On the higher, spiritual level we have an inner freedom and this freedom is unlimited.

Unlimited freedom can only come where there is nothing to fear or defend, right?

If you have something to be afraid of or to lose or to protect, you want to restrict everyone's freedom, including your own, so that things will remain safe, don't you?

The material/ego self – literally your bodyguard! – has an entirely fear-based outlook, since its only job is to make sure your material self seems to be safe, secure and comfortable, and in control of your environment. We can learn to recognize and appreciate the good job the ego self is doing – it will always be determined to do a good job! – and it will be of benefit to us as long as it is the servant of our higher/spiritual nature. The ego self belongs to the world of limitations because it is a world of beginnings and endings – nothing here lasts forever.

POINTS TO PONDER

Can you fully appreciate the excellent job your ego is doing and still guide it from your higher nature?

Do you need to try to kill off or get rid of this ego nature? Would you be able to even if you tried?

☺ If you don't learn which side of your nature should be in control, your life will resemble someone on a horseback ride who forgets that he was supposed to ride the horse, not vice-versa! Don't let your horse ride you; it wasn't in your design specifications. Look about and see what it does to the world – all those horses riding around in style!

17

The universe of unlimited powers and potentialities that is 'folded within' our material/ego selves is our higher/spiritual nature – the part of ourselves that is a bridge between this world and the eternal. This is where our most exciting powers and possibilities lie! No matter how well we train our minds and how far we advance spiritually, there are always more perfections and possibilities to look forward to because this realm has no end, places no value on anything that does end, and – since it has nothing to lose and can't die – needs never be afraid (except of being far from love).

This 'universe folded within' us is referred to in many different ways: Universe, God, Beloved, Self and Love. When Bahá'u'lláh says to turn our sight unto ourselves to find God abiding within, He is not referring to the essence of the unknowable Creator of all but an attribute of that Creator that ties us directly to Him – that allows the Source of love to be within us just as the sun is within a mirror that's turned to it.

MEMORIZE

Love is the true self of the soul, for God Himself is love.

Grundy, *Ten Days in the Light of 'Akká*, p. 82

POINTS TO PONDER

What is the true self of your soul?

Does this imply that you can come to know God by coming to know the 'true self of your soul', which is love?

It can be very helpful with an enormous concept such as the one contained in the word 'God' to recognize the limits of our understanding. Later in this guide we'll look at the paradox of God being entirely unknowable and the fact that we were created to 'know and love God'. For now, it might be helpful to substitute the word 'Love' for God when you're pondering a quotation.

Try thinking: 'I'm here to learn to know and love Love – all-inclusive, selfless, impartial Love.' Does that seem at least possible? This is the kind of love that 'Abdu'l-Bahá demonstrated every day in every act, so we have an example of what 'God' looks like in action on this earth.

> The love He personified was not blind but observant, not impersonal but warm and tender; it was a continual attitude of unobtrusive care.
>
> Gail, 'Proem' to 'Abdu'l-Bahá, *Memorials of the Faithful*, p. xii

READING

'Abdu'l-Bahá tells us that 'happiness is from the love of God' ('Abdu'l-Bahá, *Promulgation of Universal Peace*, p. 335) and that the entire world of existence was created from happiness – we were created from, for and of love and happiness:

> Know thou that there are two kinds of happiness – spiritual and material.
>
> As to material happiness, it never exists; nay, it is but imagination, an image reflected in mirrors, a spectre and shadow. Consider the nature of material happiness. It is something which but slightly removes one's afflictions; yet the people imagine it to be joy, delight, exultation and blessing. All the material blessings, including food, drink, etc., tend only to allay thirst, hunger and fatigue. They bestow no delight on the mind nor pleasure on the soul; nay, they furnish only the bodily wants. So this kind of happiness has no real existence.
>
> As to spiritual happiness, this is the true basis of the life of man because life is created for happiness, not for sorrow; for pleasure, not for grief. Happiness is life eternal. This is a light which is not followed by darkness. This is an honour which is not followed by shame. This is a life that is not followed by death. This is an existence that is not followed by annihilation. This great blessing and precious gift is obtained by man only through the guidance of God . . .
>
> This happiness is the fundamental basis for which man is created, worlds are originated, the contingent beings have existence and the world of God appears like unto the appearance of the sun at midday.

This happiness is but the love of God . . .
Were it not for this happiness the world of existence would
not have been created.

'Abdu'l-Bahá, in Divine Art of Living, p. 29

VIEWPOINT

With our inner, spiritual powers we always possess the powers
and possibilities of true freedom: for instance, these powers
allow us to be happy even if our bodies are in prison. No one has
the ability to take away our inner freedom if we learn how to
develop, nurture and use it. This is our 'reward' for the correct
application of our free will.

READING

Man is the only creature who can receive reward because he
has the power of choice – whether he will show forth love or
withhold it. He has the power to choose immortal life or to
reject it, while the animals have no qualities that are
immortal.

'Abdu'l-Bahá, quoted in Goodall and Cooper,
Daily Lessons Received at 'Akká, p. 33

VIEWPOINT

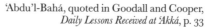

This gift of choice (also known as free will) comes with a built-in,
inescapable responsibility: you can choose to develop your
loving capacity and to benefit the world, or you can choose not
to use it and be more selfish and cruel and destructive than any
other creature – because you are given greater powers than any
other creature. With your every thought and action (or *in*action
and thought*less*ness), you're making choices – even if you're not
aware that you're choosing. Being unaware that you are always
making choices can be dangerous to yourself and to others.

If you don't learn how to
use free will, you'll find it's
pretty costly for
something that's free!

You are always free to choose to be loving.

This never means passive acceptance of injustice, either
towards yourself or others – in fact, it requires a passionate
commitment to justice. The concepts of love and justice –
greatly misunderstood in the world today – will be explored

throughout this book. So much to discover! The words 'love' and 'justice' in the higher sense create intention, which must be translated into action.

READING

> . . . in the choice of good and bad actions he is free, and he commits them according to his own will . . . the inaction or the movement of man depend upon the assistance of God. If he is not aided, he is not able to do either good or evil . . . So this condition is like that of a ship which is moved by the power of the wind or steam; if this power ceases, the ship cannot move at all. Nevertheless, the rudder of the ship turns it to either side, and the power of the steam moves it in the desired direction . . .
>
> In the same way, in all the action or inaction of man, he receives power from the help of God; but the choice of good or evil belongs to the man himself.
>
> 'Abdu'l-Bahá, *Some Answered Questions*, pp. 248–50

POINTS TO PONDER

If you're like a steamship, and you're moving, can it be assumed that you're being assisted?

No matter what the situation is, what choice always belongs to you?

How can we know what a 'bad' or 'evil' action is? Discuss or write in your journal.

VIEWPOINT

Our entire creation and purpose is to experience and express love in this world and beyond. If we don't express this capacity for love by loving God (all-encompassing, ever-expanding, unselfish love), we *will* express it by loving our lower nature and material pursuits, which leads to all the sadness and misery we are now witnessing on earth – all the addictions, power plays and degrading pursuits and insecurities.

All things are beneficial if joined with the love of God; and
without His love all things are harmful, and act as a veil
between man and the Lord of the Kingdom.

'Abdu'l-Bahá, *Selections from the Writings of 'Abdu'l-Bahá*, p. 181

beneficial promoting a
favourable result,
enhancing well-being

POINTS TO PONDER

If our power is about whether to act in a loving manner or to
withhold love, would a 'bad' or 'evil' action be one that was
lacking in love and a 'good' action be one that developed or
enhanced the spirit of love?

On a spiritual level, would 'beneficial' always imply drawing
closer to the Source of love – increasing capacity for the
experience and expression of love?

EXERCISE

Choose something that attracts you and consider how it is
beneficial if joined with the love of God (inclusive, impartial
love) and a veil between you and love if you have other motives.
Try this with washing dishes or mowing the lawn – is the
outcome for you (and probably everyone around you!) different
if you're doing it lovingly rather than resentfully?

6

You Choose the Path and the Pace

Free will is a great and terrible power. It was given to you so you could perfect yourself and expand your capacity for and expression of the love of God – so you could take off and fly freely above the material world on wings of love. Desire is an aspect of our loving capacity that either becomes the wind beneath our wings or the mud that weighs down and holds us on the ground. As with everything, desire is neither good nor bad – it all depends on *intention*.

Our will is independent of our knowing and loving capacities. For example, when desire is present, knowing what is best for us doesn't always guarantee that we will choose to act on that knowledge – in fact, we might do the opposite if we think it will be easier or more fun. For our own benefit, we can use our knowledge to form conscious intentions and use our will to move us to action. We'll explore more about what these words mean and imply later in the book.

> As a man thinkest in his heart, so is he.
>
> Proverbs 23:7

VIEWPOINT

Thinking and knowing in the heart is the source and foundation for the knowing that always includes volition and action. Love can only show up by being applied: application is essential. 'Essential' means 'of the essence' and essence is not material – and therefore with everything we do – smiling, singing, sewing on buttons, scrubbing floors or building a financial empire or curing AIDS or cancer – its only importance and lasting value is

volition willingness to act

as an expression of love – if it is doing this, it is a good and worthwhile thing to do.

'Abdu'l-Bahá says this in other words when He says that any accomplishment is achieved through 'knowledge, volition and action' ('Abdu'l-Bahá, *Promulgation of Universal Peace*, p. 157).

Volition involves discovering a motivating force within yourself that directs your actions – not an outside force.

EXERCISES

Write down three conditions that are needed to accomplish anything.

Is it really 'volition' if someone has to force you to do something, or you're unwilling to do it? Discuss and write in your journal.

Choose a specific incident from your past in which you felt forced or manipulated into doing something – even if it was 'for your own good' or 'good for you'. How did you feel? How would that experience have been different if you had been inspired or assisted to do it of your own volition? Will recognizing the effect on yourself of such actions change the way you attempt to influence someone else?

Give an example of something you have accomplished, pointing out the knowledge, the volition and the action.

Consider carefully and then in your journal write something you intend to accomplish; point out the intention or desired outcome, and the knowledge and action that will be required (of course, the first knowledge that is required is the knowledge of what you want to accomplish – what is your desired outcome).

☺ Bob Harris's 'Quick & Easy Transformation Formula':

Step 1 (Knowledge) Know that kindness is a good thing

Step 2 (Volition) Now that you're motivated, think of ways you want to be kind

Step 3 (Action) Perform acts of kindness

It's simple but not always easy: as long as we choose love over hate and unity over separation, we're doing it right.

VIEWPOINT

Attraction brings intention, which 'Abdu'l-Bahá says brings attainment – its all about loving, but there are so many ways to get distracted from and extremely confused about the purpose of all this loving! Red Grammer sings, 'Push comes to shove and I lose track of love, I'm blind by the light of day . . .' That sums it up beautifully! We forget our purpose and our loving spirits wander around in darkness on a gorgeous sunny day.

Our spiritual nature is what enables us to go beyond the conditions of our lower nature, which we share with the animals, and which, because of our super-natural powers, can result in world-destroying horrors. With our spiritual powers, we can love beyond the world of limitations and can develop our spiritual nature – the source of limitless perfections and possibilities.

Compare life to driving a car which is always speeding along, never stopping. Learning about making choices from our spiritual nature is like learning to steer and maintain a safe vehicle. Not doing this is like a speeding car without a driver: your ego waits for the chance to take the wheel and drive you into walls and off cliffs. As you practise, driving will begin to seem easy and you may be tempted to look down and fiddle with the cassette player: **CRASH!**

If you become unconscious of the fact that there is a result to every thought and action – that choices are involved in all you do – your ego will make the choices. In fact, there will never be a time when you can just quit steering. There is no spiritual auto-pilot, especially during this time when we have no support from the outside world for living a spiritually based life.

☺ Uh-oh! The devil made me do it!

Love always implies knowledge, volition and action. If these are not present, what we have is fantasy or imagination or something else, but it's not love expressed from our higher nature. Any accomplishment is achieved through these three things, so just having knowledge, volition and action doesn't automatically mean we'll accomplish what we think we want to accomplish (a brainwish). You may truly want to be loving but you may love being right more than you love being kind – what happens then? To be effective, volition must be trained by the knowledge of the will of God and be heartfelt. Your ego/lower nature can *always* overcome a brainwish – and if you have no discipline in understanding the will of God, anything your ego is attracted to can seem loving. This is what is meant by 'knowledge of the love of God' – we need to *know* how and what God loves before we can know the kind of amazing, healing love we're capable of. Otherwise we're stuck with a pathetic shadow of love which the ego will produce in endless variety. Thoughts, feelings and behaviour = knowledge, volition and action.

I desire that each of you become so great that each may guide a nation. Now the friends must endeavour to attain such stations so as to teach the people . . . Divine qualities are unlimited. For this reason you must not be satisfied with one quality, but must try to attain all. Each of us must improve himself, that he may attain nothing short of the best. When one stops, he descends. A bird, when it is flying, soars; but as soon as it stops, it falls. While man is directed upward, he develops. As soon as he stops, he descends. Therefore I wish the beloved of God always to ascend and develop.

There exist in man two powers. One power uplifts him. This is divine attraction, which causes man's elevation. In all grades of existence he will develop through this power. This belongs to the spirit. The other power causes man to descend. This is the animal nature. The first attracts man to the Kingdom. The second brings him down to the contingent world. Now we must consider which of these will gain more power. If the heavenly power overcome, man will become heavenly, enlightened, merciful; but if the worldly power overcome, he will be dark, satanic, and like the animal. Therefore he must develop continually. As long as the heavenly power is the great force, man will ascend.

contingent depending (on something else)

'Abdu'l-Bahá, quoted in *The Diary of Juliet Thompson*, pp. 24–5

Ever been grounded? Bahá'u'lláh refers to the 'birds of human hearts' and tells us what will happen if, fueled by desire, the bird takes off on the wings of free will with the ego navigating. He says that we were given the power of flight (our spiritual powers) so we all 'may be sanctified from the mire of self and desire, and be made worthy to soar in the atmosphere of God's love.'

Wings that are besmirched with mire can never soar.

Bahá'u'lláh, *Epistle to the Son of the Wolf*, p. 131

What else but desire would get us stirred up in our search for the Beloved. Bahá'u'lláh warns us not to let our egos fly us into the ground:

O Son of Desire!
How long wilt thou soar in the realms of desire? Wings have

I bestowed upon thee, that thou mayest fly to the realms of mystic holiness and not the regions of satanic fancy.

Bahá'u'lláh, *Hidden Words*, Persian no. 79

Ye are even as the bird which soareth, with the full force of its mighty wings and with complete and joyous confidence, through the immensity of the heavens, until, impelled to satisfy its hunger, it turneth longingly to the water and clay of the earth below it, and, having been entrapped in the mesh of its desire, findeth itself impotent to resume its flight to the realms whence it came. Powerless to shake off the burden weighing on its sullied wings, that bird, hitherto an inmate of the heavens, is now forced to seek a dwelling-place upon the dust. Wherefore, O My servants, defile not your wings with the clay of waywardness and vain desires, and suffer them not to be stained with the dust of envy and hate, that ye may not be hindered from soaring in the heavens of My divine knowledge.

Bahá'u'lláh, *Gleanings*, p. 327

The mystic poet Rúmí reminds us that desire *and* muddy wings are an important part of our flying lessons (☺ in fact, if you've never noticed the effects of mud on your wings, you've probably never even tried to fly!):

> Birds make great sky circles in their freedom.
> How do they learn it?
> They fall,
> and falling,
> they are given wings.

VIEWPOINT

The ego/lower nature is unable to do anything but draw you to love the things *it's* attracted to. Without a point of orientation for our higher/spiritual nature, we're pretty much stuck with whatever the ego defines as worthwhile – because we *are* creatures designed for desire and love. In Bahá'u'lláh, as in Christ, Buddha and all the Manifestations of God, we can find the perfect mirror of the source and the object of our spirit's desire.

Rúmí in the Mathnawi says:

> If Love withholds
> Its strengthening care
> The lover is left
> like a bird without wings.

The lesson here is not in the relative dirtiness or cleanliness of the wings but in the flying. If you are not practising flying, the wings are useless, even if they are spotless! So don't worry about a little dirt or slow flight – just dust 'em off and take off again.

Ever see someone trying to learn to walk? Think about how much harder it is to learn to fly and be patient with yourself and others in this flight school called life. The main thing is not to let your wing muscles atrophy from lack of use. Suppose you had been so afraid of falling that you never learned to walk? 'Mistakes' only mean that you have more information to work with.

We'll meet up with desire again later. Take off! Fly! Even if your wings are all tattered and torn.

READINGS

> Praise be to God! man is always turned toward the heights, and his aspiration is lofty; he always desires to reach a greater world than the world in which he is, and to mount to a higher sphere than that in which he is. The love of exaltation is one of the characteristics of man.
>
> 'Abdu'l-Bahá, *Some Answered Questions*, p. 188

'Abdu'l-Bahá explains the station of humanity:

> If there were no man, the perfections of the spirit would not appear, and the light of the mind would not be resplendent in this world. This world would be like a body without a soul.
>
> This world is also in the condition of a fruit tree, and man is like the fruit; without fruit the tree would be useless.
>
> 'Abdu'l-Bahá, *Some Answered Questions*, p. 201

POINTS TO PONDER

The Bible says that we are made in the 'image and likeness of God'.

Do you think that God has a body or a colour or a gender?

Do you think that our physical qualities are what are referred to here, or our spiritual qualities such as loving-kindness and compassion?

Name some perfections of the spirit.

Do the animals have to think about what's right or wrong? Do they ever have to wonder about doing anything except eating, drinking, sleeping and walking about?

VIEWPOINT

The animals are born into a condition of perfection – they can only *be*, they can't *become*. Because they don't have the ability to make choices, they can't make mistakes – and they can't change their condition, progress or develop knowledge and true understanding. This material world is a paradise for them and they have no need to learn anything else. In the phenomenal world the tiniest bird has it easier than the best-educated person – no mortgages, no earning a living, no worry about getting old and dying! Animals do not have true freedom; they are captives of the world of nature and are guided by instincts and drives, not by thoughts and choice. Animals can be trained but they can't *decide* to be trained.

STORY

'Abdu'l-Bahá was at a luncheon party at the elegant home of Mrs Agnes Parsons during His visit to the United States in 1912. He was expected by Mrs Parsons to present His message to the leaders of society she had gathered at the table:

> But 'Abdu'l-Bahá told them a story which made them laugh. He Himself laughed heartily, and again with them when they, encouraged by the lead He had given, also told amusing stories. 'Abdu'l-Bahá and his guests were full of mirth throughout that luncheon. It was 'good to laugh', He told them; 'laughter is a spiritual relaxation'.

At this point He referred to His years in prison. Life was hard, He said, tribulations were never far away, and yet, at the end of the day, they would sit together and recall events that had been fantastic, and laugh over them. Funny situations could not be abundant, but still they probed and sought them, and laughed. Joy was not, He told them, a by-product of material comfort and affluence. Were it so, dejection would have ruled every hour of their lives in those days, whereas their souls were joyful . . .

Balyuzi, 'Abdu'l-Bahá, pp. 31–2

No riches, wealth, comfort or ease of the material world is equal to the wealth of a bird; all the areas of these plains and mountains are its dwelling, and all the seeds and harvests are its food and wealth, and all the lands, villages, meadows, pastures, forests and wildernesses are its possessions. Now, which is the richer, this bird, or the most wealthy man? for no matter how many seeds it may take or bestow, its wealth does not decrease.

Then it is clear that the honour and exaltation of man must be something more than material riches. Material comforts are only a branch, but the root of the exaltation of man is the good attributes and virtues which are the adornments of his reality. These are the divine appearances, the heavenly bounties, the sublime emotions, the love and knowledge of God; universal wisdom, intellectual perception, scientific discoveries, justice, equity, truthfulness, benevolence, natural courage and innate fortitude; the respect for rights and the keeping of agreements and covenants; rectitude in all circumstances; serving the truth under all conditions; the sacrifice of one's life for the good of all people; kindness and esteem for all nations; obedience to the teachings of God; service in the Divine Kingdom; the guidance of the people, and the education of the nations and races. This is the prosperity of the human world! This is the exaltation of man in the world! This is eternal life and heavenly honour!

'Abdu'l-Bahá, Some Answered Questions, pp. 79–80

Section II

Investigating Reality

I

Reality

Human beings are able to investigate material (physical) reality AND spiritual reality, so there are two aspects to the investigation of reality: Science helps us to investigate physical, or phenomenal, reality. It is not used to investigate spiritual reality. The tool God gives us to investigate spiritual reality is religion.

There is, in fact, only one reality – just two methods of understanding its different aspects. If something calling itself religion doesn't agree with established scientific fact, it could be superstition. Humanity has covered true religion with many man-made beliefs and practices, which is one reason why religion must be renewed from age to age. Science is capable of generating superstition too, and if science seeks to tell us that nothing exists that can't be established by our physical senses, it has ceased to be scientific and has moved into the realm of nonsense☺! Back to the cow.

☺ That same *non-sense* they claim doesn't even exist!

Lily Tomlin, a comedienne, claims that reality is 'nuthin' but a collective hunch . . . a leading cause of stress'! When humanity is completely out of touch with the Messengers of God to orient humanity to Reality, a collective hunch is about the best it can hope for. This way lies insanity – the entire structure of society built on the quicksand of collective hunches.

EXERCISE

Knowledge is a single point, but the ignorant have multiplied it.

Ḥadíth, a saying attributed to the Prophet Muḥammad or to one of the Imáms. Quoted by Bahá'u'lláh in The Seven Valleys, pp. 24–5

Discuss this thought and write, in your own words, what it means to you.

As Bahá'ís we accept as a basic tenet of our Faith that every person must 'independently and impartially investigate every form of reality' ('Abdu'l-Bahá, *Promulgation*, p. 327). Surely this does *not* mean that we must do this investigation alone and unaided – it's good to study and discuss with others – but rather that we must determine to our own satisfaction the truth or lack of it in every matter – especially if it's as important as spiritual guidance. No one else can determine what our true spiritual path will be. It must be *your* response to the truth that guides you, not someone else's expectations or force or interpretation.

POINTS TO PONDER

What does it mean to investigate 'independently' and 'impartially'? Discuss this.

Would that include independence from traditional outlooks and understandings? Lack of prejudice (judging *before* investigating)?

Can you put the responsibility for your spiritual development onto someone else – your parents, maybe, or a priest or teacher or friend?

VIEWPOINT

As there is only one reality and both science and religion are used to investigate different facets of that same reality, they are both means of arriving at truth. Cars and airplanes are both vehicles, means of transportation. If you want to go by air, you use an airplane, not a car. If you try to fly in a car, it's useless, but that doesn't mean that flying is impossible, does it? If you try to use physical science to investigate spiritual reality and it doesn't discover anything, does that mean that there's nothing to discover? Can physical science prove that love exists? If not, does that mean it doesn't?

Religion must conform to science and reason, otherwise it is superstition. God has created man in order that he may perceive the verity of existence and endowed him with mind and reason to discover truth. Therefore scientific knowledge and religious belief must be conformable to the analysis of this divine faculty in man.

'Abdu'l-Bahá quoted in Ives, *Portals to Freedom*, p. 172

God has bestowed upon man the gift of mind in order that he may weigh every fact or truth presented to him and adjudge it to be reasonable.

'Abdu'l-Bahá quoted in Ives, *Portals to Freedom*, p. 172

To say that there is conflict between science and religion is false, for 'how can the heart approve what the brain does not accept?'

'Abdu'l-Bahá, quoted in Ward, *239 Days*, p. 113

VIEWPOINT

Religion can be compared to a school; the knowledge of God is brought to humanity by special Teachers called Prophets, Messengers or Manifestations. God's school, religion, is renewed from age to age and is periodic and progressive, which means that it works like the grades or forms in school. An 'age', in this sense, usually lasts for five hundred to one thousand years.

periodic appearing at regular intervals

progressive making progress, moving forward

For example, you're in the first grade or form one for a period of time and then you progress to the second grade or form two. There you build on what you learned in first grade and have new lessons appropriate to your present stage of development.

POINTS TO PONDER

When you go into a new grade or form, you don't ever need to reject your previous teacher or what you learned in the grade before, do you? (That would be ridiculous, wouldn't it?)

Do you have any reason to fight or argue with those who are in a different grade and following a different teacher?

We're told in this age of the unification of humanity that if two people quarrel over a religious question or concept, they are both wrong: as for 'religious warfare' (a true oxymoron), we'd be better off with no religion than to go to war over a religious dispute or misunderstanding.

oxymoron putting together contradictory or incongruous terms, i.e. 'a deafening silence'

For quarreling over divine questions, see 'Abdu'l-Bahá, *Tablets of the Divine Plan*, p. 56

POINTS TO PONDER

Is it o.k. to quarrel over spiritual matters as long as you *know* you're right?

Is it o.k., in this age of unity, for nations to go to war over their versions of truth?

READING

> The keynote of the Bahá'í message is *Unity*. 'Be united, be united,' said 'Abdu'l-Bahá, addressing representatives of many humanitarian and religious bodies.
> 'Those of you who are working separately are as ants, but working together you will be as eagles; when working separately you will be as drops or little rivulets of water, but when working in union you will be a mighty river carrying the Water of Life into the barren desert places of the world; and,' He added, 'it is rather dangerous to be an isolated drop; you might be spilt or blown away.'
> Blomfield, *The Chosen Highway*, p. 4

EXERCISE

> Devotion to the tree is profitless, but partaking of the fruit is beneficial.
> 'Abdu'l-Bahá, *Promulgation of Universal Peace*, p. 151

If you were hungry, would you look for fruit on a dead or dormant tree?

Would the name of the tree or the way it looked be important to you, or would you be interested in the quality of the fruit?

In your own words, explain what the quotation above means to you if you apply it to religion.

VIEWPOINT

Because the followers of different Teachers have added man-made ideas, superstitions and practices to religion and have become more attached to the lamp than to the light, many destructive and horrible things have taken place in the name of religion. When people don't accept a new Messenger (who is always foretold by the One they follow), their progress is materially and spiritually hindered. Although the teachings they have are true, they do not have the advantage and blessing of knowing the teachings for the age in which they live. It's like refusing to move on to another grade in school when the time comes, or refusing to learn to walk when you've crawled long enough – and just try getting through today on yesterday's meals.

The basic reality of all true religion can only be truth and it is, therefore, changeless. There are, however, two types of laws brought by each Teacher:

- There are fundamental spiritual laws, which don't change but are enhanced and expanded from age to age as humanity's capacity for truth grows.

This category includes laws of morality and love. For instance, every religion has a 'Golden Rule', with slight differences in phrasing but the same meaning: Treat others as you would be treated.

- And there are secondary social laws – often dealing with questions of diet, family matters (marriage, inheritance, etc.), methods of worship and such. These secondary laws are subject to change entirely from age to age, depending on the prevailing conditions.

It is the change in these social ordinances that tests the believers greatly when the time comes to embrace a new Message. They fear that 'breaking' an earlier law will be an evil thing to do. For example, Moses made it a law that His followers never eat pork. Considering that they were a tribe of desert-dwelling people without any refrigeration, this was a very healthy, loving, sensible law. No need to explain to an unruly and disobedient humanity about diseases in the meat of pigs – just say 'No!' Those conditions no longer prevail, so we no longer have the law about pork.

READINGS

At one time the Master was asked, 'What shall I say to those who state that they are satisfied with Christianity and do not need this present Manifestation?' His reply was clear: 'Let them alone. What would they do if a former king had reigned and a new king was now seated upon the throne? They must acknowledge the new king, or they are not true subjects of the Kingdom. Last year there was a springtime. Can a man say "I do not need a new springtime this year – the old springtime is enough for me?" No! The new spring must come to fill the earth with beauty and brightness.'

Honnold, Vignettes, p. 120

'Abdu'l-Bahá says that

. . . it is necessary to have an instrument, a motive for love's manifestation, an object, a mode of expression.

We must find a way of spreading love . . .

Love is unlimited, boundless, infinite! Material things are limited, circumscribed, finite. You cannot adequately express infinite love by limited means.

The perfect love needs an unselfish instrument, absolutely freed from fetters of every kind. The love of family is limited; the tie of blood relationship is not the strongest bond. Frequently members of the same family disagree, and even hate each other.

Patriotic love is finite; the love of one's country causing hatred of all others, is not perfect love! Compatriots also are not free from quarrels amongst themselves.

The love of race is limited; there is some union here, but that is insufficient. Love must be free from boundaries!

To love our own race may mean hatred of all others, and

even people of the same race often dislike each other.

Political love also is much bound up with hatred of one party for another; this love is very limited and uncertain.

The love of community of interest in service is likewise fluctuating; frequently competitions arise, which lead to jealousy, and at length hatred replaces love.

A few years ago, Turkey and Italy had a friendly political understanding; now they are at war [1912]!

All these ties of love are imperfect. It is clear that limited material ties are insufficient to adequately express the universal love.

The great unselfish love for humanity is bounded by none of these imperfect, semi-selfish bonds; this is the one perfect love, possible to all mankind, and can only be achieved by the power of the Divine Spirit. No worldly power can accomplish the universal love.

Let all be united in this Divine power of love! Let all strive to grow in the light of the Sun of Truth, and reflecting this luminous love on all men, may their hearts become so united that they may dwell evermore in the radiance of the limitless love . . .

The animal creation is captive to matter, God has given freedom to man. The animal cannot escape the law of nature, whereas man may control it, for he, containing nature, can rise above it.

The power of the Holy Spirit, enlightening man's intelligence, has enabled him to discover means of bending many natural laws to his will. He flies through the air, floats on the sea, and even moves under the waters.

All this proves how man's intelligence has been enabled to free him from the limitations of nature, and to solve many of her mysteries. Man, to a certain extent, has broken the chains of matter.

The Holy Spirit will give to man greater powers than these, if only he will strive after the things of the spirit and endeavour to attune his heart to the Divine infinite love.

When you love a member of your family or a compatriot, let it be with a ray of the Infinite Love! Let it be in God, and for God! Wherever you find the attributes of God love that person, whether he be of your family or of another. Shed the light of a boundless love on every human being whom you meet, whether of your country, your race, your political party, or of any other nation, colour or shade of political opinion. Heaven will support you while you work in this ingathering of the scattered peoples of the world beneath the shadow of the almighty tent of unity.

You will be servants of God, who are dwelling near to Him, His divine helpers in the service, ministering to all Humanity. *All* Humanity! Every human being! *Never forget this! . . . all are equal in the sight of God!*

Remember not your own limitations; the help of God will come to you. Forget yourself. God's help will surely come!

When you call on the Mercy of God waiting to reinforce you, your strength will be tenfold.

Look at me: I am so feeble, yet I have had the strength given me to come amongst you . . . One must never consider one's own feebleness, it is the strength of the Holy Spirit of Love, which gives the power . . . The thought of our own weakness could only bring despair. We must look higher than all earthly thoughts; detach ourselves from every material idea, crave for the things of the spirit; fix our eyes on the everlasting bountiful Mercy of the Almighty, who will fill our souls with the gladness of joyful service to His command 'Love One Another'.

'Abdu'l-Bahá speaks of the distinctive characteristics of Bahá'u'lláh's Manifestation in *Promulgation*, pp. 431–7

'Abdu'l-Bahá, *Paris Talks*, pp. 36–9

POINTS TO PONDER

Can we, as humanity, just get together and decide that we're all going to get along and be peaceful from now on?

Why is a Manifestation of God essential to the process of bringing about unity and harmony in humanity?

What does it take to change yourself – never mind someone else – to bring about the necessary attraction and intention (the knowledge, volition and action)? Vision? Bonds of love for something greater than your ego/lower self?

Is it *ever* up to you to change someone else in any way?

2

'Love's in Need of Love Today'

INTRODUCTION

Stevie Wonder's song is very appropriate: Love is *definitely* in
need of love today – it seems to have been almost universally
distorted, perverted or forgotten. The only source of guidance
to our heart's desire – unlimited and infinite love and total
security – is the true religion of God, brought from age to age by
His Messengers. But religion has, for many reasons, gone out of
style.

Religion's purpose is to educate, inspire and attract us –
collectively and individually – to love; to guide us in its
expression; and to provide for its expansion, preservation and
protection. Its sphere of influence is universal, since it is spiritual
in origin and effect.

This is the age of the unification of the human race, and if
the generating impulse and effect of a movement is not love and
unity, it is not – whatever its claims – truly of God (as God =
love). We are better off without any movement that distracts us
from or interferes with the proper and all-inclusive use of our
loving capacity as human beings. God is love. Religion is love's
school. And it is good!

Maturing always brings new rights *and* responsibilities. As we
grow up, we start having to make our own decisions, and the
consequences of them become more obvious and potentially
more beneficial or harmful. Bahá'u'lláh tells us that in this age
humanity has reached a stage of maturity. Because of this, each
person must investigate the truth for himself or herself: we can
no longer depend on tradition, parents, priests, friends, teachers
or *anyone else* to define and determine truth for us. We are now
free to discover and respond to the truth for ourselves.

responsibility a duty, an
obligation

The word 'responsibility'
comes from combining
the words 'ability' and
'respond'. As we mature,
we grow in the ability to
respond and are,
therefore, given more
responsibilities.

All created things have their degree, or stage, of maturity. The period of maturity in the life of a tree is the time of its fruit bearing. The maturity of a plant is the time of its blossoming and flower. The animal attains a stage of full growth and completeness, and in the human kingdom man reaches his maturity when the lights of intelligence have their greatest power and development.

From the beginning to the end of his life man passes through certain periods, or stages, each of which is marked by certain conditions peculiar to itself. For instance, during the period of childhood his conditions and requirements are characteristic of that degree of intelligence and capacity. After a time he enters the period of youth, in which his former conditions and needs are superseded by new requirements applicable to the advance in his degree. His faculties of observation are broadened and deepened; his intelligent capacities are trained and awakened; the limitations and environment of childhood no longer restrict his energies and accomplishments. At last he passes out of the period of youth and enters the stage, or station, of maturity, which necessitates another transformation and corresponding advance in his sphere of life activity. New powers and perceptions clothe him, teaching and training commensurate with his progression occupy his mind, special bounties and bestowals descend in proportion to his increased capacities, and his former period of youth and its conditions will no longer satisfy his matured view and vision.

Similarly, there are periods and stages in the life of the aggregate world of humanity, which at one time was passing through its degree of childhood, at another its time of youth but now has entered its long presaged period of maturity, the evidences of which are everywhere visible and apparent. Therefore, the requirements and conditions of former periods have changed and merged into exigencies which distinctly characterize the present age of the world of mankind. That which was applicable to human needs during the early history of the race could neither meet nor satisfy the demands of this day and period of newness and consummation. Humanity has emerged from its former degrees of limitation and preliminary training. Man must now become imbued with new virtues and powers, new moralities, new capacities. New bounties, bestowals and perfections are awaiting and already descending upon him. The gifts and graces of the period of youth, although timely and sufficient during the adolescence of the world of mankind, are now incapable of meeting the requirements of its maturity. The playthings of childhood and infancy no longer satisfy or interest the adult mind.

From every standpoint the world of humanity is undergoing a reformation. The laws of former governments and civilizations are in process of revision; scientific ideas and theories are developing and advancing to meet a new range of phenomena; invention and discovery are penetrating hitherto unknown fields, revealing new wonders and hidden secrets of the material universe; industries have vastly wider scope and production; everywhere the world of mankind is in the throes of evolutionary activity indicating the passing of the old conditions and advent of the new age of reformation. Old trees yield no fruitage; old ideas and methods are obsolete and worthless now. Old standards of ethics, moral codes and methods of living in the past will not suffice for the present age of advancement and progress.

This is the cycle of maturity and reformation in religion as well. Dogmatic imitations of ancestral beliefs are passing. They have been the axis around which religion revolved but now are no longer fruitful; on the contrary, in this day they have become the cause of human degradation and hindrance. Bigotry and dogmatic adherence to ancient beliefs have become the central and fundamental source of animosity among men, the obstacle to human progress, the cause of warfare and strife, the destroyer of peace, composure and welfare in the world.

dogmatic given to asserting or imposing personal opinions; arrogant; forcing one's opinions on others; intolerantly authoritative

'Abdu'l-Bahá, *Promulgation*, pp. 438–9

VIEWPOINT

This is a new freedom for humanity, and it brings with it a new power and responsibility: we not only don't *have to* depend on someone else for the truth, we *are not able to*. No one else can make our spiritual choices for us and no one else can be blamed for our lack of spiritual progress. It's up to each one of us individually.

MEMORIZE

Success or failure, gain or loss, must, therefore, depend upon man's own exertions. The more he striveth, the greater will be his progress.

Bahá'u'lláh, Gleanings, pp. 81–2

READING

Personal effort is indeed a vital prerequisite to the recognition and acceptance of the Cause of God. No matter how strong the measure of divine grace, unless supplemented by personal, sustained and intelligent effort it cannot become fully effective and be of any real and abiding advantage.

Shoghi Effendi, Living the Life, p. 7

POINTS TO PONDER

Does this mean that even if your parents are Bahá'ís and you have 'grown up in the Faith' you still have to investigate and accept the truth of it for yourself or it won't be fully effective or of any real advantage to you?

If just 'growing up in a faith' or knowing a lot about it was sufficient, what would happen to your free will?

What good will someone else's knowledge and faith do you when you have decisions to make?

Will what they know do you any good when you're alone and distressed?

STORY

One day in London the Master gave His listeners an unusual, imaginative, yet realistic dialogue between the Prophets and men: 'Always, man has confronted the Prophets with this: "We were enjoying ourselves, and living according to our own opinions and desires. We ate; we slept;

we sang; we danced. We had no fear of God, no hope of Heaven; we liked what we were doing, we had our own way. And then you came. You took away our pleasures. You told us now of the wrath of God, again of the fear of punishment and the hope of reward. You upset our good way of life."

'The Prophets of God have always replied: "You were content to stay in the animal world. We wanted to make you human beings. You were dark, We wanted you illumined; you were dead, We wanted you alive. You were earthly, We wanted you heavenly." '

'Abdu'l-Bahá, quoted in Honnold, *Vignettes*, p. 141

VIEWPOINT

When you were a baby, you didn't necessarily see the benefits of toilet training or of developing social graces such as courtesy and consideration of others. These were things that someone else had to firmly guide you to – with the threat of punishment and the promise of reward – or you would never have enjoyed the advantages of maturity. Once you're born, you can't decide to remain in the state of an infant or a child, no matter how much you enjoy it! You must progress to youth and maturity. This is inherent in your very being and inevitable. The same is true for humanity as a whole: it must progress from age to age, like it or not!

Someone once asked 'Abdu'l-Bahá what would happen if people didn't make efforts to develop themselves spiritually. He replied, 'Nothing!'

Is nothing what you really want to have happen with your loving capacity? What happens if you are trying to learn *anything* and you don't make efforts or practice? Yeah, nothing.

POINT TO PONDER

Imagine what it would be like if you refused to learn anything and just grew up remaining in the infant's stage of development.

READING

God has given man the eye of investigation by which he may see and recognize truth. He has endowed man with ears that he may hear the message of reality and conferred upon him the gift of reason by which he may discover things for himself. This is his endowment and equipment for the investigation of reality. Man is not intended to see through the eyes of another, hear through another's ears nor comprehend with another's brain. Each human creature has individual endowment, power and responsibility in the creative plan of God. Therefore, depend upon your own reason and judgement and adhere to the outcome of your own investigation, otherwise, you will be utterly submerged in the sea of ignorance and deprived of all the bounties of God.

'Abdu'l-Bahá, *Promulgation*, p. 293

EXERCISE

After studying the paragraph above, answer these questions:

What kind of 'eye' have you been given?

What are two things you can do with this eye?

Do you think this is a physical eye?

Why did God give you ears?

Will you have to hear this message with your physical ears?

Why were you given the gift of reason?

What were you given by God as your own equipment for the investigation of reality?

Can you see through another person's eyes physically?

Will it help you grow and develop spiritually if you only 'see' through another's eyes spiritually?

What does that mean, seeing through another's eyes spiritually? Think about and discuss this.

Will it help *you* pass the test if you get someone else to study for you?

What does each human creature have?

☺ Bob Harris's 'Dreaded Mirror Test':

Stand in front of the mirror, look yourself in the eye and ask yourself:

Do I really care about the suffering of the children of the world?

Do I want my life to count?

Ponder: What is your endowment? power? responsibility? Could it be called the 'creative plan of God' because it evolves according to how we use our powers and respond to our responsibilities?

What are you supposed to depend on? What are you supposed to adhere (stick!) to?

Do you think it will be helpful to have some training and hints about how to investigate reality for yourself?

Do these spiritual powers and gifts need to be educated and trained just as your physical and mental powers do?

If you don't use these powers to investigate reality, what does 'Abdu'l-Bahá say will happen to you?

Can you name some things that you think of as bounties of God?

What kind of human being am I?

What would I like to have accomplished before I die?

Who am I?
. . . and what do I want to be tomorrow?

What would be written in my obituary today?

How would I like it to read?

Bob reminds us that *no one's* life is wasted – there are wonderful examples of things to do and things *not* to do: you can always serve as a bad example!

3

Seeking's Good ~ Finding's Better!

Having created the world and all that liveth and moveth
therein, He, through the direct operation of His
unconstrained and sovereign Will, chose to confer upon man
the unique distinction and capacity to know Him and to love
Him – a capacity that must needs be regarded as the
generating impulse and the primary purpose underlying the
whole of creation . . .

Bahá'u'lláh, Gleanings, p. 65

. . . how can mine heart, already powerless to apprehend the
significance of its own potentialities, pretend to have
comprehended Thy nature? How can I claim to have known
Thee, when the entire creation is bewildered by Thy
mystery, and how can I confess not to have known Thee,
when, lo, the whole universe proclaimeth Thy Presence and
testifieth to Thy truth? The portals of Thy grace have
throughout eternity been open, and the means of access
unto Thy Presence made available, unto all created things,
and the revelations of Thy matchless Beauty have at all times
been imprinted upon the realities of all beings, visible and
invisible.

Bahá'u'lláh, Gleanings, p. 63

This passage from
*Gleanings from the Writings of
Bahá'u'lláh* states in
beautiful language the
paradox faced by all
humans: we were created
to know and love God but
God is, essentially,
unknowable. How can
any creature know its
creator?

4

Learning the Science of the Love of God

'Wouldst thou that the mind should not entrap thee?
Teach it the science of the love of God!'
Saná'í, quoted by Bahá'u'lláh in *The Seven Valleys*, p. 52

POINTS TO PONDER

What are some ways that your mind can 'entrap' you?

Does it allow you to think that your opinions and viewpoint are the only correct way to see something?

Can it make you think that if someone is different from you, he or she is inferior or superior to you?

Does it sometimes make you very unhappy or confused about your life?

EXERCISE

Write a specific example of how your mind can entrap you.

VIEWPOINT

Scientific methods require that to prove the truth of an idea, observable and relevant data must be carefully collected, a test must be set up using experiment and observation, and the results must be predictable and reproducible – so that anyone could get the same results if they carried out the same experiments.

Maybe this is what Bahá'u'lláh means when He reminds us to teach our minds 'the science of the love of God': anyone who follows His teachings can experience the love of God themselves and the results (experiencing the love of God) will be predictable and reproducible. What an interesting and exciting promise: anyone, by following clear directions, can come to know and love God – can personally experience the love of God. This *User's Guide* is designed to help you learn the directions, so you can teach yourself the science of the love of God.

It's up to you to decide if you want to learn and experience this – no one can ever force another person's spirit to do anything, and no one can do it for you. Your spiritual growth and your faith can never be dependent on anyone but yourself. It's very nice if your family, your friends and the culture you live in support you in your spiritual choices, and it's difficult if they don't – and *still* it's entirely up to you to recognize and respond to the truth.

God doesn't need anything from us. Nothing can be added or taken away from God. Out of His love for us, He doesn't give us such a potentially ruinous gift as free will combined with human intelligence without a safety net: He sends Teachers to guide us in the training and development of our loving capacities. But, of course, it's totally up to us. He says:

> 'If ye believe, to your own behoof will ye believe; and if ye believe not, ye yourselves will suffer.'
>
> Bahá'u'lláh, *Gleanings*, p. 148

POINTS TO PONDER

Who will benefit if you choose to learn about and obey spiritual laws?

Who will suffer?

Will it hurt God if you don't believe in these teachings?

VIEWPOINT

Bahá'u'lláh has come to invite you on a wonderful journey to a place that is all you could ever hope for or imagine: a universe of powers and possibilities! He has brought you a map to real treasure, given you the rules of safe travel and warned you of dangers along the way. Remember, though: all of this will be of no use to you until *you* choose to take the journey. The best part is that this 'place' is always right within you and this treasure can *never* be taken from you.

MEMORIZE

> The Purpose of the one true God, exalted be His glory, in revealing Himself unto men is to lay bare those gems that lie hidden within the mine of their true and inmost selves.
>
> Bahá'u'lláh, *Gleanings*, p. 287

> Ye are My treasury, for in you I have treasured the pearls of My mysteries and the gems of My knowledge.
>
> Bahá'u'lláh, *Hidden Words*, Arabic no. 69

EXERCISES

What gems do you think He means? Name three possibilities.

Write down what the pearls and gems might be. Think about how pearls are produced when a grain of sand or other irritant gets in the shell of the oyster. Apply this thought to the uses of tests and irritations in your life.

Does your dual nature make you a mystery?

READING

Bahá'u'lláh pleads with us to dig ourselves out of our dark caves and come out to sparkle in the brilliance of Divine love and grace:

> Say: O people! Withhold not from yourselves the grace of God and His mercy. Whoso withholdeth himself therefrom is indeed in grievous loss. What, O people! Do ye worship the dust, and turn away from your Lord, the Gracious, the

All-Bountiful? . . . Say: The Book of God hath been sent down in the form of this Youth. Hallowed, therefore, be God, the most excellent of makers! Take ye good heed, O peoples of the world, lest ye flee from His face. Nay, make haste to attain His presence, and be of them that have returned unto Him . . . He it is Who hath created you; He it is Who hath nourished your souls through His Cause, and enabled you to recognize Him Who is the Almighty, the Most Exalted, the All-Knowing. He it is Who hath unveiled to your eyes the treasures of His knowledge, and caused you to ascend unto the heaven of certitude – the certitude of His resistless, His irrefutable, and most exalted Faith. Beware that ye do not deprive yourselves of the grace of God, that ye do not bring to naught your works, and do not repudiate the truth of this most manifest, this lofty, this shining, and glorious Revelation. Judge ye fairly the Cause of God, your Creator, and behold that which hath been sent down from the Throne on high, and meditate thereon with innocent and sanctified hearts. Then will the truth of this Cause appear unto you as manifest as the sun in its noon-tide glory. Then will ye be of them that have believed in Him.

Say: The first and foremost testimony establishing His truth is His own Self. Next to this testimony is His Revelation. For whoso faileth to recognize either the one or the other He hath established the words He hath revealed as proof of His reality and truth. This is, verily, an evidence of His tender mercy unto men. He hath endowed every soul with the capacity to recognize the signs of God. How could He, otherwise, have fulfilled His testimony unto men, if ye be of them that ponder His Cause in their hearts. He will never deal unjustly with any one, neither will He task a soul beyond its power. He, verily, is the Compassionate, the All-Merciful.

Say: So great is the glory of the Cause of God that even the blind can perceive it, how much more they whose sight is sharp, whose vision is pure. The blind, though unable to perceive the light of the sun, are, nevertheless, capable of experiencing its continual heat. The blind in heart, however . . . are impotent, no matter how long the Sun may shine upon them, either to perceive the radiance of its glory, or to appreciate the warmth of its rays.

Say: O people . . . We have chosen you out of the world to know and recognize Our Self . . . Take heed lest ye allow yourselves to be shut out as by a veil from this Day Star that shineth above the dayspring of the Will of your Lord, the

recognize to identify as already known; know or be aware that something perceived has been perceived by oneself before; to realize or discover the nature of something; to be familiar with (familiar = as of family)

☺ How could you not recognize something that is your very Self?

Other quotations below will help clarify the meaning of this extremely important passage.

All-Merciful, and whose light hath encompassed both the small and the great. Purge your sight, that ye may perceive its glory with your own eyes, and depend not on the sight of any one except your self, for God hath never burdened any soul beyond its power. Thus hath it been sent down unto the Prophets and Messengers of old, and been recorded in all the Scriptures.

Strive, O people, to gain admittance into this vast Immensity for which God ordained neither beginning nor end, in which His voice hath been raised, and over which have been wafted the sweet savours of holiness and glory. Divest not yourselves of the Robe of grandeur, neither suffer your hearts to be deprived of remembering your Lord, nor your ears of hearkening unto the sweet melodies of His wondrous, His sublime, His all-compelling, His clear, and most eloquent voice.

Bahá'u'lláh, Gleanings, pp. 104–7

POINTS TO PONDER

Does His own Self refer to the Manifestation of God?

How does the Manifestation Himself establish the proof of His Reality and truth?

Is it true that a Manifestation *must* manifest the attributes of God in His life and all His actions?

If His 'Revelation' is *not* the Manifestation Himself, as He was named as the first proof, and it is *not* the words He has revealed, as these are named as the third proof, *what* could the revelation *be*? Think about this and about the meaning of the word 'reveal'.

'He hath endowed every soul with the capacity to recognize the signs of God.' Does this mean that *you* have the capacity to recognize the signs of God?

To clarify the question of what 'His Revelation' mentioned in the quotation above is, Bahá'u'lláh tells us:

Thy heart is My home; sanctify it for My descent. Thy spirit is My place of revelation; cleanse it for My manifestation.

Bahá'u'lláh, Hidden Words, Arabic no. 59

Does this mean that the 'Revelation' of God's love takes place in the spirit of every individual who is willing to receive it?

What is God's home?

How do you sanctify your heart and cleanse your spirit for the Manifestation of love?

Is this something that only has to be done once, or is it something that takes continuous practice and grows and develops over a lifetime – and beyond?

Perhaps these words of Bahá'u'lláh's will give you a clue in this treasure hunt for reality:

> God hath made My hidden love the key to the Treasure; would that ye might perceive it! But for the key, the Treasure would to all eternity have remained concealed; would that ye might believe it! Say: This is the Source of Revelation, the Dawning-place of Splendour, Whose brightness hath illumined the horizons of the world.

Bahá'u'lláh, Kitáb-i-Aqdas, para. 15

What is 'the key to the Treasure' within your inmost being?

Could you ever have found this treasure within yourself without the key of His hidden love? Ponder and discuss this.

STORY

Howard Colby Ives, an early Bahá'í in the United States, tells this story:

> I read for the first of many times these wonderful words from Bahá'u'lláh's Tablet to the Pope:
>
> > If ye believe in Me ye shall experience that which has been promised you, and I will make you the friends of my soul in the realm of My Greatness, and the

companions of My Perfection in the Kingdom of My Might forever.

Under the influence of such tremendous thoughts as these I one day asked 'Abdu'l-Bahá how it could ever be possible for me, deep in the mass of weak and selfish humanity, ever to hope to attain when the goal was so high and great. He said that it is to be accomplished little by little; little by little. And I thought to myself, I have all eternity for this journey from self to God. The thing to do is to get started.

Ives, Portals to Freedom, pp. 62–3

5

Making a Beginning

To become kinder, to make the world a better place, to have peace and security for everyone – all of these are things that most of us sincerely want, so why don't we see them in the world? Humanity is as unable to enlighten itself as a candle is unable to light itself: an outside power is required.

A careful study of humanity's passage through history will show that the bursts of progress and civilization (both material and spiritual) came as the result of a renewal of religion. Nothing else is capable of bringing about the necessary conditions in human hearts for an ever-advancing civilization. Unaided, humanity remains in an ego/fear-centred state. There is no effective solution to the problems facing us – as individuals or humanity as a whole – except the knowledge of God's will for the age in which we live.

READING

Religion, moreover, is not a series of beliefs, a set of customs; religion is the teachings of the Lord God, teachings which constitute the very life of humankind, which urge high thoughts upon the mind, refine the character, and lay the groundwork for man's everlasting honour.

Note thou: could these fevers in the world of the mind, these fires of war and hate, of resentment and malice among the nations, this aggression of peoples against peoples, which have destroyed the tranquillity of the whole world ever be made to abate, except through the living waters of the teachings of God? No, Never!

And this is clear: a power above and beyond the powers of

nature must needs be brought to bear, to change this black
darkness into light, and these hatreds and resentments,
grudges and spites, these endless wrangles and wars, into
fellowship and love amongst all the peoples of the earth.
This power is none other than the breathings of the Holy
Spirit and the mighty inflow of the Word of God.

'Abdu'l-Bahá, *Selections from the Writings of 'Abdu'l-Bahá*, pp. 52–3

EXERCISES

Take each paragraph of the quotation above and discuss it, then
answer these questions:

What is religion?

Can you name *anything* besides the teachings of God that can
bring true peace and well-being to the world?

VIEWPOINT

Mírzá Abu'l-Faḍl, a great Bahá'í scholar, said: 'Religion is
naught but a law prescribed by divine decree that guarantees the
preservation of society, through which eternal and everlasting
life can be attained' (Abu'l-Faḍl, *Letters and Essays*, p. 145). He
reminds us: 'Just as the divine Essence does not become
multiple, though it may have numerous Manifestations, even so
religion itself is the same even though it be manifest through
different laws and bestowals . . . the good and righteous revealers
of these religions were all Manifestations of a single reality that
is called the Spirit of God and His Cause' (Abu'l-Faḍl, *Letters and
Essays*, pp. 124–5). He quotes Muḥammad's book, the Qur'án:
'We make no division between any one of His Messengers'
(Qur'án 2:285).

    Mírzá Abu'l-Faḍl speaks of the effect that the renewal from
age to age of true religion can have on its followers if they accept
the Manifestation for their age: 'They have transformed their
inherited false dogmas into sound, demonstrable beliefs,
destroyed their superstitions, and perfected their faith. Their
ethics were renewed, their tastes edified, their vision set ablaze,
and their consciences set at ease. Through the light of faith,
their ignorance was turned into knowledge, their weakness into

Mírzá Abu'l-Faḍl noted
that if man hadn't
previously called
superstition religion, man
would not now call
religion superstition.

power, their treachery into trustworthiness, their evil into chastity, their estrangement into affection, their cowardice into valour, and their brutality into meekness' (Abu'l-Faḍl, *Miracles and Metaphors*, p. 33).

He singles out *guidance* as 'the sign that most clearly distinguishes the truth of a prophet or messenger – as healing is to medicine, as knowledge of planes is to geometry, as buying and selling is to commerce, and as making doors and bedsteads is to carpentry. It is by virtue of the great and noble attribute of guidance that prophets are said to prophesy, messengers to deliver God's message, and divine legislators to give laws' (Abu'l-Faḍl, *Miracles and Metaphors*, p. 156). And he again quotes Muḥammad's challenge: 'Bring a Book from God that gives better guidance than these, and follow it, if you speak truly' (Qur'án 28:48–9).

Can any other power on earth work such miracles?

See also Balyuzi, *'Abdu'l-Bahá*, pp. 282, 299, 302; and Grundy, *Ten Days in the Light of 'Akká*, pp. 33–7

POINTS TO PONDER

Ponder Muḥammad's challenge that begins: 'Bring a Book. . . .'

VIEWPOINT

Each age has its own evolution: from obscurity and overt persecution to a 'golden age' of fruition then gradual decline and preparation for the Promised One. Each Manifestation gives prophecies about His return and tells what to look for when seeking the new face of the Beloved.

READING

When a movement fundamentally religious makes a weak nation strong, changes a nondescript tribal people into a mighty and powerful civilization, rescues them from captivity and elevates them to sovereignty, transforms their ignorance into knowledge and endows them with an impetus of advancement in all degrees of development (this is not theory, but historical fact), it becomes evident that religion is the cause of man's attainment to honour and sublimity.

But when we speak of religion, we mean the essential foundation or reality of religion, not the dogmas and blind

A sincere student of history will notice the great advances in civilization during the 'golden age' of each Manifestation's Revelation. Each age is like a person or a tree: it has its own evolution from seed to full maturity and fruiting then to gradual decline and preparation

imitations which have gradually encrusted it and which are the cause of the decline and effacement of a nation.

'Abdu'l-Bahá, *Promulgation of Universal Peace*, p. 363

POINTS TO PONDER

Can man-made additions to and divisions of religion cause harm to individuals and nations? How?

What happens in the world when people don't know what their purpose is (why they were created) or forget or don't know what the rules are?

Is that happening now?

How does it affect your life every day?

For the next generation. For an exciting example of the power of a new Revelation, look at what's happened in the world of technology to facilitate the unification of humanity. Compare progress in the centuries between Caesar and George Washington: they both travelled the same way, lit their homes the same way, got news from afar basically the same way. Now look at what's happened in just the century and a half since the Bahá'í Era began! Compare how we live and travel and receive news, etc. today to 150 years ago.

VIEWPOINT

In school, as you develop more capacity, you move to higher grades or forms and new teachers. You build on what your earlier teacher helped you learn. You don't reject your first-grade teacher when you move to the second grade, do you? Your second-grade teacher teaches you things appropriate to *your* age, not everything he or she might know. As humanity advances in capacity and understanding, God sends a new Teacher (Manifestation) and more advanced lessons. The Manifestations bring teachings appropriate for humankind's stage of development, just as teachers at school teach you what you're intended and able to learn at a certain age.

The Manifestations of God bring us God's love, show us the attributes of love and give us love's laws. They are the guides and teachers for our spiritual nature. Human beings who don't know about or develop the spiritual side of their nature are like cars which are used as cupboards or chicken coops – it works, but . . .

attribute a quality or characteristic

EXERCISE

Name three attributes of love.

The Buddha, a Messenger of God, advised:

> Believe nothing merely because you have been told it, or
> because it is traditional, or because you have imagined it. But
> whatsoever, after due examination, you find to be conducive
> to the good, the welfare of all beings – that doctrine believe
> and cling to, and take as your guide.

He said:

> The gift of religion exceeds all gifts; the sweetness of religion
> exceeds all sweetness; the delight in religion exceeds all
> delights; the extinction of thirst overcomes all pain. Few are
> there among men who cross the river and reach the goal.
> The great multitudes are running up and down the shore;
> but there is no suffering for him who has crossed the river
> and finished his journey.
>
> *The Sayings of Buddha*, pp. 59–60

Christ warned that there would be many who would try to gain
personal power over people by deceiving them. He told His
followers how to distinguish good guidance from bad:

> Beware of false prophets, which come to you in sheep's
> clothing, but inwardly they are ravening wolves.
>   Ye shall know them by their fruits. Do men gather grapes
> of thorns, or figs of thistles?
>   Even so every good tree bringeth forth good fruit; but a
> corrupt tree bringeth forth evil fruit . . .
>   Wherefore by their fruits ye shall know them.
>
> Matt. 7:16–20

Bahá'u'lláh says:

> O my friend! In all circumstances one should seize upon
> every means which will promote security and tranquillity
> among the peoples of the world. The Great Being saith: In
> this glorious Day whatever will purge you from corruption
> and will lead you towards peace and composure, is indeed
> the Straight Path.
>
> Bahá'u'lláh, *Tablets of Bahá'u'lláh*, p. 171

Is a person who says he is giving guidance from God but is actually taking advantage of others' willingness to be generous for a 'good' cause like a wolf in sheep's clothing? (If you don't know this story, it's worth looking it up.)

What are the qualities of sheep that make them an appropriate comparison here?

What *is* the fruit of *all* true religion?

VIEWPOINT

God has always sent humankind guidance through Teachers or 'Manifestations'. Some of the Ones we know about are Abraham, Krishna, Buddha, Moses, Zoroaster, Christ, Muḥammad, the Báb and – for today – Bahá'u'lláh.

EXERCISES

Write down the names of nine Manifestations of God.

Write down the name of the Manifestation of God for this age.

VIEWPOINT

A 'Manifestation of God' is sent to show us God's love and His attributes and to teach us the purpose of our creation and the laws for our stage of development. The Manifestations help us develop – through our love for and obedience to them – morals and the capacity to become civilized and spiritualized. The Manifestations are to God as the rays are to the sun – the interface between human beings and God. They are validated by the effectiveness of the guidance they bring, by the transforming effect they have on the human heart – causing it to turn from selfishness to loving-kindness – and by their teachings and laws, which their followers recognize as incomparable blessings.

---

manifest to show or demonstrate plainly, to reveal

The three 'Wise Men'— the Magi – are thought to have been Zoroastrian priests who sought and found the new Manifestation, Jesus Christ, by following Zoroaster's prophecies.

The Báb, which means the 'Gate', was the Forerunner of Bahá'u'lláh. Bahá'ís believe that the Báb was the Mahdi, the Promised One awaited by the Sunní Muslims, as well as the return of the Shí'í Twelfth Imám. Bahá'u'lláh fulfils the Sunní prophecies concerning the Return of Christ.

☺ Frequently, when people first hear about the Bahá'í Faith, they ask: 'Is that one of those *eastern* religions?' Well, yes. They *all* are. Christ wasn't born in Bethlehem, Pennsylvania. The physical sun rises in the east; so does the spiritual Sun.

The Manifestations have *all* suffered greatly at the hands of a humanity which doesn't want to accept change, even though humanity itself would be the only beneficiary of that change.

'Abdu'l-Bahá told this story at the Bowery Mission when He was in New York City in 1912. The Bowery Mission was a centre where homeless and destitute men could come for shelter and food.

Tonight I am very happy for I have come here to meet my friends. I consider you my relatives, my companions; and I am your comrade . . .

When Jesus Christ appeared it was the poor who first accepted Him, not the rich . . . you are His comrades for He outwardly was poor not rich. Even this earth's happiness does not depend upon wealth . . . While Bahá'u'lláh was in Baghdád . . . He left all He had and went alone from the city, living two years among the poor. They were His comrades . . . He chose for one of His names the title of 'The Poor One', and often in His writings refers to Himself as 'Darvísh' which in Persian means 'poor'; and of this title He was very proud. He admonished all that we must be the servants of the poor, helpers of the poor, remember the sorrows of the poor, associate with them for thereby we may inherit the kingdom of heaven . . .

admonished to counsel against something; caution, warn

Jesus was a poor man. One night when He was out in the fields the rain began to fall. He had no place to go for shelter so He lifted His eyes toward heaven saying 'O Father! for the birds of the air Thou hast created nests, for the sheep a fold, for the animals dens, for the fishes places of refuge, but for me Thou hast provided no shelter; there is no place where I may lay my head; my bed consists of the cold ground, my lamps at night are the stars and my food is the grass of the field, yet who upon earth is richer than I? . . .'

And in conclusion I ask you to accept 'Abdu'l-Bahá as your servant.

'Abdu'l-Bahá quoted in Balyuzi, *'Abdu'l-Bahá*, p. 177

... the primary purpose in revealing the Divine Law ... is to bring about happiness in the after life and civilization and the refinement of character in this ...

'Abdu'l-Bahá, Secret of Divine Civilization, p. 46

POINTS TO PONDER

Why should we care about the after life when we're here on earth?

Does what went on in the womb affect the health and well-being of a baby once it's born?

Why should we care about refinement of character and what does that mean?

How does Divine Law bring about civilization in this life? Give a specific example.

What are some of the attributes of a civilized society? Name at least three.

What happens as the effect of religion declines and morals are, consequently, disregarded?

Are these things happening now?

How does this affect you personally? Be specific.

6

Progressive Revelation

To reveal His religion to humanity and to serve as guides for it,
God has sent many Teachers. We can safely follow what they *do*,
not just what they *say*, although their words, as with all else
about them, are always effective. Unfortunately, in the past the
followers of these Teachers have, through misunderstanding
and distortion of truth, changed the practices and forgotten the
true message brought by the Teachers.

Religion is revealed in stages to humanity. It is revealed in
stages to individuals, too: as more capacity is developed, more
love is revealed to and through us. In brief and simplified form:
It's all about love. It's all process. There's only now.

To end the religious division and strife that has caused so
much heartache and bloodshed in the world, Bahá'u'lláh has
clarified the role of these Manifestations and the seeming
differences that people have used as excuses to hate each other.
In this age, there is no excuse for warfare or strife of any kind.
This is the age of maturity and of the recognition of the oneness
of humanity.

POINTS TO PONDER

> Reality is one; it does not admit multiplicity or division.
> Reality is as the sun, which shines forth from different
> dawning points; it is as the light, which has illumined many
> lanterns.
>
> 'Abdu'l-Bahá, *Promulgation of Universal Peace*, p. 126

Is this same idea as expressed by the ḥadíth, 'Knowledge is a
single point, the ignorant have multiplied it'?

When religion is viewed with this in mind, what do you recognize in this paradox? Today's sun brings life today. Is it the *same* sun that appeared yesterday? And is it also a *different* sun than yesterday's?

Can you grow today's crops with yesterday's sun?

Write down what the quotation above means to you.

These Teachers are sometimes called Messengers, Prophets or Manifestations. They are all the bringers of God's message to humankind. Like the sun, they bring a message for a certain period of time – called an 'age'. An 'age' in religious terms usually lasts about five hundred to a thousand years. Each Messenger builds on what the previous Messenger taught, like teachers in a school, and each foretells (prophesies) that there will be another Messenger to follow. Each comes to bring new teachings that are appropriate for humanity's stage of development. Clinging to the former Manifestation when the next one has come is as fruitless as clinging to a previous teacher when it's time to advance to a new grade. It is the *light* that's important, not the *lamp*.

• In one age the Teacher was called Moses, who brought teachings that are passed on in a book we now call the Torah and the grade in religion was referred to as Judaism. Moses brought the concept of law to a young humanity.

• In another age the Teacher was called the Buddha (the Enlightened One) and the religion was called Buddhism. Buddha taught personal enlightenment.

• Another Teacher was Jesus Christ (the Anointed One), who brought teachings we learn of in the New Testament, and the religion became known as Christianity. Christ taught about love and personal salvation.

- Next came Islam (which means 'submission to the will of God'), taught by Muḥammad. His teachings are in a book called the Qur'án. Muḥammad brought humanity the concept of brotherhood and nations.

- Now, for this wonderful age we're living in, the Teacher is known as Bahá'u'lláh, 'the Glory of God', and the same school of religion as always is now called the Bahá'í Faith – 'Bahá'í' means 'of the Glory' or 'of Bahá'u'lláh'. Because humanity has reached a mature state, Bahá'u'lláh revealed hundreds of books to guide us. His main teaching for this age is unity.

Humanity has reached a stage of maturity, so we are ready for very special teachings. For the first time in religious history, volumes of the Manifestation's teachings were recorded during His lifetime, so their accuracy was verified by the Manifestation Himself. As we have seen, Bahá'u'lláh's main teaching is unity:

- the unity of God: there is only one God, even when people use different names – God, Dios, Alláh, etc. – these are all names for one Reality. Jews and Christians and Muslims and Bahá'ís all worship the same God.

- the unity of Religion: there is only one religion, which has gone by different names in different ages. All Manifestations or Prophets have come to guide and train people's spiritual nature with lessons appropriate for their stage of development at the time.

- the unity of humanity: there is only one human race. Its members come in many different types and colours – they are like a beautiful garden that has many different kinds and colours of flowers. Every member of humanity is created and loved by God and every person has the capacity to know and love God – we are all made for and from love.

READING

The teachings of Bahá'u'lláh are the light of this age and the spirit of this century.

Expound each of them at every gathering.
The first is investigation of truth,
The second, the oneness of mankind,
The third, universal peace,
The fourth, conformity between science and divine revelation,
The fifth, abandonment of racial, religious, worldly and political prejudices, prejudices which destroy the foundation of mankind.
The sixth is righteousness and justice,
The seventh, the betterment of morals and heavenly education,
The eighth, the equality of the two sexes,
The ninth, the diffusion of knowledge and education,
The tenth, economic questions [including a spiritual solution to the economic problems facing the world, such as extremes of wealth and poverty], and so on and so forth.

'Abdu'l-Bahá, *Selections from the Writings of 'Abdu'l-Bahá*, pp.107–8

VIEWPOINT

Because this is the age of unity, religion will not be allowed to divide into many opposing and warring sects as it did in the past. God made sure of this – how could unity come from a Faith that isn't united itself? We have, as Bahá'ís, a Covenant to protect and preserve our unity.

POINTS TO PONDER

What is a 'covenant'?

Has there ever been such a covenant between a Manifestation and His followers before?

Why is it so important in this Faith?

VIEWPOINT

No one can *change* Bahá'u'lláh's laws. When clarification of their

covenant an agreement or contract between two or more parties

Bahá'ís refer to the 'Greater Covenant', wherein God promises not to leave us without guidance and we promise to follow His Messenger for the age in which we live; and to the 'Lesser Covenant', which is unique to the Bahá'í Faith. By this Covenant, Bahá'u'lláh promises we will never be left without infallible guidance and we promise to be obedient to the laws and institutions He brought to us for our guidance. For the first time in recorded history, there is no doubt about the Manifestation's intentions or His follower's responsibilities regarding succession after His death.

meaning is needed, we agree that authoritative interpretation of the writings belongs to 'Abdu'l-Bahá and Shoghi Effendi. We agree to settle all disputes through consultation (because none of us is as smart as all of us!) and to be obedient to the institutions – the Universal House of Justice and the national and local assemblies.

POINTS TO PONDER

If you have an opinion or interpretation that is very different from someone else's, what are some things you could do?

Is it o.k. to force that person to accept your opinion because you're *sure* you're right?

Even if you *are* right in your facts, is it possible to be right in the spirit of unity if you're arguing and being a cause of estrangement?

EXERCISE

In your own words, explain what 'authoritative interpretation' means and why it is so important to the preservation of the unity of the Faith.

VIEWPOINT

When Bahá'u'lláh died, He named His son 'Abdu'l-Bahá as the one we should all turn to for guidance. Bahá'u'lláh said that no one could speak as an authority about the meaning of His teachings except 'Abdu'l-Bahá. 'Abdu'l-Bahá was not a Manifestation of God, so He didn't give us any new laws but He lived a perfect life and clarified and explained His father's teachings. 'Abdu'l-Bahá means 'Servant of God'.

'Abdu'l-Bahá in turn left a Will and Testament naming His grandson Shoghi Effendi the Guardian of the Bahá'í Faith and the one to whom all should turn for clear guidance. The institution of the Guardianship – which includes all of Shoghi Effendi's writings, clarifications and explanations – is a source of infallible guidance for the Bahá'ís for the rest of this age.

'authoritative interpretation' means that the explanation (of the Bahá'í writings) has the authority of Bahá'u'lláh Himself and that all believers can be sure of it.

This does not mean that we can't each interpret the writings according to our own understanding – actually we *must* to live the life! – but it does mean that we can't force that opinion or interpretation on anyone else. Remember, when two people argue over spiritual matters, they're both wrong. All such disputes are settled by consultative bodies.

68

The Bahá'í Administrative Order was written of by Bahá'u'lláh, initiated by 'Abdu'l-Bahá and developed and expanded by Shoghi Effendi. The Administrative Order of Bahá'u'lláh is a unique and wonderful feature of His Revelation.

EXERCISE

Discuss what it will be like when we all know and live by the teachings of Bahá'u'lláh. Talk about some specific ways everyone's daily life will be better, giving specific examples.

READING

'Abdu'l-Bahá gave this overview of the history of the Bahá'í Revelation when He spoke at the home of Mr and Mrs Marshall L. Emery in New York on 18 April 1912:

Tonight I wish to tell you something of the history of the Bahá'í Revelation.

The Blessed Perfection, Bahá'u'lláh, belonged to the nobility of Persia. From earliest childhood He was distinguished among His relatives and friends. They said, 'This child has extraordinary power.' In wisdom, intelligence and as a source of new knowledge, He was advanced beyond His age and superior to His surroundings. All who knew Him were astonished at His precocity. It was usual for them to say, 'Such a child will not live', for it is commonly believed that precocious children do not reach maturity. During the period of youth the Blessed Perfection did not enter school. He was not willing to be taught. This fact is well established among the Persians of Tihran. Nevertheless, He was capable of solving the difficult problems of all who came to Him. In whatever meeting, scientific assembly or theological discussion He was found, He became the authority of explanation upon intricate and abstruse questions presented.

Until His father passed away, Bahá'u'lláh did not seek position or political station notwithstanding His connection with the government.

This occasioned surprise and comment. It was frequently said, 'How is it that a young man of such keen intelligence and subtle perception does not seek lucrative appointments?

precocity, precocious
unexpectedly advanced or well developed

As a matter of fact, every position is open to him.' This is an historical statement fully attested by the people of Persia.

He was most generous, giving abundantly to the poor. None who came to Him were turned away. The doors of His house were open to all. He always had many guests. This unbounded generosity was conducive to greater astonishment from the fact that He sought neither position nor prominence. In commenting upon this His friends said He would become impoverished, for His expenses were many and His wealth becoming more and more limited. 'Why is he not thinking of his own affairs?' they inquired of each other; but some who were wise declared, 'This personage is connected with another world; he has something sublime within him that is not evident now; the day is coming when it will be manifested.' In truth, the Blessed Perfection was a refuge for every weak one, a shelter for every fearing one, kind to every indigent one, lenient and loving to all creatures.

He became well-known in regard to these qualities before the Báb appeared. Then Bahá'u'lláh declared the Báb's mission to be true and promulgated His teachings. The Báb announced that the greater Manifestation would take place after Him and called the Promised One 'Him Whom God shall make manifest', saying that nine years later the reality of His own mission would become apparent. In His writings He stated that in the ninth year this expected One would be known; in the ninth year they would attain to all glory and felicity; in the ninth year they would advance rapidly.

Between Bahá'u'lláh and the Báb there was communication privately. The Báb wrote a letter containing three hundred and sixty derivatives of the root Bahá. The Báb was martyred in Tabriz; and Bahá'u'lláh, exiled into Iraq in 1852, announced Himself in Baghdad. For the Persian government had decided that as long as He remained in Persia the peace of the country would be disturbed; therefore, He was exiled in the expectation that Persia would become quiet. His banishment, however, produced the opposite effect. New tumult arose, and the mention of His greatness and influence spread everywhere throughout the country. The proclamation of His manifestation and mission was made in Baghdad. He called His friends together there and spoke to them of God.

At one point He left the city and went alone into the mountains of Kurdistan, where He made His abode in caves and grottoes. A part of this time He lived in the city of Sulaymaniyyih. Two years passed during which neither His friends nor family knew just where He was.

Although Bahá'u'lláh was solitary, secluded and unknown in His retirement, the report spread throughout Kurdistan that this was a most remarkable and learned Personage, gifted with a wonderful power of attraction. In a short time Kurdistan was magnetized with His love. During this period Bahá'u'lláh lived in poverty. His garments were those of the poor and needy. His food was that of the indigent and lowly. An atmosphere of majesty haloed Him as the sun at midday. Everywhere He was greatly revered and beloved.

After two years He returned to Baghdad. Friends He had known in Sulaymaniyyih came to visit Him. They found Him in His accustomed environment of ease and affluence and were astonished at the appointments of One Who had lived in seclusion under such frugal conditions in Kurdistan.

The Persian government believed the banishment of the Blessed Perfection from Persia would be the extermination of His Cause in that country. These rulers now realized that it spread more rapidly. His prestige increased; His teachings became more widely circulated. The chiefs of Persia then used their influence to have Bahá'u'lláh exiled from Baghdad. He was summoned to Constantinople by the Turkish authorities. While in Constantinople He ignored every restriction, especially the hostility of ministers of state and clergy. The official representatives of Persia again brought their influence to bear upon the Turkish authorities and succeeded in having Bahá'u'lláh banished from Constantinople to Adrianople, the object being to keep Him as far away as possible from Persia and render His communication with that country more difficult. Nevertheless, the Cause still spread and strengthened. Finally, they consulted together and said, 'We have banished Bahá'u'lláh from place to place, but each time he is exiled his cause is more widely extended, his proclamation increases in power, and day by day his lamp is becoming brighter. This is due to the fact that we have exiled him to large cities and populous centres. Therefore, we will send him to a penal colony as a prisoner so that all may know he is the associate of murderers, robbers and criminals; in a short time he and his followers will perish.' The Sultan of Turkey then banished Him to the prison of 'Akká in Syria.

When Bahá'u'lláh arrived at 'Akká, through the power of

God He was able to hoist His banner. His light at first had been a star; now it became a mighty sun, and the illumination of His Cause expanded from the East to the West. Inside prison walls He wrote Epistles to all the kings and rulers of nations, summoning them to arbitration and universal peace. Some of the kings received His words with disdain and contempt. One of these was the Sultan of the Ottoman kingdom. Napoleon III of France did not reply. A second Epistle was addressed to him. It stated, 'I have written you an Epistle before this, summoning you to the Cause of God, but you are of the heedless. You have proclaimed that you were the defender of the oppressed; now it hath become evident that you are not. Nor are you kind to your own suffering and oppressed people. Your actions are contrary to your own interests, and your kingly pride must fall. Because of your arrogance God shortly will destroy your sovereignty. France will flee away from you, and you will be overwhelmed by a great conquest. There will be lamentation and mourning, women bemoaning the loss of their sons.' This arraignment of Napoleon III was published and spread.

epistle a letter, especially a formal one

Read it and consider: one prisoner, single and solitary, without assistant or defender, a foreigner and stranger imprisoned in the fortress of 'Akká, writing such letters to the Emperor of France and Sultan of Turkey. Reflect upon this: how Bahá'u'lláh upraised the standard of His Cause in prison. Refer to history. It is without parallel. No such thing has happened before that time nor since – a prisoner and an exile advancing His Cause and spreading His teachings broadcast so that eventually He became powerful enough to conquer the very king who banished Him.

His Cause spread more and more. The Blessed Perfection was a prisoner twenty-five years. During all this time He was subjected to the indignities and revilement of the people. He was persecuted, mocked and put in chains. In Persia His properties were pillaged and His possessions confiscated. First, there was banishment from Persia to Baghdad, then to Constantinople, then to Adrianople, finally from Rumelia to the prison fortress of 'Akká.

During His lifetime He was intensely active. His energy was unlimited. Scarcely one night was passed in restful sleep. He bore these ordeals, suffered these calamities and difficulties in order that a manifestation of selflessness and service might become apparent in the world of humanity;

that the Most Great Peace should become a reality; that
human souls might appear as the angels of heaven; that
heavenly miracles would be wrought among men; that
human faith should be strengthened and perfected; that the
precious, priceless bestowal of God – the human mind –
might be developed to its fullest capacity in the temple of the
body; and that man might become the reflection and likeness
of God, even as it hath been revealed in the Bible, 'Let us
make man in our image'. . .

'Abdu'l-Bahá, *Promulgation of Universal Peace*, pp. 25–8

EXERCISE

Retell the history in your own words.

Section III

Spirituality

I

Making a Beginning

The great American president Abraham Lincoln once said: 'If we could first know where we are and wither we are tending, we could better judge what to do and how to do it.'

'Where there is no vision,' the Old Testament tells us, 'the people perish: but he that keepeth the law, happy is he' (Proverbs 29:18).

Bahá'u'lláh advises us 'to see the end in the beginning' – to look at where we're headed before we begin and to keep our eyes on the intended goal; to look at where the path leads *before* we set out upon it, and look towards the light in the darkness.

After we know where we are and 'whither we are tending', we need to have a vision. When we have that vision, we need only to:

MEMORIZE

. . . make a beginning, and all will come right.

'Abdu'l-Bahá, quoted in Honnold, *Vignettes*, p. 122

VIEWPOINT

'Making a beginning' actually involves all three conditions necessary for the accomplishment of anything: knowledge, volition and action. Obviously, nothing can *ever* happen if you don't make a beginning.

What must you do so all will come right?

What are the three conditions necessary in order to accomplish anything?

VIEWPOINT

So, with all this good advice, let's first figure out 'where we are and whither we are tending'. Anyone who has any of his physical senses knows that there are enormous, seemingly insoluble problems in the world today. All the news – the worldwide hunger, the dangerous situations in our neighbourhoods and schools, the instability of families, the environmental issues – creates insecurity and outright fear in our lives, even if we are of the more fortunate and protected. The teachings of the previous Messengers have been abandoned in favour of man-made divisions, factionalism and war. Their messages have been lost in the mêlée. There is no place and no person on earth exempt from the problems of the world today. It is, clearly, time for renewal of hope and truth and vision.

mêlée confused hand-to-hand fighting in a pitched battle; a violent free-for-all; a confused mingling, as of a crowd

READING

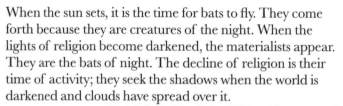

On the question of 'whither we are tending', 'Abdu'l-Bahá contrasts the way of nature and the way of spirit, and compares materialists to bats, flying about blind to light, at home in the darkness.

> When the sun sets, it is the time for bats to fly. They come forth because they are creatures of the night. When the lights of religion become darkened, the materialists appear. They are the bats of night. The decline of religion is their time of activity; they seek the shadows when the world is darkened and clouds have spread over it.
>
> 'Abdu'l-Bahá, *Promulgation of Universal Peace*, pp. 179–80

Materialism is a belief in the supremacy of material existence and that humanity, unaided by the power of God, can solve its problems and create paradise on earth; it reduces humanity to the material/ego state and doesn't allow for the transcendent spiritual state of freedom found in true religion.

From the materialists' point of view, we get such observations as 'It's human nature to make war'. True religion leads us to the realization that this is the least of human nature – that, in fact, we yearn for love and harmony in our deepest and truest being.

READING

How strange . . . it seems that man, notwithstanding his endowment with this ideal power, will descend to a level beneath him and declare himself no greater than that which is manifestly inferior to his real station. God has created such a conscious spirit within him that he is the most wonderful of all contingent beings. In ignoring these virtues he descends to the material plane, considers matter the ruler of existence and denies that which lies beyond . . . In fact from this standpoint the animal is the greater philosopher because it is completely ignorant of the Kingdom of God, possesses no spiritual susceptibilities and is uninformed of the heavenly world . . .

Alas that humanity is completely submerged in imitations and unrealities, notwithstanding that the truth of divine religion has ever remained the same. Superstitions have obscured the fundamental reality, the world is darkened, and the light of religion is not apparent. This darkness is conducive to differences and dissensions; rites and dogmas are many and various . . . True religion is the source of love and agreement amongst men, the cause of the development of praiseworthy qualities, but the people are holding to the counterfeit and imitation, negligent of the reality which unifies . . . They follow superstitions inherited from their fathers and ancestors . . . Therefore, the realm of the religionist has gradually narrowed and darkened, and the sphere of the materialist has widened and advanced . . .

'Abdu'l-Bahá, *Promulgation of Universal Peace*, pp. 178–9

rites the prescribed or customary form for conducting a religious or other solemn ceremony; a ceremonial act or series of acts

dogmas opinions accepted or fixed by an authority (such as the Church); principles, beliefs or statements that are authoritative, sometimes arrogantly, asserted as absolute truth

79

Whither are we tending? It's clear that if we continue as we are headed now, we're tending towards inevitable disaster. No political, scientific or technological efforts – even the best-funded and most enlightened – can hope to pull us out of this gallop to destruction.

As all these problems are, at their root, spiritual, the only effective remedy for them must be a spiritual one. For instance, suppose we take just one problem: starvation in developing countries. Countless millions of dollars have been applied to this problem, science and technology have been available, good-hearted efforts have been launched, yet no solution is in sight.

However, if we were spiritually enlightened and aware in our deepest being of God's teaching that we are all members of the same human family, there would never, ever be a problem with starvation anywhere on earth. Would you let your family starve when you had plenty of food? This is a problem created by greed and unenlightened self-interest – *all* problems are. There is plenty of food in the world for everyone but it is not distributed fairly. We are all required to become conscious if this is to change. There's a saying: 'If you're not part of the solution, you're part of the problem.' True.

☺ On our own, the only thing that stands between us and near-certain destruction is our wits – and we're swiftly approaching the end of them! This is *not* adequate protection.

Another paradox: by giving up our unen-lightened self-interest and greed, we *all* have more-abundant and secure lives, which is obviously in our best self-interest!

MEMORIZE

Vision must be restored where hope is lost, confidence built where doubt and confusion are rife.

The Universal House of Justice, Riḍván Message, 1988

POINTS TO PONDER

If *you're* feeling hopeless, what do you need to restore?

Is this inner vision or outer vision?

Does inner vision affect what you see (focus on, perceive?) with your outer vision?

Have you ever 'seen' a situation clearly one way, and then later, when your understanding changed, 'seen' it another? Recall an example of this from your own life.

How do you restore vision and build confidence? Think of at least two specific ways.

How can this be done in the world?

Can it be done in the world if we don't do it as individuals?

VIEWPOINT

Humanity is perishing from a lack of vision and few have been found who will happily keep the law. The vision *and* the law for us today – and for the next thousand years – are in Bahá'u'lláh's teachings: the vision and the law are love and unity.

The remedy to every problem facing humanity is available in the teachings of the Bahá'í Faith. We have – right now – all we need to build 'the kingdom of God on earth'. The decision to participate in the construction project belongs to every individual and must be renewed and practised with every choice we make, every action we take, with the purification of our deepest motives.

At this time in the history of the world, there is an urgent need for us to give up everything that we think we are and all we think we know, to drop all of our petty defences, suspicions and masks of separateness so we can join together with divine attraction to love and heal ourselves and our severely endangered planet. Let's learn to love Love more than we love self and fear. By maintaining our hatreds and divisions, our worst fears have already come upon us and there is no peace or security to be found – this is the best the material/ego nature of man can produce.

MEMORIZE

. . . let us join together to hasten forward the Divine Cause of unity, until all humanity knows itself to be one family, joined together in love.

'Abdu'l-Bahá, *Paris Talks*, p. 123

POINTS TO PONDER

Do you *really know* that humanity is one family and that it's not only *possible* but *inevitable* that we *will* know ourselves to be one family joined together in love?

Is there a difference between the lack of war and true peace? Discuss or write about this in your journal.

Can political power, technology or sincere citizen groups bring about such a peace without the unifying bond of a common love for the Manifestation of God for today? Why or why not?

Who created the vision of world unity in our minds and hearts where no such vision was before in the history of humanity?

For a comprehensive and inspiring explanation of the vision Bahá'u'lláh brought of the future of humanity, see Shoghi Effendi, *World Order of Bahá'u'lláh*, pp. 202–6 and Shoghi Effendi's brilliant summary of the Bahá'í Faith in the introduction to *Call to the Nations*.

READING

> There is no time to lose. There is no room left for vacillation. Multitudes hunger for the Bread of Life. The stage is set. The firm and irrevocable Promise is given. God's own Plan has been set in motion. It is gathering momentum with every passing day. The powers of heaven and earth mysteriously assist in its execution. Such an opportunity is irreplaceable. Let the doubter arise and himself verify the truth of such assertions. To try, to persevere, is to insure ultimate and complete victory.
>
> Shoghi Effendi, *Messages to America*, p. 17

POINTS TO PONDER

If you doubt that Bahá'u'lláh has brought the truth for this age, and that His guidance is good, what can you do to verify it?

Does the word 'arise' imply knowledge, volition and action?

When you arise, where do you begin?

Would you have to accept something as truth and actually implement it in your life for a while to really prove it right or wrong?

What is your goal? Be specific. Discuss it or write about it in your journal.

Is it necessary for you to verify Bahá'u'lláh's claims for yourself or can you go by someone else's evaluation?

What is required to ensure 'ultimate and complete victory'?

VIEWPOINT

When you set out to seek truth, one provision for the journey that's very helpful is: Be sure you allow for accepting it when you find it.

Many people have so much invested in being seekers that they actually have no intention of finding what they're supposed to be seeking. Seeking, in fact, is very popular right now; finding is not – it's generally looked upon with great suspicion and denial. To continue to seek something after you've found is like gasping for air when you could just breathe. Don't get so caught up in the drama of the quest that you lose sight of its realization. There is a wise saying: 'When the sun rises, put out the lamp.'

READING

The Báb makes the following astonishing statement:

> Regard not the all-sufficing power of God as an idle fancy. It is that genuine faith which thou cherishest for the Manifestation of God in every Dispensation. It is such faith which sufficeth above all the things that exist on the earth, whereas no created thing on earth besides faith would suffice thee.
>
> The Báb, *Selections from the Writings of the Báb*, p.123

POINTS TO PONDER

What is 'the all-sufficing power of God'?

Think and discuss how it could be *your faith* that is the all-sufficing power of God.

☺ Abdu'l-Bahá tells us if we're not sure about Bahá'u'lláh's teachings about peace, we can try peace for a while; if we don't like it, we can always go back to making war! So, try love and happiness for a while. If you don't enjoy them, you can always go back to hatred and misery!

'At this hour the morn of knowledge hath arisen and the lamps of wayfaring and wandering are quenched' Bahá'u-'lláh, *Seven Valleys*, p. 16).

Bahá'u'lláh is warning the mystics that the coming of the Manifestation makes further search unnecessary.

Is it possible to have full access to and understanding of your own capacity for selfless love without the guidance of the Manifestation of God for this age?

Would your ego/animal nature subdue its inclinations for anything less than love?

If you were following a previous Manifestation, would you have the assurance of the oneness of humankind, or would you only be required to try to love your fellow believers?

☺ Understanding this is a good way to use a lifetime – starting now!

READING

> The first sign of faith is love. The message of the holy divine Manifestations is love; the phenomena of creation are based upon love; the radiance of the world is due to love; the well-being and happiness of the world depend upon it. Therefore, I admonish you that you must strive throughout the human world to diffuse the light of love. The people of this world are thinking of warfare; you must be peacemakers. The nations are self-centred; you must be thoughtful of others rather than yourselves.
>
> 'Abdu'l-Bahá, *Promulgation of Universal Peace*, p. 337

POINTS TO PONDER

What is the first sign of faith?

What is the message of the holy divine Manifestations?

What do the well-being and happiness of the world depend upon?

What can you do all day every day to make the world a better place?

VIEWPOINT

Abdu'l-Bahá tells us that we were created to love. If we don't learn to love God and develop spiritual qualities, our loving capacity will be used by our fearful, ego selves; we'll become selfish and both cause and experience unhappiness. This is what causes wars and all the other problems that we're facing: we love from our physical, ego selves more than we love from our spiritual selves.

MEMORIZE

So we're told:

> When the love of God is established, everything else will be realized.
>
> 'Abdu'l-Bahá, *Promulgation of Universal Peace*, p. 239

POINTS TO PONDER

Are you beginning to understand how this happens?

Do you see *your* part in bringing about the 'kingdom of God [love] on earth'?

Can we bring about this kingdom without developing our spiritual natures?

Is 'turning to God' for assistance a passive thing or must we actively turn our spiritual capacities towards the source of love to be replenished and strengthened?

READING

Jesus Christ tells us this in the Bible:

> And seek not ye what ye shall eat, or what ye shall drink, neither be ye of doubtful mind . . . But rather seek ye the kingdom of God; and all these things shall be added unto you.
>
> Luke 12:29–31

A few of the things included in the 'everything else' that 'Abdu'l-Bahá and Christ are talking about are mutual helpfulness and loving-kindness, trustworthiness, happiness, fearlessness, peacefulness and self-respect – not to mention true prosperity and no more wars! Aren't these things everyone wants?

EXERCISE

Discuss how making the love of God and seeking the 'kingdom of God' – the kingdom of love, mercy, etc. – your priority will cause everything else to be realized.

POINTS TO PONDER

Is the 'love of God' an action or just a lovely idea?

Is it possible to have a content, secure society without such qualities as kindness, truthfulness and honesty?

What are some of the problems in our society today – things you hear about on the news every day?

Can those problems be solved if people don't change the way they do things and their outlook on what's most important in their lives?

Can science or technology change the way you treat other people or what goes on in your heart?

How do we serve God?

Is there any value to love that remains entirely unexpressed?

2

What is 'Spirituality'?
(and Why Should I Want It?)

INTRODUCTION

Why should you want spirituality? Only you can answer this. Give yourself time to consider the question 'Why should I want to be spiritual?' Ask yourself, as Howard Colby Ives did when considering why He should believe in Bahá'u'lláh: '. . . why should I believe in anyone or anything except as a means, an incentive, a dynamic for the securing of a fuller, deeper, more perfect life? Does the cabinet-maker's apprentice ask himself why he should believe in the master wood-worker? He wants to know how to make these raw materials into things of beauty and usefulness' (Ives, *Portals to Freedom*, p. 42).

MEMORIZE

When His love is there, every bitterness turneth sweet, and every bounty rendereth a wholesome pleasure.
'Abdu'l-Bahá, *Selections from the Writings of 'Abdu'l-Bahá*, p. 181

POINTS TO PONDER

Is there any value to you in a gift that you don't appreciate?

What are some gifts that become precious to you with the love of God?

Is consciousness and gratitude required before *anything* can be precious to you?

How about family, friends, daily chores, opportunities to learn and grow and develop understanding – would even 'tests' become precious with the love of God?

A 'Mrs C' was an early believer who went to 'Akká. She belonged to a wealthy and fashionable group of people in New York. Her life had been conventional and rather unsatisfying. She had been a sincere Christian, but somehow had not gained much comfort from her religion. She had become somewhat melancholy. While travelling abroad, she had learned about 'Abdu'l-Bahá. She eagerly grasped His message and headed to the prison-city. Having arrived, she was fascinated by everything, most especially by the Master. She noticed that 'Abdu'l-Bahá always greeted her with 'Be happy!' The other members of the party were not addressed in the same way by Him. This troubled her. Finally she asked someone to ask the Master why He addressed her in this way. With 'His peculiarly illuminating smile', He replied, 'I tell you to be happy because we can not know the spiritual life unless we are happy!'

Then Mrs C's dismay was complete, and her diffidence vanished with the fullness of her despair.

'But tell me, what is the spiritual life?' she cried, 'I have heard ever since I was born about the spiritual life, and no one could ever explain to me what it is!'

'Abdu'l-Bahá looked at His questioner again with that wonderful smile of His, and said gently: 'Characterize thyself with the characteristics of God, and thou shalt know the spiritual life!' – few words, but they were sufficient. Mrs C began to wonder what 'Abdu'l-Bahá meant. The characteristics of God? They must be such attributes as love and beauty, justice and generosity.

All day long her mind was flooded with the divine puzzle, and all day long she was happy. She did not give a thought to her duties, and yet when she arrived at the moment of her evening's reckoning, she could not remember that she had left them undone.

At last she began to understand. If she was absorbed in Heavenly ideals, they would translate themselves into deeds necessarily, and her days and nights would be full of light. From that moment she never quite forgot the divine admonition that had been granted her: 'Characterize thyself with the characteristics of God!'

And she learned to know the spiritual life.

Ford, quoted in Honnold, *Vignettes*, pp. 133–4

POINTS TO PONDER

Would developing your spiritual capacities always improve your material life as well?

Think of some specific examples of this and discuss them with others or write them in your journal.

READING

Here is some advice from 'Abdu'l-Bahá on how to increase your spiritual, loving capacity:

> The first thing to do is to acquire a thirst for Spirituality, then Live the Life! Live the Life! Live the Life! The way to acquire this thirst is to meditate upon the future life. Study the Holy Words, read your Bible, read the Holy Books, especially study the Holy Utterances of Bahá'u'lláh; Prayer and Meditation, take much time for these two. Then will you know this Great Thirst, and then only can you begin to Live the Life!
>
> 'Abdu'l-Bahá quoted in *Star of the West*, vol. 19, no. 3, p. 69

VIEWPOINT

Without thirst, you wouldn't remember to drink, and fluids are essential to material existence. A thirst for spirituality reminds you to drink from the oceans of love and mercy that surround you and are as essential for your true well-being as water is for your physical well-being. We're living in a pretty dehydrated world! Everyone's going around parched like they've been eating bags of potato chips and can't find a drink – crawling through some spiritual desert when there's actually lovely, pure water everywhere.

☺ Question: What's the difference between ignorance and apathy?

Answer: I don't know and I don't care!

Bahá'u'lláh and 'Abdu'l-Bahá tell us that the more we thirst, the greater our capacity becomes: the greater the attraction, the greater the attainment.

MEMORIZE

> Knowledge is love. Study, listen to exhortations, think, try to understand the wisdom and greatness of God. The soil must be fertilized before the seed can be sown.
>
> 'Abdu'l-Bahá quoted in *Star of the West*, vol. 20, no. 10, p. 314

READINGS

> The flame of the fire of love, in this world of earth and water, comes through the power of attraction and not by effort and striving . . . only the light of the Divine Beauty can transport and move the spirits through the force of attraction.
>
> 'Abdu'l-Bahá, *Some Answered Questions*, p. 130

> Every body calleth aloud for a soul.
>
> Bahá'u'lláh quoted in Shoghi Effendi, *Advent of Divine Justice*, p. 82

> Spirituality . . . is unity, the love of God, praiseworthy morals and the virtues of the human world.
>
> 'Abdu'l-Bahá, *Promulgation of Universal Peace*, p. 165

VIEWPOINT

The purpose of spirituality is to turn the raw materials that you possess into things of beauty and usefulness and everlasting joy – into loving action. The love of God is not something you *have* or *chase*, it's something you *do* and *are* and it results from cultivating a spirit of attraction. Knowing that you have these spiritual powers and that you can use them to experience states of joy

Ignorance: you don't know about water or thirst, you just suffer.

Lethargy: you're too lazy to wonder why you're so thirsty or whether you could overcome it.

Apathy or *indifference*: you know you're thirsty but you don't really care; you look around and say 'Who cares if there's no water, at least I've got my chips!'

☺ So, if you desire more, desire more!

and wonder (knowledge), and wanting to experience these states (volition), leads to the action of creating a state of attraction through meditation and prayer.

MEMORIZE

Spirituality is the possession of a good, pure heart. When the heart is pure, the Spirit enters, and our growth is natural and assured. Everyone is better informed of the condition of his own soul than the soul of others. Our responsibility to God increases with our years.

'Abdu'l-Bahá quoted in Grundy, *Ten Days in the Light of 'Akká*, p. 18

EXERCISE

In your own words, write in your journal why you would like to develop your spiritual/loving capacity and how your experience of life will change as you do.

READING

How to attain spirituality is indeed a question to which every young man and woman must sooner or later try to find a satisfactory answer . . . Indeed the chief reason for the evils now rampant in society is a lack of spirituality . . . The universal crisis affecting mankind is, therefore, essentially spiritual in its causes . . . It is this condition . . . into which society has fallen, that religion seeks to improve and transform . . . For the core of religious faith is that mystic feeling that unites man with God. This state of spiritual communion can be brought about and maintained by means of meditation and prayer. And this is the reason why Bahá'u'lláh has so much stressed the importance of worship. It is not sufficient for a believer merely to accept and observe the teachings. He should, in addition, cultivate the sense of spirituality which he can acquire chiefly by the means of prayer . . .

The believers, particularly the young ones, should therefore fully realize the necessity of praying. For prayer is absolutely indispensable to their inner spiritual development, and this, already stated, is the very foundation

mystic mysterious and awe-inspiring; spiritually allegorical or symbolic; of hidden meaning

communion act of communicating; the act of sharing thoughts, feelings, etc.; fellowship

and purpose of the Religion of God.

Letter of Shoghi Effendi to an individual believer, 8 December 1935
in *Compilation of Compilations*, pp. 237–8

POINTS TO PONDER

Is the 'mystic' feeling a mystery because of our dual nature? What makes a relationship with God so mysterious?

How can this state of spiritual communion be brought about and maintained?

Has Bahá'u'lláh stressed the importance of worship because He wants us to develop a state of spiritual communion?

READINGS

The world has become a new world. The darkness of night which has enveloped humanity is passing. A new day has dawned. Divine susceptibilities and heavenly capacities are developing in human souls under the training of the Sun of Truth. The capacities of souls are different. Their conditions are various. For example, certain minerals come from the stony regions of the earth. All are minerals, all are produced by the same sun, but one remains a stone while another develops the capacity of a glittering gem or jewel. From one plot of land tulips and hyacinths grow; from another, thorns and thistles. Each plot receives the bounty of the sunshine, but the capacity to receive it is not the same. Therefore, it is requisite that we must develop capacity and divine susceptibility in order that the merciful bounty of the Sun of Truth intended for this age and time in which we are living may reflect from us as light from pure crystals.

The bounties of the Blessed Perfection are infinite. We must endeavour to increase our capacity daily, to strengthen and enlarge our capabilities for receiving them, to become as perfect mirrors. The more polished and clean the mirror, the more effulgent is its reflection of the lights of the Sun of Truth. Be like a well-cultivated garden wherein the roses and variegated flowers of heaven are growing in fragrance and beauty. It is my hope that your hearts may become as ready ground, carefully tilled and prepared, upon which the divine showers of the bounties of the Blessed Perfection may descend and the zephyrs of this divine springtime may blow with quickening breath. Then will the garden of your hearts bring forth its flowers of delightful fragrance to refresh the nostril of the heavenly Gardener.

'Abdu'l-Bahá, *Promulgation of Universal Peace*, pp. 23–4

O ye friends of God! True friends are even as skilled physicians, and the Teachings of God are as healing balm, a medicine for the conscience of man. They clear the head, so that a man can breathe them in and delight in their sweet fragrance. They waken those who sleep. They bring awareness to the unheeding, and a portion to the outcast, and to the hopeless, hope.

If in this day a soul shall act according to the precepts and the counsels of God, he will serve as a divine physician to mankind, and like the trump of Israfíl [believed to be the angel appointed to sound the trumpet on the Day of Resurrection to raise the dead], he will call the dead of this contingent world to life; for the confirmations of the Abhá Realm are never interrupted, and such a virtuous soul hath, to befriend him, the unfailing help of the Company on high. Thus shall a sorry gnat become an eagle in the fullness of his strength, and a feeble sparrow change to a royal falcon in the heights of ancient glory.

'dead' in this sense means 'spiritually dead', as when Christ said: 'Let the dead bury their dead.'

Wherefore, look not on the degree of your capacity, ask not if you are worthy of the task: rest ye your hopes on the help and loving-kindness, the favours and bestowals of Bahá'u'lláh – may my soul be offered up for His friends! Urge on the steed of high endeavour over the field of sacrifice, and carry away from this wide arena the prize of divine grace.☺

☺ You have to be present to win!

'Abdu'l-Bahá, *Selections from the Writings of 'Abdu'l-Bahá*, p. 23

The intention is capacity.

'Abdu'l-Bahá quoted in Brown, *Memories of 'Abdu'l-Bahá*, p. 64

POINTS TO PONDER

Your lower self (or material/animal/ego nature) can be compared to a horse and your higher self (or spiritual nature) can be compared to the rider.

If the rider is not in control of the horse, what will happen?

Does the rider hate the horse or think it's evil?

If so, what will happen? Will the horse cooperate?

Can the rider be kind and considerate to the horse and take care of its needs without letting the horse get out of control?

Would this be better than abusing or ignoring the horse? Would it be better than letting the horse be abusive?

EXERCISES

Think of an example from your life that shows what happens if you let the horse (your lower nature) get out of control.

Discuss or write in your journal an example of a time when the rider (your higher nature) handled the horse properly.

VIEWPOINT

Prayer and meditation, by putting you in touch with your spiritual nature and your higher aspirations and goals, are ways of getting to know God and yourself; giving you riding lessons, so that you can gallop through your daily life without letting the horse ride on *your* back! Real power is being in control of yourself, not of other people. Ego power seeks to control, manipulate and dominate others. The power of love seeks to purify and strengthen your own motives and your relationships with others.

POINTS TO PONDER

What does ego power seek?

What does the power of love seek?

What is real power?

Do you have to control or change anyone else in order to have real power?

Discuss why this is so and give examples from your life.

What does love seek to purify and strengthen?

Will lots of money or fame bring you happiness if you aren't in control of yourself and your thoughts? Isn't it because people want to feel safe and loved and in control of their lives that they want money and fame? Of course, they can lose their money and fame (and being able to order others around is not real power and definitely not real love), and when they die, the money and fame won't mean anything, will it? Love is the ultimate power because it's something you *are* and *do* – not something you *have* (so you can't lose it – you can only lose touch with it). It never needs to use force and it conquers all. What else can rein in the ego?

POINTS TO PONDER

'Abdu'l-Bahá says: '. . . in the human world there is no greater power than the love of God' ('Abdu'l-Bahá, *Promulgation of Universal Peace*, p. 257).

When the ego is in control, can its job as your bodyguard backfire?

Will the ego kill you out of fear of not being the best or the strongest, which it wants to be so it can keep you safe?

How about wars? We fight them 'to protect our peace'! We all cherish peace of mind, yet isn't the ego constantly searching for signs and portents of danger, robbing us of that which we most cherish?

'Abdu'l-Bahá points out that we're fighting over our own tombs when we're warring over control and boundaries! We fight and die over a piece of earth that we'll be buried under in the end. The ego has no problem saying, 'I'll beat you even if it kills me' while convincing us it's all for our own protection. Or of making us miserable in an effort to make us happy, and endangering us to keep us safe!

> Transformation and confirmation are powers which belong to God alone.
>
> Ḥájí Mírzá Ḥaydar-ʿAlí, *Delight of Hearts*, p. 82

Just as a candle can't light itself and an eye can't create its own illumination, we can't enlighten our spirits with selfless love without God's assistance. Such assistance is sent in the form of divine Teachers who appear from age to age. Each individual is capable of and responsible for responding to this assistance personally.

POINTS TO PONDER

Does *anything* but spirituality (love, mercy, kindness) have the power to transform selfishness into self*less*ness?

Would selfishness ever even know that selflessness existed without something greater than itself to demonstrate the possibility?

Can a mirror reflect the sun if it's turned towards the ground or kept in a dark room?

Without a knowledge of God, how would we learn to ask, 'How can I be loving in this situation?' rather than 'How can I be right (or best or strongest or 'baddest'!)?

VIEWPOINT

Because religion has become unpopular and its influence has diminished in society, people think that everyone just knows right from wrong and can choose to act in a moral way. In fact, what knowledge remains of right and wrong and morals is *still* coming from the foundation laid down by religion, even though we now reject religion itself. Its influence is so great on us that we notice it no more than a fish notices water.

For every one of you his paramount duty is to choose for
himself that on which no other may infringe and none usurp
from him. Such a thing – and to this the Almighty is My
witness – is the love of God, could ye but perceive it.

infringe to violate;
disregard; go beyond the
limits of something;
trespass

Build ye for yourselves such houses as the rain and floods
can never destroy, which shall protect you from the changes
and chances of this life.

usurp to seize and hold by
force and without legal
right or authority

Bahá'u'lláh, Gleanings, p. 261

POINTS TO PONDER

Is there any true security in the material world?

Is there anything material, including your life, that can't be
taken from you?

Is Bahá'u'lláh referring to building ourselves spiritual homes?
What materials and tools would you use to build a spiritual
home that 'would protect you from the changes and chances of
this life'?

Isn't it interesting that love and kindness and mercy never end
and hatred and meanness and fear do? It pays to watch what you
invest your life in! Look for what will last and pay great
dividends.

VIEWPOINT

It *is possible* for you to know security and love and enlightened
self-discipline – which is the ability to guide your thoughts and
feelings in your own and others' best interests – whenever you
choose to do so. This personal sovereignty – being master of
your own kingdom – is what life is about. Thus it's necessary to
have knowledge that such a thing is possible (knowledge), to
create and nurture an attraction to spiritual realities (volition)
and to make efforts to remove all barriers between your heart
and the recognition and experience of the love of God (action –
removing the barriers usually means refocusing your thoughts)

so you can enjoy 'that mystic feeling' that unites you with God. This is why Bahá'u'lláh has said we must pray and meditate every day – so we can have a tangible experience of God's love, which, wondrously, was why we were created.

☺ Who says spirit isn't *tangible*? Only 'til it touches them!

EXERCISE

Want to prove this for yourself? 'Abdu'l-Bahá tells us how to achieve a *personal, tangible* experience of God's love (much more on how to do this coming up). Follow these instructions:

> Verily, I say unto thee, that if for the appearance of that Divine Essence thou desirest to have a definite proof, an indisputable testimony and a strong, convincing evidence, thou must prepare thyself to make thy heart empty and thine eye ready to look only toward the Kingdom of God. Then, at that time, the radiance of that widespread effulgence will descend upon thee successively, and that motion rendered thee by the Holy Spirit will make thee dispense with any other strong evidence that leadeth to the appearance of this Light, because the greatest and strongest proof for showing the abundance of the Spirit to the bodies is the very appearance of its power and influence in those bodies.
>
> 'Abdu'l-Bahá, *Bahá'í World Faith*, p. 369

POINTS TO PONDER

What does this law about prayer and meditation mean? (There's lots more information about this coming up.)

Who benefits if I obey this law – Bahá'u'lláh, God, or me?

Why should I do it?

How do I do it?

What will happen to me if I don't do it?

Will God be angry at me?

READING

> . . . man should know his own self and recognize that which leadeth unto loftiness or lowliness, glory or abasement, wealth or poverty.
>
> Bahá'u'lláh, *Tablets of Bahá'u'lláh*, p. 35

POINTS TO PONDER

If we didn't know these things, how could we decide whether or not we would cherish them in our lives?

Are there people in the world today who don't seem to know themselves or to recognize what leads to loftiness or lowliness?

Are they likely to put ego concerns first, causing themselves and others misery?

Does just knowing what leads to loftiness or lowliness, glory or abasement, wealth or poverty mean that you'll *have* to choose to take the high road? Could you still choose lowliness, abasement or poverty if you wanted? Of course! So what have you got to lose by knowing?

to recognize to 'know again'

Our higher, spiritual nature already *knows* God's attributes, otherwise how could they be *recognized*? Of course, if God's attributes *are* our higher, spiritual nature, how could we *not* recognize them wherever we see them?

Hint: if the attributes of God seem invisible, weird or unfamiliar (as in 'not of your family') to you, you're looking through your material eyes.

There's a bumper sticker that says: 'Misery is optional.' So is joy – and how sad if we don't know that!

MEMORIZE

Memorize this passage from the *Hidden Words* of Bahá'u'lláh: see if it answers most of the questions about why we are to pray and meditate.

> *O Son of Being!*
> Love Me, that I may love thee.
> If thou lovest Me not,
> My love can in no wise reach thee.
> Know this, O servant.'
>
> Bahá'u'lláh, *Hidden Words*, Arabic no. 5

POINTS TO PONDER

Who does the word 'Me' refer to? (Notice that it's capitalized?)

Does this mean that if you don't love Bahá'u'lláh (or God), He will stop loving you?

Or could it mean that if you forget to love God, He'll still be loving you but you won't *know* it, so you won't receive it?

If someone loves you very much but you don't know it, does it help you feel happier or stronger?

If you are created to receive God's love so that you can grow and develop spiritually (not to mention that we all just want to be loved!) what happens if you forget to reach out for it? Is it like leaving your spirit in a dark cupboard or forgetting that it requires spiritual nourishment just as your body needs food?

Muḥammad tells us that what we do for religion, we do for ourselves. Certainly. We're the ones that benefit, aren't we?

3

Here I Am – What Now?

INTRODUCTION

For this age, Bahá'u'lláh is the Manifestation of God. 'Bahá'u'lláh' means 'the Glory of God'.

In His writings, teachings and the example of His life are lessons to help us find true meaning, purpose and fulfilment in our lives. It is essential that we find these things – if we don't find them in our spiritual nature, we'll look for them everywhere else. Meaning, purpose and fulfilment are as necessary to humans as air and food and water are. You know the truth of the song 'Lookin' for love in all the wrong places'.

Bahá'u'lláh makes it easy for us to know our purpose. He tells us:

MEMORIZE

The purpose of God in creating man hath been, and will ever be, to enable him to know his Creator and to attain His Presence. To this most excellent aim, this supreme objective, all the heavenly Books and the divinely-revealed and weighty scriptures unequivocally bear witness.

Bahá'u'lláh, *Gleanings*, p. 70

Bahá'u'lláh also gave us His son, 'Abdu'l-Bahá, as an example for us to follow – a model of a perfect human being.

POINTS TO PONDER

Does the word 'man' mean all of humanity or just the guys?

Does it include you, personally?

Why were *you* created?

As Bahá'ís (followers of Bahá'u'lláh) we learn that our purpose as humans is 'to carry forward an ever-advancing civilization' and that, as individuals, we were created to know and love God – 'to know [our] Creator and to attain His Presence'.

> That the heart is the throne, in which the Revelation of God the All-Merciful is centred, is attested by the holy utterances which We have formerly revealed.
>
> Among them is this saying: 'Earth and heaven cannot contain Me; what can alone contain Me is the heart of him that believeth in Me, and is faithful to My Cause' . . . It is waywardness of the heart that removeth it far from God, and condemneth it to remoteness from Him. Those hearts, however, that are aware of His Presence, are close to Him, and are to be regarded as having drawn nigh unto His throne.
>
> Bahá'u'lláh, *Gleanings*, p. 186

MEMORIZE

> The whole duty of man in this day is to attain that share of the flood of grace which God poureth forth for him.
>
> Bahá'u'lláh, *Gleanings*, p. 8.

POINTS TO PONDER

Who has total control over what you do with your heart – you or God? (or maybe your mother or father or best friend?)

What do you think 'grace' means in the second quotation above?

Is a 'duty' something that you are responsible for doing?

What is *your* whole duty?

What would it feel like to attain *your* share of the 'flood of grace'?

How would it change your daily life?

Why do you think Bahá'u'lláh says your 'whole duty' is to receive this wonderful blessing?

If you don't receive it, how will you be able to share it with the world?

Write in your journal what you can do to make sure that you receive the 'flood of grace' every day.

4

Getting to Know God
(= Falling in Love with Love)

INTRODUCTION

What do you do if you want to get to know people?

You spend time with them, pay attention to them, find out what they're like (their attributes), learn something of what they do and how they act.

Prayer and meditation are ways of getting to know God. Reading about the Manifestations of God and how they lived and what they taught is another way to get to know what God is like. Through stories about them and about 'Abdu'l-Bahá we can see God's will and attributes in daily action and we can look to these attributes as a guide for our daily lives.

Getting to know God (Love, the Best-Beloved) is how you get to know your true self – where your fulfilment as a human being lies. Living entirely on an animal/material level, though it has its good points, really doesn't leave us happy and satisfied.

READING

Could ye apprehend with what wonders of my munificence and bounty I have willed to entrust your souls, ye would, of a truth, rid yourselves of attachments to all created things, and would gain a true knowledge of your own selves – a knowledge which is the same as the comprehension of Mine own Being.

Bahá'u'lláh, *Gleanings*, pp. 326–7

When you are entrusted with something, you don't really own it. You are 'holding it in trust': that is, it belongs to another but you are expected to care for it appropriately and as though it were your own. What then can it mean that the 'wonders of munificence [great and plenteous generosity] and bounty' are entrusted to our souls?

104

What are some wonders of God's bounty entrusted to your soul?

Does 'ridding yourself of attachment to all created things' mean that you have to get rid of or push away all the lovely material things in life? Or could it mean not to allow our 'attachments' to stop us from developing our souls or to distract us from our purpose (which is Love, not just love)?

A true knowledge of which aspect of our selves – our physical or our spiritual natures – would be the same as the comprehension of God's own Being?

MEMORIZE

> Turn thy sight unto thyself, that thou mayst find Me standing within thee, mighty, powerful, and self-subsisting.
>
> Bahá'u'lláh, *Hidden Words*, Arabic no. 13

POINTS TO PONDER

How do you 'Turn thy sight unto thyself' and find God 'standing within thee'?

Is there a 'spiritual' sight that doesn't require our physical eyes and doesn't look at physical things?

Are you able to 'see' love with this spiritual sight, even though it seems invisible materially?

What do you 'look for' when you are searching for God?

How will you know when you find God within?

EXERCISE

See how many attributes of God you can think of and write them in your journal.

5

Who am I, Anyway?

INTRODUCTION

Horace Holley, in the introduction to his book *Religion for Mankind*, says: 'For religion in its purity reveals God, and only God can reveal man to himself.' This is a good sentence to remember. If it weren't for true religion, we would not even have formed the concept of good and evil, right and wrong because we would still be in an animal state – unspiritualized and uncivilized, unaware of ourselves.

   Notice that Holley says 'religion in its purity'. 'Abdu'l-Bahá explains that 'when we speak of religion, we mean the essential foundation or reality of religion, not the dogmas and blind imitations which have gradually encrusted it and which are the cause of the decline and effacement of a nation' ('Abdu'l-Bahá, *Promulgation of Universal Peace*, p. 363).

POINTS TO PONDER

Discuss what 'the essential foundation or reality of religion' means. Does it mean the teachings and lives of the Manifestations of God? Does it include the divisions and human-added ideas about what those teachings mean?

How do dogmas and blind imitations cause the decline of a nation?

What happens to morals and virtues such as trustworthiness and kindness when religion's real meaning is lost or buried under the rust of man-made ideas, petty arguments and separations?

What happens when people adopt a religion just because their parents did or it looks good or it's a good way to meet people? Can the religion help them develop spiritually if they're only participating for those reasons, or is that putting religion on the same level as a card game – nice, but it won't change your life? If you go to school just because you have to and you never study or listen to the lessons, can you benefit from going to school?

VIEWPOINT

Without teachers, we couldn't be trained or develop. This is true of our physical, mental *and* spiritual powers. Religion is our spiritual school and the Manifestations of God are our spiritual Teachers. If we did not have these Teachers, we wouldn't know of our true, spiritual selves. If we only know our lower/animal nature, we never develop fully as human beings. By sending us spiritual Teachers, God shows us who we really are.

Without true religion, humanity would remain in the animal state. Humanity in its animal state is much more dangerous than other animals because humans have the higher powers, such as thought and comprehension. These powers allow humans to be extremely destructive when they aren't trained and developed properly.

READING

If the animals are savage and ferocious, it is simply a means for their subsistence and preservation. They are deprived of that degree of intellect which can reason and discriminate between right and wrong, justice and injustice; they are justified in their actions and not responsible. When man is ferocious and cruel toward his fellowman, it is not for subsistence or safety. His motive is selfish advantage and wilful wrong. It is neither seemly nor befitting that such a noble creature, endowed with intellect and lofty thoughts, capable of wonderful achievements and discoveries in sciences and arts, with potential for ever higher perceptions and the accomplishment of divine purposes in life, should seek the blood of his fellowmen . . .'

'Abdu'l-Bahá, *Promulgation of Universal Peace*, p. 352

What is the difference between a savage animal and a savage human being?

Why is more expected of a human?

Religion is not something you *believe*: it is something that you *live* every day. Religion is the cause of civilization and the foundation of all human virtues. Religion's purpose is to educate, inspire and attract us to love, to guide us in its proper expression, to provide for its expansion and preservation and to remove all the barriers to the awareness of love's presence.

Kahlil Gibran, a mystic poet and author, knew and loved 'Abdu'l-Bahá and spent much time with Him and the Bahá'ís in New York City. Gibran said of 'Abdu'l-Bahá: 'For the first time I saw form noble enough to be the receptacle for [the] Holy Spirit!' (Quoted in Honnold, *Vignettes*, p. 178).

In his book, *The Prophet*, Gibran writes about religion.

> And an old priest said, Speak to us of Religion.
> And he said:
> Have I spoken this day of aught else?
> Is not religion all deeds and all reflection,
> And that which is neither deed nor reflection, but a wonder and a surprise ever springing in the soul, even while the hands hew the stone or tend the loom?
> Who can separate his faith from his actions, or his belief from his occupations?
> Who can spread his hours before him, saying, 'This for God and this for myself; This for my soul, and this other for my body?
> All your hours are wings that beat through space from self to self.
> He who wears his morality but as his best garment were better naked.

The wind and the sun will tear no holes in his skin.

And he who defines his conduct by ethics imprisons his song-bird in a cage.

The freest song comes not through bars and wires.

And he to whom worshipping is a window, to open but also to shut, has not yet visited the house of his soul whose windows are from dawn to dawn.

Your daily life is your temple and your religion.

Whenever you enter into it take with you your all.

Take the plough and the forge and the mallet and the lute,

The things you have fashioned in necessity or for delight.

For in revery you cannot rise above your achievements nor fall lower than your failures.

And take with you all men:

For in adoration you cannot fly higher than their hopes nor humble yourself lower than their despair.

And if you would know God be not therefore a solver of riddles.

Rather look about you and you shall see Him playing with your children.

And look into space; you shall see Him walking in the cloud, outstretching His arms in the lightning and descending in rain.

You shall see Him smiling in flowers, then rising and waving His hands in trees.

Gibran, *The Prophet*, pp. 84–6

MEMORIZE

Is not the object of every Revelation to effect a transformation in the whole character of mankind, a transformation that shall manifest itself both outwardly and inwardly, that shall affect both its inner life and external conditions? For if the character of mankind be not changed, the futility of God's universal Manifestation would be apparent.

Bahá'u'lláh, quoted in Shoghi Effendi, *World Order of Bahá'u'lláh*, p. 25

The word 'Revelation' in this context can refer to two levels of Divine Revelation: one is the Revelation of the Manifestation to humanity as a whole, the other takes place within each individual's heart whenever it is turned with intention to the Manifestation and filled with the appreciation of His attributes.

POINTS TO PONDER

What is a Revelation? What happens when something is revealed?

Why do you think that it's capitalized here?

What do you think 'the character of mankind' is? Is mankind's character suffering from a lack of guidance right now? How?

Do the Manifestations of God force people to make changes or do they attract hearts so that people choose for themselves to grow and develop?

How do you think a transformation of the character of mankind will affect people's inner lives? Give two examples.

How do you think a transformation of the character of mankind will affect external conditions? Give an example.

MEMORIZE

'Abdu'l-Bahá tells us that

> The purpose of the appearance of the Manifestations of God is the training of the people. That is the only result of Their mission, the real outcome.
> 'Abdu'l-Bahá, *Promulgation of Universal Peace*, p. 437

training to draw, to entice or attract, rear and instruct; to drill. Training is *never* passive and is *always* a process; one can't be trained without actively and consciously participating.

VIEWPOINT

Some of the processes Bahá'u'lláh trains us in are:

1. Learning that our purpose is love and unity

2. How to remove our ego-generated perceptions of separation

3. How to expand and develop appropriate, all-inclusive and beneficial expressions of love and unity in our lives every day.

It's all about love, it's all process, and there's only now. Don't worry about what you've done or will do – or how you've done or will do it – just be loving now.

MEMORIZE

Shoghi Effendi explains:

> Self has really two meanings, or is used in two senses, in the Bahá'í writings; one is self, the identity of the individual created by God. This is the self mentioned in such passages as 'he hath known God who hath known himself, etc.' The other self is the ego, the dark, animalistic heritage each one of us has, the lower nature that can develop into a monster of selfishness, brutality, lust and so on. It is this self we must struggle against, or this side of our natures, in order to strengthen and free the spirit within us and help it to attain perfection.
>
> Shoghi Effendi, quoted in *Lights of Guidance*, p. 113

Shoghi Effendi, 'Abdu'l-Bahá's grandson, was named by Him as the Guardian of the Bahá'í Faith, the one to turn to for authoritative interpretation of the Bahá'í teachings and for infallible guidance to preserve the unity of the Faith.

infallible incapable of making a mistake; entirely dependable; incapable of failing; certain

READING

'Abdu'l-Bahá tells us:

> In man there are two natures; his spiritual or higher nature and his material or lower nature . . . In his material aspect he expresses untruth, cruelty and injustice; all these are the outcome of his lower nature. The attributes of his Divine nature are shown forth in love, mercy, kindness, truth and justice, one and all being expressions of his higher nature. Every good habit, every noble quality belongs to man's spiritual nature, whereas all his imperfections and sinful actions are born of his material nature. If a man's Divine nature dominates his human nature, we have a saint.
>
> Man has the power both to do good and to do evil; if his power for good predominates and his inclinations to do wrong are conquered, then man in truth may be called a saint. But if, on the contrary, he rejects the things of God and allows his evil passions to conquer him, then he is no better than a mere animal.
>
> 'Abdu'l-Bahá, *Paris Talks*, p. 60

EXERCISES

Give some examples of your lower nature's inclinations to do wrong ('wrong' and 'evil' could be anything loveless).

Give some examples of your higher, spiritual nature's inclinations.

STORY

When a reporter of the New York *Globe* visited 'Abdu'l-Bahá in Haifa, He gave her this message: 'Tell my followers that they have no enemies to fear, no foes to hate. Man's only enemy is himself.'

Honnold, *Vignettes*, p. 10

READING

Ultimately all the battle of life is within the individual.

Shoghi Effendi, in *Compilation of Compilations*, p. 12

POINTS TO PONDER

Discuss what you think Shoghi Effendi means in this quotation.

Does it indicate that we don't have to overcome or resist 'evil' anywhere but in our own character and choices?

How do we arm ourselves for this 'battle'? Are the laws and teachings of the Manifestations our weapons?

Do you think that we were given two natures so that we could get spiritual exercise and become strong?

If we didn't have any lower/material nature, what would happen to our special human gift of free will? Could it even exist?

Do animals have the ability and privilege to recognize and choose between right and wrong?

VIEWPOINT

If we didn't have free will, we could only *be*, we couldn't *become*.

Bahá'u'lláh asks us this question to help us be aware of the reality of human existence (remember this?):

> Dost thou reckon thyself a puny form,
> When within thee a universe is folded?'
>
> Quoted by Bahá'u'lláh in *Seven Valleys*, p. 34

POINTS TO PONDER

Here are some things to discuss and think about:

What could it mean, that within you is folded a *universe?* Do you think it's talking about your body or your spirit?

Remember the quotation that you memorized that begins, 'Turn thy sight unto thyself that thou mayst find Me standing within thee' as you think about this quotation.

The mystic poet Rúmí wrote a lovely verse about this. He says:

> I am so small I can barely
>   be seen.
> How can this great love be
>   inside me?
> Look at your eyes. They
>   are small,
> but they see enormous
>   things.

READING

Shoghi Effendi tells us:

> The more we search for ourselves, the less likely we are to find ourselves; and the more we search for God, and to serve our fellow-men, the more profoundly will we become acquainted with ourselves, and the more inwardly assured. This is one of the great spiritual laws of life.
>
> Shoghi Effendi, *Lights of Guidance*, pp. 114–15

MEMORIZE

In the *Four Valleys*, Bahá'u'lláh quotes from the Qur'án to warn us:

> And be ye not like those who forget God, and whom He hath therefore caused to forget their own selves. These are the wicked doers.
>
> Quoted by Bahá'u'lláh in *Four Valleys*, p. 52 (Qur'án 59:19)

wicked evil, depraved, bad, sinful, harmful, offensive

113

In your own words, explain what the above quotation means and give an example of how forgetting God could make you forget yourself and make you a 'wicked doer'. Write the example in your journal.

READING

Here's another quotation from the *Four Valleys* that seems to say something different:

> 'O my Lord, how shall we reach unto thee?' And the answer came, 'Leave thyself behind, and then approach Me.'
>
> Quoted by Bahá'u'lláh in *Four Valleys*, p. 55

POINTS TO PONDER

Is the 'self' referred to here the lower/ego nature? Can we approach God physically?

What do you do to 'leave [your]self behind' to approach God?

What does it mean to approach God?

Another way of thinking about finding yourself is to think about your self as a beautiful lamp:

- Can you really understand what you are if you don't let light shine through you?

VIEWPOINT

By letting God's light (the light of your higher/spiritual nature) shine through you, you can discover the reason you were given a physical body too. The lamp is nice but not much good if it doesn't give light. Life is about the light, not about messing with the lamp or making it fancier. When you're unhappy, you can bet you're looking at the lamp instead of the light.

6

Requisites of Spiritual Growth

INTRODUCTION

If we want to have healthy bodies, we have to eat enough of the right things and take enough exercise and rest. Physicians and nutritionists recommend that we eat certain amounts from each food group in order to obtain the balance of nutrients our bodies require to stay healthy. These are called the 'basic minimum daily requirements'. If we ignore these physical requirements long enough, we will suffer poor health.

We also need to have our spiritual 'minimum daily requirements' if we want to be spiritually healthy. The Universal House of Justice has outlined them for us (be sure to notice all the qualifiers, i.e. *pure-hearted* devotion).

READING

Bahá'u'lláh has stated quite clearly in His Writings the essential requisites for our spiritual growth, and these are stressed again and again by 'Abdu'l-Bahá in His Talks and Tablets.

One can summarize them briefly in this way:

1. The recital each day of one of the Obligatory Prayers with pure-hearted devotion.

2. The regular reading of the Sacred Scriptures, specifically at least each morning and evening, with reverence, attention and thought.

3. Prayerful meditation on the teachings, so that we may

See the section in this *User's Guide* regarding Obligatory Prayer

understand them more deeply, fulfil them more faithfully, and convey them more accurately to others.

4. Striving every day to bring our behaviour more into accordance with the high standards that are set forth in the Teachings.

5. Teaching the Cause of God.

6. Selfless service in the work of the Cause and in the carrying on of our trade or profession.

From a letter written on behalf of the Universal House of Justice to a National
Spiritual Assembly, in *Lights of Guidance*, p. 540

EXERCISE

Memorize the above requisites of spiritual growth. It might be helpful to think of the first three as inner or personal requirements and the last three as outer or social requirements. Be sure to notice *how* we should do these things.

VIEWPOINT

These six daily requisites for spiritual growth require the use of all of our capacities: our five physical senses, which we share with the animals, and our five spiritual senses. Knowing what these are and how to use and develop them is important to our well-being, material and spiritual, so keep reading!

7

Powers: Natural and Super-Natural

INTRODUCTION

When we discuss our two natures, we are referring to many powers and senses, all of which can be used to develop and express our loving capacity and to enhance our material life on earth. If you don't learn how you're supposed to use these powers and what they're for, you'll use them incorrectly: they won't be in your control, so they could cause sadness and harm to yourself and others, even if you don't intend it. Most of the sadness and harm done in the world is not intentional. Unless the intention is to love, we are not living a conscious, intentional life.

These powers are not 'good' or 'bad' in themselves. It is only the way that you use them that creates 'good' (those that we intend) or 'bad' (those that we didn't intend) outcomes. For example, think back to the car and driver. The car is a great tool – it allows you to travel, get to work, visit distant friends, etc. But if you aren't in control of it and someone gets run over, is the *car* 'bad'?

READING

In her diary, Juliet Thompson notes what 'Abdu'l-Bahá had to say about physical and spiritual development:

> We do not deprecate physical development, for the sound mind should work through a sound body, but We think that the people of the West are too much concerned with mere physical development. They forget the need of spiritual development . . .

Man thinks too much of perfecting the body . . . but of what use is it to him without the perfecting of the spirit? No matter how much he develops his muscles and sinews he will never become as strong as the ox, as brave as the lion or as big as the elephant! Physically he is an animal, yet inferior to the animals, for animals acquire their sustenance with the greatest ease, whereas man has to toil incessantly, to labour with infinite pain, for a mere livelihood. So, in the physical realm, the beast is nobler than man. But man is distinguished from the beast by his spiritual gifts and these he should develop with the other, *both together*. There should be the perfect balance, the spiritual *and* the physical. A man whose ideal side only is developed is also imperfect. We do not deprecate comfort. If I could find a better house than this I would certainly move into it. But man should not think of comfort alone . . .

Do you think if it had not been for spiritual assurance I could have been happy all those years in prison? Think of it, forty years! . . . forty years is the average American life. I spent My American life in prison. Yet all that time I was on the heights of happiness. Many believers in Persia have been forced to give up everything: their possessions, their families, and in the end, their lives, but they never lost their happiness.

Remember Christ, when they placed the crown of thorns on His head. At that very moment, as the thorns wounded His brow, He looked down the vista of the centuries and beheld innumerable kings bowing their jewelled crowns low before that crown of thorns. Do you think He did not *know*, that he could not *foresee?* . . . When they spat in the face of Christ . . . when they made a mock procession and carried Him around the streets, *He* felt no humiliation.

Diary of Juliet Thompson, pp. 341–3

The powers that we share with the animals are our physical/outer senses. These include sight, hearing, taste, touch and smell. These powers will die when our bodies die. They are tools to be used during our life on earth.

Discuss some ways our physical/outer powers can be misused and harm ourselves or others. Find at least two examples.

Imagine some good ways you can use and enjoy each of these powers. Find at least two examples.

VIEWPOINT

There are also five spiritual or inner powers that make us truly human and separate us from the animals. These prepare and enable us to attain the highest degrees of material and spiritual civilization. These are powers of the soul and will not disintegrate. The spiritual powers are also tools. They allow us to be happy, sad, mean, mad, kind, and enable us to learn, to love . . . to make choices! They are what make you a human *being*.

The spiritual/inner powers are:

1. The common faculty
2. Imagination
3. Thought
4. Comprehension
5. Memory

Super-natural powers
powers above the
ordinary powers of nature

The common faculty

The common faculty (sympathetic nervous system) is the intermediary (go-between) between the five physical senses and the inner powers; it conveys whatever the physical senses discern to the inner powers.

This is the faculty that allows our physical experiences to affect us spiritually, and vice versa. For instance, beautiful music, delightful fragrances and lovely surroundings all affect our spirits; however, even when we are deprived of material comfort and loveliness, our spirits can so affect us that we experience no discomfort or ugliness, even materially. We see people every day who share the same material environment but experience entirely different realities.

As this physical frame is the throne of the inner temple, whatever occurs to the former is felt by the latter. In reality that which takes delight in joy or is saddened by pain is the inner temple of the body, not the body itself. Since this physical body is the throne whereon the inner temple is established, God hath ordained that the body be preserved to the extent possible, so that nothing that causeth repugnance may be experienced. The inner temple beholdeth its physical frame, which is its throne. Thus, if the latter is accorded respect, it is as if the former is the recipient. The converse is likewise true.

There is a story that Muḥammad once stopped in the middle of revealing a passage because one of the believers near Him had dirty fingernails.

The Báb, *Selections from the Writings of the Báb*, p. 95

In His Most Holy Book, the *Kitáb-i-Aqdas*, and throughout His writings, Bahá'u'lláh speaks of the importance of fragrances, of cleanliness, music, beauty and nature – all physical things which greatly affect the spirit.

The power of the imagination

The power of the imagination conceives and forms images of things.

One of the spiritual powers is the power of imagination, the forming of pictures in the mind, the ability to create new images or ideas. This is an amazing power and, 'Abdu'l-Bahá tells us, one of the most difficult to train. With this glorious power we can create and uncover interior images of wonders (or horrors) and visions otherwise inconceivable; images of such a powerful reality that they affect us physically, emotionally and spiritually.

The imagination is the *source of* and *remedy for* most of our fears, delusions and spiritual challenges, as well as our ability to reach heights of certitude and joy.

Imagination is one of our greatest powers and a most difficult one to rule. Imagination is the father of superstition

. . . We are led astray by imagination, even in violation of will and reason. It is our test power. We are tested by our ability to control and subdue it . . . Imagination is our greatest misleader. We hold to it until it becomes fixed in memory. Then we hold to it the stronger, believing it to be fact. It is a great power of the soul but without value unless rightly controlled and guided.

'Abdu'l-Bahá quoted in Grundy, *Ten Days in the Light of 'Akká*, p. 30

POINTS TO PONDER

Does 'Abdu'l-Bahá say in the quotation above that what you *remember* about an experience may be created by your imagination?

When you look at some of your more painful experiences in this light, does it give you any ideas for re-viewing them and releasing their present negative effect on you?

VIEWPOINT

If we use this power in the wrong way (or simply don't steer it in the right way), we have 'vain imagination'.

vain not successful, not having the desired effect or the intended outcome; without real value; empty, worthless

Since these powers were given to us to enable us to know and love God and to carry forward an ever-advancing civilization, that must be the intended outcome and any other use of them could be considered 'vain'. Like using the airplane for a chicken coop (it works, but . . .).

POINTS TO PONDER

What were all of our spiritual and physical powers given to us for?

What does 'vain imagination' imply?

The power of thought

The power of thought reflects on the realities of things. Of thoughts, 'Abdu'l-Bahá says:

> The reality of man is his thought, not his material body. The thought force and the animal force are partners. Although man is part of the animal creation, he possesses a power of thought superior to all other created beings.
>
> If a man's thought is constantly aspiring towards heavenly subjects then does he become saintly; if on the other hand his thought does not soar, but is directed downwards to centre itself upon the things of this world, he grows more and more material until he arrives at a state little better than that of a mere animal.
>
> Thoughts may be divided into two classes:
>
> (1st) Thought that belongs to the world of thought alone.
> (2nd) Thought that expresses itself in action.
>
> Some men and women glory in their exalted thoughts, but, if these thoughts never reach the plane of action they remain useless: the power of thought is dependent on its manifestation in deeds.
>
> 'Abdu'l-Bahá, *Paris Talks*, pp. 17–18

POINT TO PONDER

Does all action require getting up and moving around, or can an *attitude* of love – a smile or the warmth of one's voice – be an action?

READING

From the Buddhist teachings:

> We are what we think,
>   having become what we thought,

Like the wheel that follows the cart-pulling ox,
Sorrow follows an evil thought.

And joy follows a pure thought,
    like a shadow faithfully tailing a man.
We are what we think,
    having become what we thought.

How will hate leave him if a man forever thinks,
'He abused me, he hit me, he defeated me, he robbed
    me'?

Will hate ever touch him if he does not think,
'He abused me, he hit me, he defeated me, he robbed me'?

There is only one eternal law:
Hate never destroys hate; only love does.

Dhammapada, quoted in Jurney, Gems of Guidance, pp. 69–70

The power of comprehension

The power of comprehension comprehends the reality of things.

VIEWPOINT

Our capacity for comprehension develops greatly as we apply all of our powers to our spiritual development. 'Abdu'l-Bahá says,

> . . . no happiness is sweeter than spiritual comprehension of the divine teachings.
>
> 'Abdu'l-Bahá, Promulgation of Universal Peace, p. 460

POINTS TO PONDER

Is our capacity for comprehension of the reality of things affected by the other spiritual powers, i.e. will what we understand about something depend upon what we think, imagine and/or remember?

Could this be why we're told to leave behind all acquired knowledge and ideas if we are to experience the reality of the Presence of God?

In my solitude
I have seen things very
    clearly
that were not true.
Antonio Machado

The power of memory

The power of memory retains and stores whatever a person imagines, thinks and comprehends.

It's important to remember that memory is entirely subjective and depends on your focus: what you remember is no more than what you perceived at the time of your experience. Think of your memory as a video camera. It only records what you point it at and even then the picture is filtered through your expectations – your thoughts, which create your reality. This is helpful to know because if you are experiencing blockages to your loving capacity owing to memories of loveless experiences in the past, you can learn to change how you experience those events in the present by changing your perception of them. More later. Remember: God is love, therefore love is the only true reality.

It's all about love; it's all process; there is only *now*. There will, in fact, never, *ever* come a time that isn't *now*.

We re-create the past with what we choose to focus our memory on, which becomes how we (re)experience our past – the reality of which is only in our memory now – and we build our future now with our focus (perceptions, expectations, intentions, beliefs). Every thought and memory and imagination prepares our minds to receive what we perceive. The trick is to focus this power of recall on what will preserve the past so it enriches the present and improves the future.

> You walking, your footprints *are*
>   the road, and nothing else;
>   there is no road, walker,
>   you make the road by walking.
> By walking you make the road,
>   and when you look backward,
>   you see the path that your feet

For more on spiritual/inner powers see 'Abdu'l-Bahá, *Some Answered Questions*, pp. 210–11

☺ You can start building memories *right now*, memories of being with Bahá'u'lláh and 'Abdu'l-Bahá.

124

will never step on again.
        There *is* no road,
            only wind-trails on the sea.
Antonio Machado

POINTS TO PONDER

How would the world be different today if all of us knew how to
– and chose to! – use our powers properly?

Does it do any good to know what these powers are for if you
still don't use them properly? if your daily actions don't change?

Just as you can't decide how anyone else can use his powers,
you are the only one who can decide how you will use your powers.

EXERCISES

Think about one day in your life and how it would be different if
everyone were using their powers to be loving and kind: discuss
or write in your journal.

Think about times when your inner/spiritual powers made you
sad, or angry or scared, etc. If you are in a class, discuss this. If
you aren't write about this in your journal.

☺ Now, when someone says, 'It's all in your head,' you'll agree – that's the *only* place something has the power to do great harm or great good for you! If it's negative, how much better to have it out there breaking down your door.

Now discuss how you could have changed each experience to
one that would make you feel stronger, happier, kinder, etc. by
using these same spiritual powers.

Practice some possible ways of using these powers to deal with
things that have been difficult for you in the past. Write down
one thing that you *will* change.

READINGS

All souls come into this world through the Bounty of God
and have equal right of Development. The soul is affected by
its hereditary qualities, but no matter what its condition, it
never loses the possibility of being quickened by the Fire of

the Spirit of God. One brain may work quicker than another; one soul may acquire intelligence easier than another; but the power and presence of the Spirit does not depend upon mental capacity . . . The soul or mental intelligence awakes in the mother's womb. Spirit enters when the conscience is quickened and the soul awakes to eternal Realities . . . Therefore, as all souls have capacity for enkindlement by the Spirit and as we may all be assisted by Its Divine Power, we must *will* to receive it.

'Abdu'l-Bahá quoted in Grundy, *Ten Days in the Light of 'Akká*, p. 42

Unless a man give his whole thought to a subject, he cannot comprehend it fully. He must give his mind to the thing, be free, and then he will understand it. You will know it fully. When a pupil enters the school first, he will not understand a thing at all, but when he persists in his studies, he will learn his first lessons. Even so it is with the Kingdom of God. When a person enters, when he concentrates his thought and is steadfast, he will learn good lessons, very good lessons indeed.

'Abdu'l-Bahá quoted in Brown, *Memories of 'Abdu'l-Bahá*, p. 83

The understanding of His words and the comprehension of the utterances of the Birds of Heaven are in no wise dependent upon human learning. They depend solely upon purity of heart, chastity of soul, and freedom of spirit.

Bahá'u'lláh, *Kitáb-i-Íqán*, p. 211

STORY

While 'Abdu'l-Bahá was in London He stayed at the home of Lady Blomfield, where He met many important personages and received visitors.

. . . a man, obviously battered by the world, came . . . without prior appointment. He had walked thirty miles to be there, and asked to see Lady Blomfield. He had a tragic tale to tell: 'I was not always as you see me now, a disreputable, hopeless object. My father is a country rector and I had the advantage of being at a public school. Of the various causes which led to my arrival at the Thames embankment as my only home, I need not speak to you. Last evening I had decided to put an end to my futile, hateful life, useless to God and man. Whilst taking what I had intended should be my last walk, I saw 'a Face' in the window of a newspaper shop. I stood looking at the face as if rooted to the spot. He seemed to speak to me, and call me to him. I read that he is here, in this house. I said to myself, 'If there is in existence on earth that personage, I shall take up again the burden of my life' . . . 'Is he here? Will he see me? Even me?' Lady Blomfield said that of course He would.

'Abdu'l-Bahá Himself opened the door to the wretched tramp, His hand extended, His welcome warm and affectionate. Every word, every gesture indicated that 'Abdu'l-Bahá was indeed pleased and delighted to have this unexpected visitor. Other visitors, suitably dressed for a social call, looked surprised and astonished. The tramp, his head bowed, sat on a low chair next to 'Abdu'l-Bahá, Who took his hand and stroked his matted hair, and spoke to him: 'Be happy! Be happy! Do not be filled with grief when humiliation overtaketh thee. The bounty and power of God is without limit for each and every soul in the world. Seek for spiritual joy and knowledge, then, though thou walk upon this earth, thou wilt be dwelling within the divine realm. Though thou be poor, thou mayest be rich in the Kingdom of God.'

When the man rose to go, he was no longer a dejected tramp. To Lady Blomfield he said: 'Please write down for me His words. I have attained all I expected, and even more.'

Balyuzi, 'Abdu'l-Bahá, pp. 345–6

VIEWPOINT

A good way to be sure you learn to apply these powers appropriately is by learning how to practise some of the six daily requisites for spiritual growth. Once you've attained *knowledge* of your spiritual nature, *volition* to have it develop and unfold, and are *willing* to take *action*, the most effective beginning is probably in getting to know your higher/spiritual self through meditation and prayer: to learn to experience 'that mystic feeling that unites man with God' whenever you will it.

POINTS TO PONDER

Is it possible for *everyone* to unfold and develop spiritually?

Do you have to be clever or born into a nice, educated family for this to happen?

Will this enkindlement just happen to you, or must you do something?

Section IV

Meditation and Prayer

I

Meditate? Me?

What would I have to do? Chant or wear weird clothes? Sit in odd positions? You could. However, Shoghi Effendi tells us:

READINGS

There are no set forms of meditation prescribed in the teachings, no plan, as such, for inner development. The friends are urged – nay enjoined – to pray, and they also should meditate, but the manner of doing the latter is left entirely to the individual . . .

The inspiration received through meditation is of a nature that one cannot measure or determine. God can inspire into our minds things that we had no previous knowledge of, if He desires to do so.

Shoghi Effendi, *Lights of Guidance*, pp. 455–6

One hour's reflection is preferable to seventy years of pious worship.

Quoted by Bahá'u'lláh in *Kitáb-i-Íqán*, p. 238

Verily, by His remembrance the eye is cheered and the heart is filled with delight.

Bahá'u'lláh, *Kitáb-i-Aqdas*, para. 31

Bahá'u'lláh says there is a sign (from God) in every phenomenon: the sign of the intellect is contemplation and the sign of contemplation is silence, because it is impossible for a man to do two things at one time – he cannot both speak and meditate.

'Contemplation' comes from the root words that mean 'to build the temple'. When you contemplate, think of it as building a place of worship in your mind and heart.

It is an axiomatic fact that while you meditate you are speaking with your own spirit. In that state of mind you put certain questions to your spirit and the spirit answers: the light breaks forth and the reality is revealed.

You cannot apply the name 'man' to any being void of this faculty of meditation; without it he would be a mere animal, lower than the beasts.

Through the faculty of meditation man attains to eternal life; through it he receives the breath of the Holy Spirit – the bestowal of the Spirit is given in reflection and meditation.

The spirit of man is itself informed and strengthened during meditation; through it affairs of which man knew nothing are unfolded before his view. Through it he receives Divine inspiration, through it he receives heavenly food.

Meditation is the key for opening the doors of mysteries. In that state man abstracts himself: in that state man withdraws himself from all outside objects; in that subjective mood he is immersed in the ocean of spiritual life and can unfold the secrets of things-in-themselves. To illustrate this, think of man as endowed with two kinds of sight; when the power of insight is being used the outward power of vision does not see.

This faculty of meditation frees man from the animal nature, discerns the reality of things, puts man in touch with God.

This faculty brings forth from the invisible plane the sciences and arts. Through the meditative faculty inventions are made possible, colossal undertakings are carried out; through it governments can run smoothly. Through this faculty man enters into the very Kingdom of God.

Nevertheless some thoughts are useless to man; they are like waves moving in the sea without result. But if the faculty of meditation is bathed in the inner light and characterized with divine attributes, the results will be confirmed.

The meditative faculty is akin to the mirror; if you put it before earthly objects it will reflect them. Therefore if the spirit of man is contemplating earthly subjects he will be informed of these.

But if you turn the mirror of your spirits heavenwards, the heavenly constellations and the rays of the Sun of Reality will be reflected in your hearts, and the virtues of the Kingdom will be obtained.

Therefore let us keep this faculty rightly directed – turning it to the heavenly Sun and not to earthly objects – so that we may discover the secrets of the Kingdom, and comprehend the allegories of the Bible and the mysteries of the spirit.

May we indeed become mirrors reflecting the heavenly realities, and may we become so pure as to reflect the stars of heaven.

'Abdu'l-Bahá, Paris Talks, pp. 174–6

MEMORIZE

Turn your faces away from the contemplation of your own finite selves and fix your eyes upon the Everlasting Radiance; then will your souls receive in full measure the Divine power of the Spirit and the Blessings of the Infinite Bounty.

'Abdu'l-Bahá, Paris Talks, p. 166

POINT TO PONDER

What do you understand by the words 'faces' and 'eyes' in this quotation?

VIEWPOINT

Meditation, as described by Bahá'u'lláh, requires only two simple things:

- silence

- speaking with your own spirit

The first requirement is silence. Meditation is *not* a team sport. Each of us needs to meditate in private without distractions (such as the TV, intruding voices or music). Find the quiet place inside yourself where you can be silent and peaceful. Everyone has this place, so if you can't find it right away, just keep trying. This is where you go to experience being in God's Presence – your contact point with your true self, where your nobility and highest aspirations reside. Practise doing this – it gets much easier if you practise it every day.

Here's a lovely poem by Rilke to remind us not to *grasp* at answers and truths:

Be patient toward all
that is unsolved in your
heart
and try to love
the questions themselves
like locked rooms
or books that are written
in a foreign tongue.

The point is
to live everything.
Live the questions now.

Perhaps you will then
gradually,
without noticing it,
live your way
some distant day
into the answers.

Rainer Maria Rilke

☺ The actor/director Woody Allen says that 90% of life is just showing up. True: you must be conscious and present to partake of it.

I am trying to cultivate a lifestyle that does not require my presence.

Cartoonist Gary Trudeau

Jalálu'd-Dín Rúmí, the greatest of all Persian mystic poets, wrote these lines to describe how to reach this state of meditative silence and attraction:

> In thy soul of love build thou a fire
> And burn all thoughts and words entire.
>
> Rúmí quoted by Bahá'u'lláh in *Seven Valleys*, p. 28

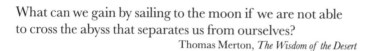

VIEWPOINT

The second step in meditation is speaking with your own spirit (your higher/spiritual nature).

> What can we gain by sailing to the moon if we are not able
> to cross the abyss that separates us from ourselves?
>
> Thomas Merton, *The Wisdom of the Desert*

In this state we do not require anything else to fulfil and complete us.

> *Enough.* These few words are enough.
> If not these words, this breath.
> If not this breath, this sitting here.
> This opening to the life
> we have refused
> again and again
> until now.
> Until now.
>
> David Whyte

If you can worry, you can meditate: worrying is a form of not-necessarily-beneficially-directed meditation whereby you focus on a single point, forgetting or ignoring everything else around you. Now, every time you notice that you're worrying, be gratefully reminded that you know how to meditate and can focus on strength and love instead of weakness and fear.

Next time you notice that you're worrying, what can you do? If you're feeling weak and fearful, what attributes can you focus on for relief?

2

'Speak to My Spirit'
(What Does It Mean?)

INTRODUCTION

'Could ye but apprehend', Bahá'u'lláh tells us, 'with what wonders of My munificence and bounty I have willed to entrust your souls, ye would, of a truth, rid yourselves of attachment to all created things, and would gain a true knowledge of your own selves – a knowledge which is the same as the comprehension of Mine own Being' (Bahá'u'lláh, *Gleanings*, pp. 326–7).

So speaking to our own spirits – our higher nature – through prayer and meditation is how we commune with God and get to know what wonders are in our souls.

commune to have close, intimate communication; to share; feel in close touch with

In meditation, you take the time to turn the mirror of your heart to the sunshine of God's love and presence within you. When you do this, you don't have to *make* the mirror shine – it will automatically glow. You won't have to wonder whether God loves you – you will be absolutely certain. The mirror doesn't have to wonder whether it's turned to the sun or not: either there's light or there's not!

VIEWPOINT

All it takes to have His attributes appear in you – to attain His Presence – is to turn the mirror of your heart to Him and let it glow! By meditating on His attributes, they appear in your heart. Notice that these are not referred to as *your* attributes – the only way you can have them is by *reflecting* them, and as often as you choose to reflect them and reflect upon them, you'll have them.

What are some of the attributes of God?

What do you have to do to have these attributes appear in you?

Do they 'appear in you' when you imagine, think about or remember them with consciousness and intention?

Do you have to be a perfect person to attain the Presence of the Beloved?

READING

In the *Hidden Words* we read:

> *O Son of Love!*
> Thou art but one step away from the glorious heights above and from the celestial tree of love. Take thou one pace and with the next advance into the immortal realm and enter the pavilion of eternity. Give ear then to that which hath been revealed by the pen of glory.
>
> Bahá'u'lláh, *Hidden Words*, Persian no. 7

POINT TO PONDER

Could the two steps of meditation be a way of understanding the two steps mentioned in this Hidden Word?

3

What Is *Prayer?*

INTRODUCTION

Prayer, 'Abdu'l-Bahá says, is 'conversation with God' (quoted in *Lights of Guidance*, p. 541, no. 1836).

Conversation means 'friendly talk' or 'the informal exchange of ideas using spoken words'. There are always at least two sides to a conversation.

POINTS TO PONDER

What do you like about conversations?

How do you like the other person to treat you?

Suppose the other person talks and asks you for things but doesn't pay any attention when you try to speak to him or her – or he doesn't even stop talking long enough to see if you're listening. Is that really conversation?

If you do that when you talk to God, are you having a conversation?

Now suppose that you're with a really good friend and you seem to know what each other feels, sometimes even without words. Is that conversation?

Can you have a conversation with someone who doesn't speak your language? Can you become friends, get to know each other, and share ideas and information anyway?

How can we have a conversation with God?

READINGS

Hearing God's side of the conversation:

> . . . we must not be rigid about praying; there is not a set of
> rules governing it; the main thing is we must start out with
> the right concept of God, the Manifestation, the Master, the
> Guardian – we can turn, in thought, to anyone of them
> when we pray. For instance you can ask Bahá'u'lláh for
> something, or thinking of Him, ask God for it. The same is
> true of the Master or the Guardian. You can turn in thought
> to either of them and then ask their intercession, or pray
> direct to God. As long as you don't confuse their stations,
> and make them all equal, it does not matter how you orient
> your thoughts.
>
> From a letter written on behalf of Shoghi Effendi, *Lights of Guidance*, p. 456

Why pray? 'Abdu'l-Bahá wrote to an American believer:

> As to thy question, 'Why pray? What is the wisdom thereof,
> for God has established everything and executes all affairs
> after the best order and He ordains everything according to
> a becoming measure and puts things in their places with the
> greatest propriety and perfection – therefore what is the
> wisdom in beseeching and supplicating and in stating one's
> wants and seeking help?' Know thou, verily, it is becoming of
> a weak one to supplicate to the strong One and it behoveth a
> seeker of bounty to beseech the glorious, bountiful One.
> When one supplicates to his Lord, turns to Him and seeks
> bounty from His ocean this supplication is by itself a light to
> his heart, an illumination to his sight, a life to his soul and an
> exaltation to his being.
>
> Therefore during thy supplications to God and thy
> reciting, 'Thy name is my healing', consider how thy heart is
> cheered, thy soul delighted by the spirit of the love of God
> and thy mind attracted to the kingdom of God! By these
> attractions one's ability and capacity increase. When the
> vessel is widened the water increaseth and when the thirst
> grows the bounty of the cloud becomes agreeable to the
> taste of man. This is the mystery of supplication and the
> wisdom of stating one's wants.

'Abdu'l-Bahá also said,

> God will answer the prayer of every servant if that prayer is
> urgent.
>
> Honnold, Vignettes, p. 147

POINTS TO PONDER

What is the 'mystery of supplication and the wisdom of stating
one's wants'?

What do these attractions bring about?

READINGS

Bahá'u'lláh pleads for us to come near and commune with Him
in this Hidden Word:

> *O Moving Form of Dust!*
> I desire communion with thee, but thou wouldst put no trust
> in Me. The sword of thy rebellion hath felled the tree of thy
> hope. At all times I am near unto thee, but thou art ever far
> from Me. Imperishable glory I have chosen for thee, yet
> boundless shame thou hast chosen for thyself. While there is
> yet time, return, and lose not thy chance.
>
> Bahá'u'lláh, Hidden Words, Persian no. 21

communion sharing; a mutual participation in anything; interchange of thoughts, purposes, etc.; fellowship. This is conversation and more – this is friendship and comfortable, familiar companionship

> There is very little Divine love in the world to-day, but a great
> deal of intellectual reasoning, which is an entirely different
> thing, and springs from the mind and not the heart . . . We
> liken God to the Sun, which gives us all our life. So the Spirit
> of God reaches us through the Souls of the Manifestations.
> We must learn to commune with Their Souls . . . This is the
> true mysticism, and the secret, inner meaning of life which
> humanity has at present, drifted so far from.
>
> Shoghi Effendi, Unfolding Destiny, pp. 406–7

POINTS TO PONDER

If you *know* that God wishes to commune with you, and you

prefer to fill your time with everything *but* communing with God, what are the consequences of your choice?

When you spend your reflective powers and energy worrying and fretting about things instead of experiencing the ecstasy and love of God, what choices are you making and what will be the effect in your life?

What does Bahá'u'lláh mean by the word 'return', in His quotation above?

The measurement of time has to do with the material world. During your life on earth, there is a concept of time and you are given free will. Are you going to run out of time and free will before you begin to develop and enjoy your loving capacities?

READING

'Abdu'l-Bahá says:

> When we pray to God a feeling fills our hearts. This is the language of the spirit which speaks to God.
>   When in prayer we are freed from all outward things and turn to God, then it is as if in our hearts we heard the voice of God. Without words we speak, we communicate, we converse with God and hear the answer.
>
> <div align="right">'Abdu'l-Bahá quoted in Moffett, <i>Du'a</i>, p. 58</div>

POINTS TO PONDER

How do you think you 'free yourself from all outward things'?

Do you find that when you are very interested in something (a book, a TV show, your own thoughts, a conversation, making something, etc.), you don't notice that all sorts of things are going on around you? Why does this happen? Is this similar to being 'freed from all outward things' when in prayer?

When 'Abdu'l-Bahá was in New York, He called to Him an ardent Bahá'í and said, 'If you will come to Me at dawn tomorrow, I will teach you to pray.'

Delighted, Mr M arose at four and crossed the city, arriving for his lesson at six. With what exultant expectation he must have greeted this opportunity! He found 'Abdu'l-Bahá already at prayer, kneeling by the side of the bed. Mr M followed suit, taking care to place himself directly across.

Seeing that 'Abdu'l-Bahá was quite lost in His Own reverie, Mr M began to pray silently for his friends, his family and finally for the crowned heads of Europe. No word was uttered by the quiet Man before him. He went over all the prayers he knew then, and repeated them twice, three times – still no sound broke the expectant hush.

Mr M surreptitiously rubbed one knee and wondered vaguely about his back. He began again, hearing as he did so, the birds heralding the dawn outside the window. An hour passed, and finally two. Mr M was quite numb now. His eyes, roving along the wall, caught sight of a large crack. He dallied with a touch of indignation but let his gaze pass again to the still figure across the bed.

The ecstasy that he saw arrested him and he drank deeply of the sight. Suddenly he wanted to pray like that. Selfish desires were forgotten. Sorrow, conflict, and even his immediate surroundings were as if they had never been. He was conscious of only one thing, a passionate desire to draw near to God.

Closing his eyes again he set the world firmly aside, and amazingly his heart teemed with prayer, eager, joyous, tumultuous prayer. He felt cleansed by humility and lifted by a new peace. 'Abdu'l-Bahá had taught him to pray!

The 'Master of 'Akká' immediately arose and came to him. His eyes rested smilingly upon the newly humbled Mr M. 'When you pray,' He said, 'you must not think of your aching body, nor of the birds outside the window, nor of the cracks in the wall!'

He became very serious then, and added, 'When you wish to pray you must first know that you are standing in the presence of the Almighty.'

Honnold, *Vignettes*, pp. 148–9

READINGS

'Abdu'l-Bahá tells us that

> Prayer is both attitude and word . . . It is like a song; both words and music make the song. Sometimes the melody will move us, sometimes the words.
>
> 'Abdu'l-Bahá, quoted in Moffett, *Du'a*, p. 55

'Attitude' is a way of thinking, acting or feeling; 'move' in this quotation means to stir a person's feelings.

'Abdu'l-Bahá said of the spirit of prayer:

> We are like flutes and all these tunes are from Him.
>
> 'Abdu'l-Bahá quoted in Ward, *239 Days*, p. 107

POINT TO PONDER

Can a flute play itself? Think about this beautiful metaphor.

VIEWPOINT

Bahá'u'lláh has given us many, many beautiful words to use in our prayers. His words are a great treasure. The writings of the Manifestations are the most important words we will ever read.

POINTS TO PONDER

But is just reading or saying these words *really* prayer?

Can these words be speaking 'the language of the spirit' even if we are not moved?

God hears the voice of your heart. Is it enough to *say* that you are happy and that you love Him, or will you communicate with Him better and receive your share of grace if you *feel* your love and gratitude and take the time to feel His love for you?

4

Speaking the 'Language of the Spirit'

INTRODUCTION

Just as it takes a lot of practice to learn any language, it takes practice to learn the 'language of the spirit' so that we can have a conversation with God whenever we wish.

Luckily, God – unlike your friends or your parents – is always there for you. All you have to do to be with Him is take the time to know you *are* with Him.

> I have put duality away,
> I have seen the two worlds are one;
> One I seek, One I know,
> One I see, One I call.
> He is the first, He is the last,
> He is the outward, he is the inward.
> Rúmí

MEMORIZE

> You are always in the Presence of God. Open the windows
> of your soul so *His* Presence may be within you.
> 'Abdu'l-Bahá, quoted in Grundy, *Ten Days in the Light of 'Akká*, p. 41

POINT TO PONDER

What can you do to 'open the windows of your soul'? Discuss and write an example in your journal.

To converse with God, you only need to be willing to concentrate your mind and heart on Him – it's always your choice. God will never force you to be aware of His Presence or to become spiritual in your outlook.

MEMORIZE

> God Himself cannot compel the soul to become spiritual. The exercise of a free human will is necessary.
>
> 'Abdu'l-Bahá quoted in Grundy, *Ten Days in the Light of 'Akká*, p. 6

> Will is the centre or focus of human understanding. We must *will* to know God . . . The will is what we do, the understanding is what we know. Will and understanding must be one in the Cause of God. Intention brings attainment.
>
> 'Abdu'l-Bahá quoted in Grundy, *Ten Days in the Light of 'Akká*, p. 31

> Be still, and know that I am God.
>
> Psalm 46:10

When you're feeling scared or distressed, try being still and thinking of God – it's the best (and sometimes the *only*) remedy.

VIEWPOINT

We've been given many powers as human beings: all of them are given to us by God to assist us to fulfil our purpose on earth which Bahá'u'lláh tells us is to know and worship God.

These powers can bring us happiness or make us miserable (as you've probably already noticed!). They can make us caretakers of the world or enable us to destroy it. If we don't learn what these powers are for, so that we can direct and apply them properly, it's as if we were riding in a speeding car with no driver.

Our powers *will* be used and expressed, so it's up to each of us to decide *how* we will use them. We can't just expect them to work properly; they must be trained and developed. To be happy, we need to learn to live with conscious intention. There won't ever be a time when we can quit our spiritual driving – who else would you want at the wheel of your experience of life?

. . . only in the remembrance of God can the heart find rest.

'Abdu'l-Bahá, *Selections from the Writings of 'Abdu'l-Bahá*, p. 96

5

Attaining the Presence of God

Bahá'u'lláh says:

> The purpose of God in creating man hath been, and will
> ever be, to enable him to know his Creator and to attain His
> Presence.
>
> Bahá'u'lláh, *Gleanings*, p. 70

EXERCISE

Here's a practical use for your imagination. Just imagine . . .

- your favourite person – from any time in your life – to be
  with or to visit.

- what this person is like and why you like him or her so
  much.

- you are with this person right now.

- what you feel like.

VIEWPOINT

When you imagine being in the presence of a friend, you don't
have any trouble knowing what it feels like because you've
already experienced it – you know the attributes of your friend.

Although we're always in the presence of God, we may not
have recognized His presence or experienced it consciously.

146

Imagining what it is like being in God's presence and seeking a God we have made up is a bit like worshipping an idol rather than God Himself. An imaginary friend is never as satisfying as a real friend, is it?

To be in God's presence, to have a 'conversation' in the 'language of the spirit', we need to know what God's attributes are and how to respond to His presence. We are told we can find God's presence within our own selves, so He can't be too far away! As Bahá'u'lláh says:

> Turn thy sight unto thyself, that thou mayest find Me standing within thee, mighty, powerful and self-subsisting.
>
> Bahá'u'lláh, *Hidden Words*, Arabic no. 13

READINGS

> Thou, both End and Origin
> Thou without and Thou within —
> From every eye Thou hidest well
> And yet in every eye dost dwell.
>
> Rúmí, quoted by 'Abdu'l-Bahá in *Memorials of the Faithful*, p. 31

> It is my hope that thou wilt attain unto the true meeting with Him, which is to behold Him with the inner, not the outer eye.
>
> 'Abdu'l-Bahá, *Selections from the Writings of 'Abdu'l-Bahá*, p. 66

> Turn to God, supplicate humbly at His threshold, seeking assistance and confirmation, that God may rend asunder the veils that obscure your vision. Then will your eyes be filled with illumination, face to face you will behold the reality of God and your heart become completely purified from the dross of ignorance, reflecting the glories and bounties of the Kingdom.
>
> 'Abdu'l-Bahá, *Promulgation of Universal Peace*, p. 293

POINTS TO PONDER

Could the 'dross of ignorance' disguise itself as knowledge?

Could your perception of 'reality' be a veil to your perceiving Reality?

What if you decide to try this – can it do any harm at all?

If you fear this experience, is it because your ego would experience it as a loss of control over your perceptions?

If 'Abdu'l-Bahá were still alive and you could visit Him, what would you do to prepare to be in His Presence?

How would you prepare your mind and heart?

What would it feel like to have Him loving you and so happy to see you – holding His arms open for you and saying, 'Welcome! Welcome!'?

VIEWPOINT

'Abdu'l-Bahá's perfect eye sees only your perfections: all else is overlooked as being part of the process, just as you take no notice of any lack of maturity in a child – it has no significance at all. You are seen, accepted and loved exactly as you are. He is with you right now. Allow yourself to experience 'Abdu'l-Bahá loving you *now*.

By using your imagination to focus your mind on 'Abdu'l-Bahá and His attributes, which are the attributes of God and which 'Abdu'l-Bahá showed in all His acts, your mind will not be as likely to want to wander away somewhere else or to keep chattering at you while you're conversing with God.

Bahá'u'lláh gave us 'Abdu'l-Bahá to demonstrate the attributes of God to us – to be our example of how God wants us to be. Being with 'Abdu'l-Bahá and feeling His attributes in your heart will help you become sure of God and His love for you.

READING

Shoghi Effendi mentions using one's imagination this way:

> If you find you need to visualize someone when you pray,
> think of the Master. Through Him you can address
> Bahá'u'lláh. Gradually try to think of the qualities of the

Manifestation, and in that way a mental form will fade out, for after all the body is not the thing, His Spirit is there and is the essential, everlasting element.

Shoghi Effendi quoted in *Lights of Guidance*, p. 458

EXERCISES

Practise feeling the attributes of 'Abdu'l-Bahá until you are sure He is with you in your heart. This will help you experience and learn the attitude of prayer.

Tell, or write in your journal, one of your favourite stories about 'Abdu'l-Bahá. Point out what attributes of God it demonstrates.

Reading and hearing stories about Bahá'u'lláh, Jesus and 'Abdu'l-Bahá, as well as about the heros, heroines and early believers of the Faith, will help you experience God's love. You will become more conscious and confident of God's love and will better understand how you can use your love for Him to be a happy, strong and secure human being.

6

Attitude

The attitude of prayer is very important.

Would you go to see and talk to a very special person without preparing yourself properly?

Before you pray and meditate, take a moment to prepare yourself physically and spiritually until you become aware that you are in God's Presence. Practise washing your heart and mind just as you wash your hands and face.

READING

> Prayer is communion with God . . . Its efficacy is conditional upon the freedom of the heart from extraneous suggestions and mundane thoughts. The worshipper must pray with a detached spirit, unconditional surrender of the will, concentrated attention and a magnetic spiritual passion.
>
> 'Abdu'l-Bahá, *Star of the West*, vol. 8, no. 4, p. 44

POINTS TO PONDER

What is prayer?

What are the conditions that make prayer effective?

Give some examples of extraneous suggestions and mundane thoughts.

How must the worshipper pray?

VIEWPOINT

What if you don't *feel* like praying?

Surely there are times when you don't feel like brushing your teeth, or looking both ways when you cross the street but you choose to do these things anyway because you know they're good for you, keep you safe, save you from pain.

When you don't feel like praying, remind yourself that it is good for *you* – for your own spiritual health and happiness. And just choose to do it!

READING

As to how to acquire it when you are not in a receptive mood and are immersed in worldly affairs, the Master said: 'Finally, the power of will may be depended upon to draw you into this condition or state of ecstasy. By force of will and effort of mind, man turns his attention to God, to His Knowledge, His wonderful creation, His wisdom, His Omnipotence; and then thinking deeply and fervently and frequently of Him, he attains at last to the state of love, of desire for prayer and finally of supreme ecstasy.'

'Abdu'l-Bahá, quoted in Moffett, *Do'a* [1933 ed.], pp. 81–2

ecstasy a state of exalted delight; a state of joy experienced very intensely; exaltation, rapture

POINT TO PONDER

What can you do if you don't feel like praying?

• Remember the quotation: 'as all souls have capacity for enkindlement by the Spirit and as we may all be assisted by Its Divine Power, we must *will* to receive it.'

'Abdu'l-Bahá quoted in Grundy, *Ten Days in the Light of 'Akká*, pp. 41–2

☺ Isn't it marvellous what complicated and perverse creatures we are that we require a *law* to remind us to experience ecstasy daily!

READINGS

Your deepest presence is in every small contracting
    and expanding
the two as beautifully balanced and coordinated
    as birdwings.
Muhammad says,

'I come before dawn
     to chain you and drag you off.'
It's amazing, and funny, that you have to be pulled away
     from being tortured, pulled out
into this Spring garden
     but that's the way it is.

Rúmí, The Essential Rumi, p. 174

To a correspondent, 'Abdu'l-Bahá wrote:

> Thou hast asked the wisdom of prayer. Know thou that
> prayer is indispensable and obligatory, and man under no
> pretext whatsoever is excused from performing the
> [obligatory] prayer unless he be mentally unsound, or an
> insurmountable obstacle prevent him. The wisdom of
> prayer is this: That it causeth a connection between the
> servant and the True One, because in that state (i.e. prayer)
> man with all heart and soul turneth his face towards His
> Highness the Almighty, seeking His association and desiring
> His love and compassion. The greatest happiness for a lover
> is to converse with his beloved, and the greatest gift for a
> seeker is to become familiar with the object of his longing;
> that is why with every soul who is attracted to the Kingdom
> of God, his greatest hope is to find an opportunity to entreat
> and supplicate before his Beloved, appeal for His mercy and
> grace and be immersed in the ocean of His utterance,
> goodness and generosity.
>
>   Besides all this, prayer . . . is the cause of awakening and
> mindfulness and conducive to protection and preservation
> from tests.

Honnold, Vignettes, p. 148

POINTS TO PONDER

Is it o.k. just to skip prayer if you're feeling pretty good and don't
have anything in particular to ask for anyway? Why?

Are spiritual laws as binding upon us as physical laws are?
Would you think it o.k. to disobey the law of gravity if you didn't
feel like you needed it?

Thinking of the things that we would do and the feelings we would have if we were going to see Bahá'u'lláh or 'Abdu'l-Bahá helps us get in the right spirit to be with them in prayer and meditation.

Bahá'u'lláh tells us in His Book of Laws (Kitáb-i-Aqdas) how important the spirit is:

> . . . were a man to read a single verse with joy and radiance it would be better for him than to read with lassitude all the Holy Books of God, the Help in Peril, the Self-Subsisting.
> Bahá'u'lláh, Kitáb-i-Aqdas, para. 149

lassitude a state of exhaustion; lack of energy; weariness

He also says in the *Hidden Words*:

> Rejoice in the gladness of thine heart, that thou mayest be worthy to meet Me and to mirror forth My beauty.
> Bahá'u'lláh, *Hidden Words*, Arabic no. 36

What does 'worthy' mean?

How can we be worthy to meet the source of love and purity if we must already be loving and pure?

Remember times when you have rejoiced.

Remember what it feels like to feel worthy.

Have you ever felt that you wouldn't be worthy to meet Bahá'u'lláh?

What do you think now?

To be worthy to meet Bahá'u'lláh, would you have to be very, very good, or would you only have to rejoice that God loves you and you love Him?

If you are angry or unhappy, are you able to mirror forth God's beauty?

Does this affect not only yourself but everyone you meet, and possibly even everyone they meet?

READING

> It is the Spirit behind the words which is really important.
> Shoghi Effendi, quoted in *Compilation of Compilations.* vol. 2, p. 341

POINTS TO PONDER

What does the word 'spirit' mean in these quotations?

Do you have the power to call forth this 'spirit' and to change your 'reality'?

VIEWPOINT

The point is the effect that prayer has on your spirit, thus on the transformation of your character, thus on the transformation of the world.

7

Reverence and Gratitude

Bahá'u'lláh's laws regarding prayer and meditation are to encourage us to make taking a 'paradise break' habitual.

Meditation and communion are our bridge between the limited, material world and the infinite, spiritual world. By practising daily we build confidence in this connection and experience the reality of powers and possibilities we could not otherwise imagine. We begin to set our priorities from our genuine values rather than from the suggestions of our fearful ego nature.

Reverence is showing with thoughts and actions that you have great respect for something; showing honour and awareness of the importance of something. Reverence is the quality of spirit that separates what is most important to and cherished by us from that which is ordinary and unworthy.

One important way to experience reverence is by being very still inside and allowing yourself to feel the love and beauty around you. If you take a little time every day consciously to practise reverence, you will be able to feel God's presence. Being present (it's all about love, it's all process and there is only now!) for communion removes you from the realm of the limited for a visit to the limitless. Reverence makes the experience of 'now' the experience of perfection. Every moment has the possibility of perfection, awaiting only our perception and awareness of it. Reverence is expressed in acts of kindness – even very small acts can be acts of reverence.

POINTS TO PONDER

Can just being still and feeling grateful be an *act* of reverence?

☺ Don't forget that you are a human *being*, not a human *doing*! Your state of *being* will determine the effectiveness and quality of your *doing*.

155

If you are filled with gratitude, is there any room for sadness or worry?

EXERCISES

Discuss how you would show reverence in the following situations (note that reverence is expressed differently in different cultures):

- during prayers

- when someone asks you to help with something that you don't really like doing

- when you have a picnic and have trash to dispose of

- when you are near a lovely garden

- when you're handling Bahá'í books

Write in your journal some ways you can develop your experience of reverence every day.

I pray that my capacity may be widened so that I may appreciate more and love more.

Juliet Thompson

VIEWPOINT

Gratitude is a feeling of thankfulness. If we don't feel gratitude, having every wonderful thing in the world is of no use. If you do something special for someone and he ignores it, don't you feel like he didn't *really* get it? The same is true if you don't appreciate something – especially if you don't appreciate the blessings God gives you.

POINTS TO PONDER

Think of a time when you felt very, very grateful. Did you feel happy and want to do nice things for others?

Is the feeling of gratitude *itself* a great blessing?

What can you do to increase your feelings of gratitude?

EXERCISE

Write two things in your journal that you can do every day to increase your feelings of gratitude.

VIEWPOINT

If you have no feelings of reverence and gratitude, you're not really conscious. With intention and effort, you will find that the state of reverence is so natural and so much a part of consciousness that you'll be amazed you were ever unaware of it. Without reverence and gratitude, you receive no benefits or blessings. Your reverence and gratitude create the value of anything – you, yourself, must realize (make real) the value.

Want your life to be filled with precious things and glorious moments? *Realize* that your life *is* filled with precious things and glorious moments.

realize to comprehend correctly; to make real or actualize; bring into reality

MEMORIZE

In this day, to thank God for His bounties consisteth in possessing a radiant heart, and a soul open to the promptings of the spirit. This is the essence of thanksgiving.
'Abdu'l-Bahá, *Selections from the Writings of 'Abdu'l-Bahá*, p. 179

If we are not happy and joyous at this season, for what other season shall we wait and for what other time shall we look?
'Abdu'l-Bahá in *Bahá'í World Faith*, p. 351

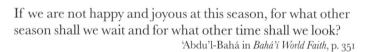

READING

As for offering thanks by speaking out or writing, although this is indeed acceptable, yet when compared with that other thanksgiving, it is only a semblance and unreal; for the essential thing is these intimations of the spirit, these emanations from the deep recess of the heart. It is my hope that thou wilt be favoured therewith.
'Abdu'l-Bahá, *Selections from the Writings of 'Abdu'l-Bahá*, p. 179

intimation hinted or indirect communication; suggestion, announcement, proclamation

emanation a coming forth as from a source or origin; something given out by a substance

157

Curtis Kelsey was in the Holy Land when 'Abdu'l-Bahá died. After Shoghi Effendi recovered from the initial shock of being appointed Guardian, he 'noticed Curtis in the street and asked that he join him in a walk on Mount Carmel Avenue, which led to the Shrine of the Báb'.

Curtis knew that it wasn't going to be an ordinary walk, for the young man walking beside him was now more than a faithful grandson of 'Abdu'l-Bahá: he was the Guardian. Maybe, he wondered, the Guardian would give him a special assignment, Curtis didn't know what to expect.

As they walked up the road, children were dancing in the shadows cast over the street by the floodlight perched at the base of the Shrine. Electricity was new to the people of Haifa. No one had it in their homes. Seeing shadows in the evening was odd; and the children turned them into a form of recreation. Of course, none of them knew that the man who made the shadows possible was in their midst and beside him was the 'sign of God' on earth.

As they walked up the mountain, Shoghi Effendi turned to Curtis and thanked him for the wonderful work he had done in installing the three electrical plants and pointed out how much the Master appreciated his efforts.

The praise made Curtis uncomfortable; and he blushed, saying, 'Well, Shoghi Effendi, I was very happy doing the work for the Master, and I want no credit.'

The Guardian stopped walking and looked into Curtis' eyes and said firmly, 'Nevertheless appreciation goes with your service.'

When Curtis tried to make light of his work, the Guardian grew firmer, making an issue of the importance of sincerely thanking a person for the services he renders. For Curtis it was an important lesson. After that experience, he always made sure to share his gratitude with the person who did work for him, however small the task.

Rutstein, *He Loved and Served*, pp. 104–5

We sometimes see in Bahá'í communities that services are overlooked or taken for granted. 'They should do it for Bahá'u'lláh', it is said, 'and not for praise or recognition.' Well, this is true, and they probably *did*. But as recipients of favours we should express loving thanks. It benefits everyone when sincere appreciation and gratitude are expressed. The gift – whatever it is, from a sunny morning to a worldly treasure – isn't truly received unless one gives thanks.

appreciation gratefulness or gratitude; an increase in value (does it increase your sense of value to be appreciated and to appreciate others?)

Lady Blomfield relates this story of 'Abdu'l-Bahá's time in London:

The following touching incident took place one day when we were seated at table with the Master.

A Persian friend arrived who had passed through 'Iṣhqábád. He presented a cotton handkerchief to 'Abdu'l-Bahá, Who untied it, and saw therein a piece of dry black bread, and a shrivelled apple.

The friend exclaimed: 'A poor Bahá'í workman came to me: "I hear thou goest into the presence of our Beloved. Nothing have I to send, but this my dinner. I pray thee offer it to Him with my loving devotion."'

'Abdu'l-Bahá spread the poor handkerchief before Him, leaving His own luncheon untasted. He ate of the workman's dinner, broke pieces off the bread, and handed them to the assembled guests, saying: 'Eat with me of this gift of humble love.'

Blomfield, The Chosen Highway, pp. 161–2

MEMORIZE

Render continual thanks unto God so that the confirmations of God may encircle you all.

'Abdu'l-Bahá, Promulgation of Universal Peace, p. 189

Be thou happy and well pleased and arise to offer thanks to God, in order that thanksgiving may conduce to the increase of bounty.

'Abdu'l-Bahá, Divine Art of Living, p. 52

POINTS TO PONDER

Where do you receive the 'confirmations of God'?

What are some examples of the confirmations of God?

See 'Angels' (= confirmations of God) in section 9.

Is thanksgiving *itself* a bounty and a blessing?

Does being thankful (filled with thanksgiving) increase our loving capacities?

Praise is simply drawing back the curtains
to let his qualities in
The sun,
of course, remains apart
from what I say.

What the sayer of praise is really praising is
himself, by saying implicitly,
'My eyes are clear.'

Likewise, someone who criticizes is criticizing
himself, saying implicitly, 'I can't see very well
with my eyes so inflamed.'
. . .

Awe is the salve
that will heal our eyes.

Rúmí

VIEWPOINT

The more we practise feeling reverence and gratitude, the more
we will find our lives filled with blessings and happiness. This is a
promise from God.

8

Different Ways to Pray

INTRODUCTION

There are many different kinds of prayer and ways of being in a prayerful state. The best prayer is when you're conversing with God just because you love Him and are feeling grateful that He loves you.

READINGS

In the highest prayer, men pray only for the love of God, not because they fear Him or hell, or hope for bounty or heaven . . . When a man falls in love with a human being, it is impossible for him to keep from mentioning the name of his beloved. How much more difficult is it to keep from mentioning the Name of God when one has come to love Him . . . The spiritual man finds no delight in anything save in commemoration of God.

'Abdu'l-Bahá, quoted in Esslemont, *Bahá'u'lláh and the New Era*, p. 90

> . . . if my human throat were not so narrow,
> I would praise you as you should be praised,
> in some language other than this word-language,
> but a domestic fowl is not a falcon.
> We must mix the varnish we have
> and brush it on.
>
> Rúmí

STORY

One day a despondent little Jewish girl, all in black, was brought into the Master's presence. With tears flowing, she told Him her tale of woes: her brother had been unjustly imprisoned three years before – he had four more years to serve; her parents were constantly depressed; her brother-in-law, who was their support, had just died. She claimed the more she trusted in God the worse matters became. She complained, '. . . my mother reads the Psalms all the time; she doesn't deserve that God should desert her so. I read the Psalms myself, – the ninety-first Psalm and the twenty-third Psalm every night before I go to bed. I pray too.'

Comforting and advising her, 'Abdu'l-Bahá replied, 'To pray is not to read Psalms. To pray is to trust in God, and to be submissive in all things to Him. Be submissive, then things will change for you. Put your family in God's hands. Love God's will. Strong ships are not conquered by the sea, – they ride the waves. Now be a strong ship, not a battered one.'

'Abdu'l-Bahá quoted in Honnold, *Vignettes*, pp. 132–3

READING

'Abdu'l-Bahá once posed the question, 'Why should it be necessary for [a person] to repeat prayers aloud and with the tongue?' He then answered:

> One reason for this is that if the heart alone is speaking, the mind can be more easily disturbed. But repeating the words so that the tongue and heart act together enables the mind to become concentrated. Then the whole man is surrounded by the spirit of prayer and the act is more perfect.
>
> 'Abdu'l-Bahá, *Star of the West*, vol. 8, no. 4, p. 46

POINTS TO PONDER

What language do we use for prayer?

Where is God?

Why should we say prayers aloud?

The prayers found in Bahá'í prayer books are not just words. They were *specifically revealed* and constitute infallible guidance for humankind. The words are beautiful: don't let that make you believe beauty is their only value.

Here is what Bahá'u'lláh says about reading or saying prayers out loud:

> Intone, O My servant, the verses of God that have been received by thee, as intoned by them who have drawn nigh unto Him, that the sweetness of thy melody may kindle thine own soul, and attract the hearts of all men. Whoso reciteth, in the privacy of his chamber, the verses revealed by God, the scattering angels of the Almighty shall scatter abroad the fragrance of the words uttered by his mouth, and shall cause the heart of every righteous man to throb. Though he may, at first, remain unaware of its effect, yet the virtue of the grace vouchsafed unto him must needs sooner or later exercise its influence upon his soul. Thus have the mysteries of the Revelation of God been decreed by virtue of the Will of Him Who is the Source of power and wisdom.
>
> Bahá'u'lláh, *Gleanings*, p. 295

Most of the time, however, our prayers won't be in words. We can be in a prayerful state at any time. 'Abdu'l-Bahá said, 'Prayer need not be in words but in thought and attitude' ('Abdu'l-Bahá, *Compilation*, vol. 2, p. 236). The idea is to remove everything that comes between you and the realization that you're in God's presence: create an attitude in your heart and an atmosphere in your surroundings that will be conducive to this realization. This is not a matter of struggling, it is a matter of attraction:

The flame of the fire of love, in this world of earth and water, comes through the power of attraction and not by effort and striving.

'Abdu'l-Bahá, *Some Answered Questions*, p. 130

. . . strive that your actions day by day may be beautiful prayers.

'Abdu'l-Bahá, *Paris Talks*, p. 81

POINTS TO PONDER

Will God be able to 'speak' to your heart if your prayer is only in words that you're saying because you 'have to'?

What are some things you can do to create attraction in your own heart?

Why are we told that 'the flame of the fire of love . . . comes through the power of attraction, and not through effort and striving' but also told to 'strive' to make our actions 'beautiful prayers'?

Think of some examples from your daily life where you can strive to make your actions beautiful prayers. Can doing homework, cleaning up, washing dishes and working together in the right attitude be beautiful prayers?

Can you think of something that you *have* to do that you can turn into a beautiful prayer?

MEMORIZE

We should do little things as well as great things for the Love of God.

'Abdu'l-Bahá, quoted in Grundy, *Ten Days in the Light of 'Akká*, p. 6

9

Does God Always Answer Prayers?

READING

God will answer the prayer of every servant if that prayer is urgent. His mercy is vast, illimitable. He answers the prayers of all His servants . . . it is natural that God will give to us when we ask Him. His mercy is all-encircling.

But we ask for things which the divine wisdom does not desire for us, and there is no answer to our prayer. His wisdom does not sanction what we wish. We pray, 'O God! Make me wealthy!' If this prayer were universally answered, human affairs would be at a standstill . . . it is evident that it would not be well for us if all prayers were answered. The affairs of the world would be interfered with, energies crippled and progress hindered. But whatever we ask for which is in accord with divine wisdom, God will answer. Assuredly!

'Abdu'l-Bahá, *Promulgation of Universal Peace*, pp. 246–7

POINTS TO PONDER

How can you be assured that what you ask for will be answered?

How can you know what God's will for this age is?

EXERCISE

By reading and studying the writings of Bahá'u'lláh we can find out what 'divine wisdom' and 'God's will' are, so we can learn to pray for things that are *sure* to be answered!

Remember: it's entirely up to you to realize (which is to make real) that your prayers have been answered; don't keep grasping for something that is in your hand. As you discover what it is you're really seeking, you'll be able more readily to recognize that you have received it.

Write down some of the things that you *know* are in accord with God's wisdom.

Sometimes if we pray for something that would not be best for us or for someone else, the prayer will be answered, but the answer will be 'No!'

We know that if we pray to become close to God, to grow spiritually, to attain virtues, to be of service – these prayers will always be answered with a 'Yes!'

Bahá'u'lláh tells us: 'Thou disappointest no one who hath sought Thee, nor dost Thou keep back from Thee any one who hath desired Thee' (Bahá'u'lláh, *Prayers and Meditations*, p. 250).

STORY

Love Dogs

One night a man was crying,
   Allah! Allah!
His lips grew sweet with the praising,
   until a cynic said,
'So! I have heard you
   calling out, but have you ever
   gotten any response?'

The man had no answer to that.
He quit praying and fell into a confused sleep.

He dreamed he saw Khidr, the guide of souls,
   in a thick, green foliage.

'Why did you stop praising?'

'Because I've never heard anything back.'

'This longing you express *is* the return message.
   Your pure sadness that wants help is the secret cup.
   Listen to the moan of a dog for its master.
   That whining is the connection.

There are love-dogs
no one knows the names of.

Give your life
to be one of them.

Rúmí, translated by Coleman Barks

READING

The true worshipper, while praying, should endeavour not so
much to ask God to fulfil his wishes and desires, but rather to
adjust these and make them conform to the Divine Will.
Only through such an attitude can one derive that feeling of
inner peace and contentment which the power of prayer
alone can confer.

Letter written on behalf of Shoghi Effendi, *Compilation*, vol. 2, p. 240

VIEWPOINT

It's helpful to realize that when we ask for God's help, we're
usually asking Him to correct our thinking and to heal our
perceptions – to let us see with His perfect eye, which beholds
only perfections, rather than with our imperfect ones that see a
lot to complain and want and worry about, and to re-orient our
heart which has wandered away from love.

The prayers revealed by Bahá'u'lláh, 'Abdu'l-Bahá and the
Báb remind us that we're asking to have our hearts returned to
the complete joy and safety of God's love – that's the only place
we have all we need and are entirely happy and satisfied, no
matter what's going on around us on the material plane. By
returning to love, to the Presence of God, all prayers are
answered and there is nothing to want.

READING

Shoghi Effendi suggested to a believer these five steps of finding
a solution to a problem through prayer. This statement is a
'pilgrim's note' and cannot claim the same authority as the
sacred text.

First Step – Pray and meditate about it. Use the prayers of the manifestations, as they have the greatest power. Then remain in the silence of contemplation for a few minutes.

Second Step – Arrive at a decision and hold this. This decision is usually born during the contemplation. It may seem almost impossible of accomplishment but if it seems to be an answer to a prayer or a way of solving the problem, then immediately take the next step.

Third Step – Have determination to carry the decision through. Many fail here. The decision, budding into determination, is blighted and instead becomes a wish or a vague longing. When determination is born, immediately take the next step.

Fourth Step – Have faith and confidence that the power will flow through you, the right way will appear, the door will open, the right thought, the right message, the right principle or the right book will be given to you. Have confidence, and the right thing will come to your need. Then, as you rise from prayer, take at once the fifth step.

Fifth Step – . . . Act as though it had all been answered. Then act with tireless, ceaseless energy. And as you act, you, yourself, will become a magnet, which will attract more power to your being, until you become an unobstructed channel for the Divine power to flow through you. Many pray but do not remain for the last half of the first step. Some who meditate arrive at a decision, but fail to hold it. Few have the determination to carry the decision through, still fewer have the confidence that the right thing will come to their need. But how many remember to act as though it had all been answered? How true are these words – 'Greater than prayer is the spirit in which it is uttered, and greater than the way it is uttered is the spirit in which it is carried out.'

Cited in Principles of Bahá'í Administration, pp. 90–1

POINT TO PONDER

Can you literally change the outcome of something by affirmation and expectation?

EXERCISE

Many prayers are affirmations. Look through your prayer book
and see how many you can find.

10

Is Longer Better?

The most acceptable prayer is the one offered with the utmost spirituality and radiance; its prolongation hath not been and is not beloved by God. The more detached and purer the prayer, the more acceptable is it in the presence of God.

The Báb, *Selections from the Writings of the Báb*, p. 78

Pride not yourselves on much reading of the verses or on a multitude of pious acts by night and day; for were a man to read a single verse with joy and radiance it would be better for him than to read with lassitude all the Holy Books of God, the Help in Peril, the Self-Subsisting. Read ye the sacred verses in such measure that ye be not overcome by languor and despondency. Lay not upon your souls that which will weary them and weigh them down, but rather what will lighten and uplift them, so that they may soar on the wings of Divine verses towards the Dawning-place of His manifest signs; this will draw you nearer to God, did ye but comprehend.

Bahá'u'lláh, Kitáb-i-Aqdas, para. 149

lassitude weariness; not inclined to exert or interest oneself; lack of energy

languor lack of energy or alertness; faintness; fatigue

despondency downhearted; dejection

When we are praying, is the length of the prayer important? Or the spirit in which we pray?

Could feelings of guilt, fear and unworthiness be in the category of 'that which will weary and weigh down' our souls?

Will thinking about our faults and failures be helpful when we want to pray?

What are some of 'His manifest signs'?

What are some things that lighten and uplift your soul? Do you consciously use these things when you're praying?

II

Special Times for Prayers

In the next section we'll look at the joy and benefits of praying the obligatory prayers Bahá'u'lláh has given us. Here we are concerned with our ordinary prayers.

Both Bahá'u'lláh and 'Abdu'l-Bahá suggest that there are special times for us to pray, to seek guidance from God and to remember Him.

READINGS

> Recite ye the verses of God every morn and eventide. Whoso faileth to recite them hath not been faithful to the Covenant of God and His Testament, and whoso turneth away from these holy verses in this Day is of those who throughout eternity have turned away from God. Fear ye God, O My servants, one and all.
>
> Bahá'u'lláh, Kitáb-i-Aqdas, para. 149

> At the dawn of every day he [the true seeker] should commune with God, and, with all his soul, persevere in the quest of his Beloved.
>
> Bahá'u'lláh, *Gleanings*, p. 265

> Prayer verily bestoweth life, particularly when offered in private and at times, such as midnight, when freed from daily cares.
>
> 'Abdu'l-Bahá, *Selections from the Writings 'Abdu'l-Bahá*, p. 202

> Supplicate to God, pray to Him and invoke Him at midnight and at dawn. Be humble and submissive to God and chant the verses of thanksgiving at morn and eve . . .
>
> 'Abdu'l-Bahá, *Bahá'í World Faith*, p. 359

12

Obligatory Prayer

Bahá'ís of 15 years and older are able to take on the
responsibilities of adulthood. Two of the special benefits and
responsibilities of adult Bahá'ís are obligatory prayer and
fasting.

Bahá'u'lláh revealed three obligatory prayers for our use
daily (as well as one obligatory prayer to be said when someone
dies). No obligatory prayer is more powerful than any other
obligatory prayer and we are free to choose whichever one we
like to use on any particular day. The Long Obligatory Prayer
may be said at anytime in the 24 hours. The Medium
Obligatory Prayer is to be said three times a day, in the morning,
at noon and in the evening. The Short Obligatory Prayer is to be
said anytime between noon and sunset.

There are certain preparations to be made before saying our
obligatory prayer. The prayer is said in private and before the
prayer we perform 'ablutions', which simply means we
reverently wash our hands and face, remembering to prepare
our hearts at the same time. We also turn towards the Shrine of
Bahá'u'lláh to remind ourselves that we are seeking His
Presence.

obligatory compulsory;
required to be done, as a
duty

Those things that are
essential for our spiritual
development, Bahá'u'lláh
has made obligatory.

For more information on
all aspects of obligatory
prayer see Kitáb-i-Aqdas,
paragraphs 6, 8–10,
12–14, 18; Questions and
Answers 14, 21, 51, 58–67,
77, 81–3, 86, 93; and notes
3–8, 12–17, 20–2, 34.

READINGS

The reason why privacy hath been enjoined in moments of
devotion is this, that thou mayest give thy best attention to
the remembrance of God, that thy heart may at all times be
animated with His Spirit, and not be shut out as by a veil
from thy Best Beloved. Let not thy tongue pay lip service in
praise of God while thy heart be not attuned to the exalted

summit of Glory, and the Focal Point of communion.

The Báb, *Selections from the Writings of the Báb*, pp. 93–4

The obligatory prayers are binding inasmuch as they are conducive to humility and submissiveness, to setting one's face towards God and expressing devotion to Him. Through such prayer man holdeth communion with God, seeketh to draw near unto Him, converseth with the true Beloved of one's heart, and attaineth spiritual stations.

'Abdu'l-Bahá, *Compilation*, vol. 2, p. 232

Know thou that in every word and movement of the obligatory prayer there are allusions, mysteries, and a wisdom that man is unable to comprehend, and letters and scrolls cannot contain.

'Abdu'l-Bahá, *Compilation*, vol. 2, p. 233

These daily obligatory prayers, together with a few other specific ones, such as the Healing Prayer, the Tablet of Aḥmad, have been invested by Bahá'u'lláh with a special potency and significance, and should therefore be accepted as such and be recited by the believers with unquestioning faith and confidence, that through them they may enter into a much closer communion with God, and identify themselves more fully with His Laws and precepts.

Shoghi Effendi, in *Directives of the Guardian*, p. 60

Concerning the directions given by Bahá'u'lláh for the recital of certain prayers, Shoghi Effendi wishes me to inform you that these regulations – which by the way are very few and simple – are of a great spiritual help to the individual believer, in that they help him to fully concentrate when praying and meditating. Their significance is thus purely spiritual.

Letter written on behalf of Shoghi Effendi, in *Compilation*, vol. 2, p. 237

MEMORIZE

This is the Short Obligatory Prayer to be said between noon and sunset after washing your hands and face and turning towards the Shrine of Bahá'u'lláh (Bahjí).

I bear witness, O my God, that Thou hast created me to

know Thee and to worship Thee. I testify, at this moment, to my powerlessness and to Thy might, to my poverty and to Thy wealth.

There is none other God but Thee, the Help in Peril, the Self-Subsisting.

Bahá'u'lláh, Kitáb-i-Aqdas, pp. 100–1

POINTS TO PONDER

What does to 'bear witness' mean?

Do the way you think, the way you live your life and interact with others 'bear witness' and 'testify' to your love for Bahá'u'lláh as much as your words do?

How can you know God?

How can you worship Him?

Why do you think it's good for us to remember our powerlessness and poverty and God's might and wealth?

What do you think He's trying to teach us by having us say this prayer every day?

What does it mean when you say, 'There is none other God but Thee'?

What are some 'perils' you face every day? Do some of them come from your own lower self?

Recognizing and experiencing our powerlessness is our only access to authentic power – the power of God's love flowing through us. Removing our ego-centred, arrogant concept of power allows us this access.

13

What is 'Worship'?

This is worship: to serve mankind and to minister to the needs of the people. Service is prayer.

'Abdu'l-Bahá, *Paris Talks*, p. 177

Work done in the spirit of service is the highest form of worship.

'Abdu'l-Bahá, *Compilation*, vol. 1, p. 313

In the Bahá'í Cause arts, sciences and all crafts are (counted as) worship.

'Abdu'l-Bahá, *Paris Talks*, p. 176

POINTS TO PONDER

Do the above quotations imply that if your work is *not* done in the spirit of service, it does not suffice as worship – that you won't receive the blessings you would if it was done in a different spirit?

In order for us to experience our work as worship, do we need to do it in the spirit of loving service?

What are some examples of loving service that you do every day?

. . . that others do for you?

Can just noticing someone and smiling at him or her be a service? How about expressing gratitude for what a person does for you – is *that* a service?

Mother Teresa said that there are no great deeds – just small deeds done with great love!

Bob Harris says that many of us interpret 'Work is worship' by praying: 'O God! Let me serve Thee! Especially in an advisory capacity.'

Lady Blomfield relates this incident, which occurred while 'Abdu'l-Bahá was visiting her in London:

> A workman who had left his bag of tools in the hall was welcomed with smiling kindness by 'Abdu'l-Bahá. With a look of sadness the man said: 'I don't know much about religious things, as I have no time for anything but my work.'
>
> 'That is well. Very well. A day's work done in the spirit of service is in itself an act of worship. Such work is a prayer unto God.'
>
> The man's face cleared from its shadow of doubt and hesitation, and he went from the Master's presence happy and strengthened, as though a weighty burden had been taken away.
>
> Blomfield, Chosen Highway, p. 152

VIEWPOINT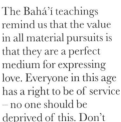

By saying 'Thou hast created me to know Thee and to worship Thee' every day, we begin to realize that to know God is to get to know His attributes within ourselves and others. This releases and enhances our loving capacity, and guides and supports us in applying it appropriately – which *is* worship. Knowledge, volition and action are all present in this sentence.

The Bahá'í teachings remind us that the value in all material pursuits is that they are a perfect medium for expressing love. Everyone in this age has a right to be of service – no one should be deprived of this. Don't labour; serve. When you serve, all labour is a labour of love!

It is a very good thing to spend some time each day relaxing and having fun as well as working. One day in Adrianople Bahá'u'lláh told His followers: 'We commanded you to follow a trade so that you may be usefully occupied and not get bored, and may earn money and invite Us to feasts.' (Balyuzi, *King of Glory*, p. 222)

14

The 'Greatest Name'

In Islam there is a tradition that among God's many names, one is the greatest; however, this name is hidden. Bahá'u'lláh teaches that the Greatest Name is 'Bahá'.

There are many forms of the Greatest Name. For example, 'Bahá'u'lláh' means 'the Glory of God'. This is the name of the Manifestation of God for this age and the Promised One of all ages.

One form of the Greatest Name that we often use is 'Alláh-u-Abhá', which means 'God the All-Glorious'. Bahá'ís frequently use this form of the Greatest Name as a greeting when they are glad to see each other. However, Shoghi Effendi has advised that we should avoid using it in front of people who might think it strange or who would be made uncomfortable by it.

In the Kitáb-i-Aqdas (paragraph 18) Bahá'u'lláh asks us to say 'Alláh-u-Abhá' 95 times each day. Before doing so we are to wash our hands and face, seat ourselves and turn to God.

Another form of the Greatest Name is Yá Bahá'u'l-Abhá, an invocation which means 'O Thou Glory of Glories'.

READINGS

'Abdu'l-Bahá tells us that:

> The Greatest Name should be found upon the lips in the first awaking moment of early dawn. It should be fed upon by constant use in daily invocation, in trouble, under opposition, and should be the last word breathed when the head rests upon the pillow at night. It is the name of

invocation an appeal made to God; calling upon God in prayer

comfort, protection, happiness, illumination, love and unity.

'Abdu'l-Bahá, in *Lights of Guidance*, p. 266

That the Most Great Name exerciseth influence over both
physical and spiritual matters is sure and certain.

'Abdu'l-Bahá, *Compilation*, vol. 1, p. 461

Section V

Detachment, Sacrifice, God's Will, Free Will

I

What is 'Detachment'?

INTRODUCTION

There are many ways to define 'detachment'. One dictionary
says 'detached' means 'separated from, objective' and that
'detachment' is 'the state of being detached'. Another says
'detachment' means 'a state of aloofness from or indifference to
other people, one's surroundings, and so on'. Detachment,
however, is a spiritual quality and, for Bahá'ís and people of
faith, means much more than these definitions. Detachment has
something to do with freedom, with justice, with being more
attached to the Will of God than to our own.

'Abdu'l-Bahá said that detachment is 'marked by the freedom
of the heart' (quoted in Balyuzi, *'Abdu'l-Bahá*, p. 9).

POINTS TO PONDER

What should one's heart be free of?

'Freedom of the heart' could mean being able to put aside all
other thoughts and concerns to commune with God. If you try
to commune with God and your mind and heart are already full
of other things, is there room for Him?

EXERCISE

How can you make room for God in your mind and heart?
Write a specific example in your journal.

The essence of detachment is for man to turn his face
towards the courts of the Lord, to enter His presence, behold
His countenance, and stand as witness before Him.

Bahá'u'lláh, *Tablets of Bahá'u'lláh*, p. 155

This is what you're doing
when you pray and
meditate!

2

True Freedom = Detachment

When people said to 'Abdu'l-Bahá how happy they were that He was now free,* He replied:

'Freedom is not a matter of place, but of condition. I was happy in that prison, for those days were passed in the path of service.

'To me prison was freedom.

'Troubles are a rest to me.

'Death is life.

'To be despised is honour.

'Therefore was I full of happiness all through that prison time.

'When one is released from the prison of self, that is indeed freedom! For self is the greatest prison.

'When this release takes place one can never be imprisoned.

'Unless one accepts dire vicissitudes, not with dull resignation, but with radiant acquiescence, one cannot attain this freedom.'

Honnold, *Vignettes*, pp. 9–10

Anybody can be happy in the state of comfort, ease, health, success, pleasure and joy; but if one will be happy and contented in the time of trouble, hardship and prevailing disease, it is the proof of nobility.

'Abdu'l-Bahá, in *Bahá'í World Faith*, p. 363

* 'Abdu'l-Bahá spent most of His life as a prisoner and exile.

vicissitudes changes of luck

dire dreadful

acquiescence agreement

☺ Mice learning detachment: Forget the cheese – let's get out of the trap!

'Attachment to the world' is the opposite of 'detachment from all else save God' ('Abdu'l-Bahá, *Selections from the Writings of 'Abdu'l-Bahá*, p. 87). Here is how Bahá'u'lláh defines 'the world':

READINGS

> Know ye that by 'the world' is meant your unawareness of him who is your Maker, and your absorption in aught else but him . . . Whatsoever deterreth you, in this Day, from loving God is nothing but the world.
>
> Bahá'u'lláh, *Gleanings*, p. 276

> By the world is meant that which turneth you aside from Him Who is the Dawning-Place of Revelation, and inclineth you unto that which is unprofitable unto you. Verily, the thing that deterreth you, in this day, from God is worldliness in its essence.
>
> Bahá'u'lláh, *Epistle to the Son of the Wolf*, p. 54

POINTS TO PONDER

What are some situations where being kind could be 'detached'?

Could the same situation – same actions, different motive – indicate your 'attachment to this world'?

What are some examples of 'attachment to this world'?

Can we become attached to being 'perfect'?
  . . . or to feeling guilty, unworthy of love?
  . . . to being angry, sad, hurt, distant?
  . . . to plans (even very good plans) that don't work out the
      way we wanted them to?
  . . . to being liked, admired, respected?
  . . . even to 'seeming' like a 'good', kind person?

Can not accepting any help be attachment?

How can we use our attachments – which are lessons in the school of life – to help us learn 'detachment from all else save God'?

VIEWPOINT

Detachment from the world also means being detached from our lower selves and focusing on our higher selves. In the section on prayer we saw that through prayer and meditation we can learn to do this.

READING

At Wandsworth Prison the Master, 'Abdu'l-Bahá, wrote in the visitors' book: 'The greatest prison is the prison of self.'

Honnold, *Vignettes*, p. 9

VIEWPOINT

Detachment, in one sense, means getting our priorities right – putting things spiritual before things material. Shoghi Effendi reminds us that

'Abdu'l-Bahá said we must sacrifice the important for the most important.

Shoghi Effendi, *Unfolding Destiny*, p. 448

So, in this sense, detachment can be a question of putting the most important before the important.

☺ When you get frenzied and find that this phenomenal world has a grip on you, here's a good quotation to remember to put things back into perspective:

. . . the whole world, in the estimation of the people of Bahá, is worth as much as the black in the eye of a dead ant . . . Abandon it unto such as have set their affections upon it, and turn thou unto Him Who is the Desire of the world.

Bahá'u'lláh, *Epistle to the Son of the Wolf*, p. 56

EXERCISE

Meditate on the following quotations. They can be helpful in orienting your priorities in a way that will best serve you.

READINGS

Say: If ye be seekers after this life and the vanities thereof, ye should have sought them while ye were still enclosed in your mothers' wombs, for at that time ye were continuously approaching them, could ye but perceive it. Ye have, on the other hand, ever since ye were born and attained maturity, been all the while receding from the world and drawing closer to dust.

Bahá'u'lláh, Gleanings, p. 127

Should anyone at any time encounter hard and perplexing times, he must say to himself, 'This too will pass'; then he will grow calm.

'Abdu'l-Bahá, quoted in Rutstein, He Loved and Served, p. 82

'This, too, will pass' is a helpful phrase when 'detachment' is a stretch.

3

Sacrifice

We usually think of sacrifice as giving something up – something that we like or need or want. The dictionary says that 'sacrifice' is 'giving something up in order to benefit another person or to gain something more important'. The word 'sacrifice' comes from the same root as the word 'sacred', so to sacrifice can be thought of as 'to make sacred'.

'Abdu'l-Bahá tells us that if we sacrifice (make sacred) our own 'conditions' we will gain a divine station:

MEMORIZE

> The mystery of sacrifice is that man should sacrifice all his conditions for the Divine Station of God. The Station of God is Mercy, Kindness, Forgiveness, Sacrifice, Favour, Grace and Giving-Life to the spirits and lighting the fire of His love in the hearts . . .
>
> 'Abdu'l-Bahá, in Lights of Guidance, p. 117

READING

> Self-sacrifice means to subordinate this lower nature and its desires to the more godly and noble side of our selves. Ultimately, in its highest sense, self-sacrifice means to give our will and our all to God to do with as He pleases. Then He purifies and glorifies our true self until it becomes a shining and wonderful reality.
>
> From a letter written on behalf of Shoghi Effendi in Compilation, vol. 2, p. 19

Sacrifice, paradoxically, means giving up something lesser for something greater or more desirable.

☺ From a skit entitled 'Just Say Yes!' at a Bahá'í summer school:

Seeker: 'Do Bahá'ís believe in animal sacrifice?'

Bahá'í: 'Sure! We believe we must learn to sacrifice our animal nature!'

189

What do you think are the human conditions that must be sacrificed?

Could these include selfishness, anger and greed?

Do all the human conditions that must be sacrificed pertain to our material/lower nature?

How does giving up our human conditions made us 'sacred'?

Is 'lighting the fire of His love in the hearts' the way to teach the Faith to ourselves and others?

EXERCISE

Acting from our higher/spiritual self makes our actions sacred. Think of some examples of times when you might need to sacrifice your lower nature's wishes in order to feel the strength and joy of nearness to God. Discuss or write about them in your journal.

VIEWPOINT

Sacrifice must always be a thoughtful, inner decision, not undertaken in response to outside pressure. When Bahá'u'lláh knows something is essential for our well-being, He makes it a law; that way we can't overlook the bounties!

One of the ways in which Bahá'u'lláh has made it possible for us to sacrifice is by asking us to contribute to the Bahá'í funds, something only Bahá'ís can do. Although giving to the funds is obligatory, it is an entirely private and personal matter, much like obligatory prayer and fasting. These obligations are to be motivated and fulfilled from love and are never under anyone else's scrutiny.

Contributing to the fund is a sacred act and is one way we can develop our spiritual being.

Contributions to this fund constitute, in addition, a practical and effective way whereby every believer can test the measure and character of his faith, and prove in deeds the intensity of his devotion and attachment to the Cause.

Letter written on behalf of Shoghi Effendi, in *Compilation*, vol. 1, p. 538

Contributing to the Fund should constitute an integral part of the spiritual life of every Bahá'í and be regarded as the fulfilment of a fundamental spiritual obligation.

Letter from the International Teaching Centre to the Counsellors,
1 December 1991

STORY

This true story is told by 'Abdu'l-Bahá about the building of the Bahá'í House of Worship in Wilmette:

One of the wondrous events that has of late come to pass is this, that the edifice of the Mashriqu'l-Adhkár is being raised in the very heart of the American continent, and numerous souls from the surrounding regions are contributing for the erection of this holy Temple. Among these is a highly esteemed lady of the city of Manchester, who hath been moved to offer her share.

Having no portion of goods and earthly riches, she sheared off with her own hands the fine, long and precious tresses that adorned her head so gracefully, and offered them for sale, that the price thereof might promote the cause of the Mashriqu'l-Adhkár.

Consider ye, that though in the eyes of women nothing is more precious than rich and flowing locks, yet notwithstanding this, that highly-honoured lady hath evinced so rare and beautiful a spirit of self-sacrifice.

And though this was uncalled for, and 'Abdu'l-Bahá would not have consented to such a deed, yet as it doth reveal so high and noble a spirit of devotion, He was deeply touched thereby. Precious though the hair be in the sight of western women, nay, more precious than life itself, yet she offered it up as a sacrifice for the cause of the Mashriqu'l-Adhkár!

'Abdu'l-Bahá, *Selections from the Writings of 'Abdu'l-Bahá*, p. 98

4

Detachment vs. Materialism vs. Prosperity

Detachment does *not* mean giving up the enjoyment of comfort and material pleasures. Bahá'u'lláh has clearly forbidden asceticism. What we need to avoid is materialism – the idea that physical well-being constitutes the greatest good and highest value in life.

asceticism keeping back from all kinds of pleasure; rigidity in devotion, sternly austere

materialism an excessive devotion to worldly rather than spiritual concerns and especially to the acquisition of material possessions

READING

Materialism is a greatly misunderstood word: many people believe that it means that they shouldn't enjoy any material things or comforts. Bahá'u'lláh puts things in perspective for us:

> Should a man wish to adorn himself with the ornaments of the earth, to wear its apparels, or partake of the benefits it can bestow, no harm can befall him, if he alloweth nothing whatever to intervene between him and God, for God hath ordained every good thing, whether created in the heavens or in the earth, for such of His servants as truly believe in Him. Eat ye, O people, of the good things which God hath allowed you, and deprive not yourselves from His wondrous bounties. Render thanks and praise unto Him, and be of them that are truly thankful.
>
> Bahá'u'lláh, *Gleanings*, p. 276

VIEWPOINT

From reading Bahá'u'lláh's writings it is clear that poverty and wretchedness are the social evils, not prosperity, which is intended to be enjoyed by everyone. Bahá'u'lláh has abolished the extremes of wealth and poverty and made the sharing of one's wealth voluntary and dependent on the spirit of generosity. Careful study of the spirit of the law of Ḥuqúqu'lláh, the 'Right of God', will provide clear guidelines for the voluntary and joyful sharing of one's excess wealth.

The Bahá'í writings tell us that we must combine our spiritual life with our material one. Right now, we cannot live without both!

READINGS

. . . if material happiness and spiritual felicity be conjoined, it will be 'delight upon delight' . . .

'Abdu'l-Bahá, *Promulgation of Universal Peace*, p. 166

It is certain that spirituality will defeat materialism, that the heavenly will subdue the human . . .

'Abdu'l-Bahá, *Selections from the Writings of 'Abdu'l-Bahá*, p. 191

☺ Trying to live and feel secure with an entirely materialistic outlook at this point in history is a lot like being beautifully dressed and rearranging the deck chairs on the sinking *Titanic* – life's impossible and very frightening but the decor is nice.

5

God's Will, Free Will

Often when people say, 'it's the will of God', they're referring to some tragic happening: a flood or hurricane, a ship sinking, a child dying. This is a very sad and burdensome perception of the will of God. God's will is spelled out for us by the Manifestations of God in each age. In this age, for instance, we know that it is God's will that each person receive his share of God's grace, that we be happy and joyful, live in harmony and unity, that we learn to respect and cherish our diversity, that we each have a right to be of service and to express ourselves spiritually and creatively, that we honour our parents and the rights of each individual in a family – these are just a few of the things we know are the will of God.

As humans, we are given free will so that we can choose to do God's will!

☺ Overheard at Bahá'í school: 'I *know* there's a God; He keeps messin' with my plans.'

At the same time, God has given us our own will, which we can choose to use as we wish. This is free will. 'Abdu'l-Bahá explains the difference between the two:

READING

> Some things are subject to the free will of man, such as justice, equity, tyranny and injustice, in other words, good and evil actions; it is evident and clear that these actions are, for the most part, left to the will of man. But there are certain things to which man is forced and compelled, such as sleep, death, sickness, decline of power, injuries and misfortunes; these are not subject to the will of man, and he is not responsible for them, for he is compelled to endure them. But in the choice of good and bad actions he is free, and he commits them according to his own will.
>
> For example, if he wishes, he can pass his time in praising

God, or he can be occupied with other thoughts. He can be an enkindled light through the fire of the love of God, and a philanthropist loving the world, or he can be a hater of mankind, and engrossed with material things. He can be just or cruel. These actions and these deeds are subject to the control of the will of man himself; consequently, he is responsible for them.

. . . in all the action or inaction of man, he receives power from the help of God; but the choice of good or evil belongs to the man himself.

'Abdu'l-Bahá, *Some Answered Questions*, pp. 248–50

VIEWPOINT

Another way of looking at free will is to remember that we always have the freedom to respond to our experiences – the choice is whether we will develop spiritually by responding from our higher, spiritual nature or whether we will allow ourselves to continue to react to life's challenges from our ego/material nature. It is God's will that we develop our spiritual capacity while on this plane of existence; that we use this life on earth as a workshop to strengthen our loving capacity with every choice we make.

MEMORIZE

Make of your will a door through which the confirmations of the Holy Spirit may enter.

'Abdu'l-Bahá, quoted in Mathews, *Not Every Sea Hath Pearls*, p. 8

EXERCISE

Find a point of reaction or resistance in yourself right now. Meditate on making your will a door through which the confirmations of the Holy Spirit may enter.

POINTS TO PONDER

What are the confirmations of the Holy Spirit?
Does this meditation change your outlook on reality?

Does it change the way you feel physically and emotionally?

VIEWPOINT

Choices, choices!

Because we are human and have both a physical/lower nature and a spiritual/higher nature and because we have free will, we can and *must* make choices. It is impossible for us to live as humans and not make choices.

We can choose to be good or evil, loving or hateful, generous or stingy. In every situation, our response depends on us – not on what has happened to us or on something that someone else has done. This is wonderful, since we *can* change ourselves but we *can't* change anyone else! When we learn this, we have superpowers that can never be taken away from us and we have learned the secret of happiness. But it isn't easy – it takes a lifetime of practice.

Providentially, choices that do not bring us closer to God will often make us sad or angry or anxious – unhappy and uncomfortable. These painful feelings are a reminder from our higher nature to turn back to the love of God.

Just as you have learned to make choices about what you want to look at, smell, hear, touch and taste, you can learn to make choices about what you want to think about, seek to comprehend, remember and imagine. You wouldn't eat something you knew was poisonous or touch something that would burn or sting you. Every child learns to avoid physical pain. If your parents told you not to touch the stove and you did it anyway, you got burned – and you learned!

The pain taught you an important lesson. But you didn't *have* to feel the pain. You could have followed your parents' instructions. Either way, however, you learned the lesson, which was beneficial to you. We learn spiritual lessons the same way. We can follow the loving guidance of the Manifestations of God for the age in which we live, or we can ignore them and learn from the pain.

The pain we feel when we ignore God's laws is just another way to help us learn a lesson. To avoid this pain, we need to learn to do it God's way! To learn to do it God's way, we can read, study and discuss the writings – there are laws, stories, examples, etc. in the books. 'Abdu'l-Bahá always did it God's

If you practise directing your thoughts like you would steer a car – making them go where you choose for them to go, you will be able to change your mood when you feel sad or angry: you will be able to control how you experience and respond to the things that happen in your life, even though you can't always control what happens to you.

providentially of or resulting from divine providence; happening as through divine intervention; divinely provided

Compare life to an ocean: we were each given some kind of craft – some a yacht, some a leaky rowboat, others maybe a rickety raft, but something to get out and experience the dynamics of the sea. The point is not the kind of craft you're given – or in fixing it up and making your rowboat look like a yacht; the point is to learn seamanship.

way, so reading lots of stories about Him can help us assimilate what 'God's way' looks like in daily life. The only way we can really 'lose the wager' is to go through life unconscious of our spiritual nature.

READING

Afflictions and troubles are due to the state of not being content with what God has ordained for one. If one submits himself to God, he is always happy. A man asked another: 'In what station are you?' The other answered: 'In the utmost happiness.' 'Where does this happiness come from?' 'Because all existing things move according to my wish. I do not find anything contrary to my desire. Therefore I have no sorrow. There is no doubt that all the beings move by the Will of God, and I have given up my own will, desiring the Will of God. Thus my will became the Will of God, for there is nothing of myself. All are moving by His Will, yet they are moving by my own will. In this case, I am very happy.'

When man surrenders himself, everything will move according to his wish.

'Abdu'l-Bahá, quoted in *The Diary of Juliet Thompson*, pp. 59–60

VIEWPOINT

Once we start having daily communication with our spiritual selves – using prayer and meditation – and practise getting our goals and motives in line with our best choices and first priorities, we will be doing things God's way. There will then be far less confusion and unhappiness in our lives.

POINTS TO PONDER

Do you have a choice about what you're thinking?

Does what you think about affect what you're feeling?
    If you believe that what you're feeling controls what you're thinking, try thinking about something else entirely and see if it changes the way you feel: your feelings show you what your thoughts are doing.

6

Actions and Reactions

As we have seen, to be human means to have free will, to be able
to make choices. If God made us so that our choices didn't
matter, or we couldn't make them, then we would no longer be
human. This ability to know right from wrong and to make
choices allows us to grow spiritually – it is what makes us human
and separates us from the animals.

When we *act* we are most like 'Abdu'l-Bahá; when we *react* we
are likely to do things that cause unhappiness, anger or
unkindness.

To tell the difference, we just have to notice how our attitudes
and actions affect others and ourselves. Actions – and these
include attitudes and intentions – will change the world for the
better and create an environment for unity and peace. Negative
reactions are what make the world an unhappy and dangerous
place. All emotions are energy that can be used by us in many
different ways. We can train ourselves to use the energy, instead
of just feeling it and reacting unconsciously.

There are situations in life when anger or sadness is an
appropriate response. The choice we have in these situations is
in deciding how we will *act* – what we will do with the energy of
the sadness or anger.

For example, if someone is abusing you or acting in a way
that is dangerous to you, the appropriate way for you to act is to
get away from the person and get to a safe place and/or to ask
for help. If they are being unfair or unjust – to us or to someone
else – we have many examples of *love in action* in such situations.
Humiliation is *not* a valid aspect of humility; spirituality, *not*
egotism, is the basis of authentic self-esteem.

Economic justice, even in small matters, was important to the Master. Once in Egypt 'Abdu'l-Bahá obtained a carriage in order that He might offer a ride to an important Páshá, who was to be His luncheon guest. When they reached their destination, the driver asked an exorbitant fee. The Master was fully aware of this and refused to pay the full amount. The driver, big and rough, grabbed His sash and 'jerked Him back and forth', demanding his unfair price. 'Abdu'l-Bahá remained firm and the man eventually let go. The Master paid what He actually owed him and informed him that had he been honest, he would have received a handsome tip instead of only the fare. He then walked away.

Shoghi Effendi, His grandson, was present when this happened. He later admitted to being very embarrassed that this should have happened in front of the Páshá. 'Abdu'l-Bahá, on the other hand, was evidently 'not at all upset', but simply determined not to be cheated.

Honnold, *Vignettes*, p. 109

If you are feeling very sad over something in your life, the appropriate thing to do might be to find a caring, wise person who treats you with respect and talk the situation over. As long as you aren't assigning blame – not trying to put the responsibility for your lack of spiritual well-being or happiness onto someone else – this is *not* backbiting or gossip. This is an appropriate and wise response to a situation. Do be *very* careful of your motives and who you choose as confidant. Frequently the best plan is to contact the Local Spiritual Assembly with a request for personal assistance. In some cases, medical or legal assistance may be required.

Being spiritual means taking proper care of yourself, physically, emotionally and spiritually.

If what you're doing is kind and loving and might have been done by 'Abdu'l-Bahá, it's action. Action makes you feel good about yourself deep down, even if it creates situations that are painful or embarrassing to your ego, such as admitting when you're wrong or when others try to humiliate you because you aren't going along with the crowd. Action is true strength, because its source is the love of God – and God's power is behind you when you act.

If what you do is less than loving and makes you or someone else unhappy or closes hearts, it's not action: it's reaction – no matter what someone else did to 'make' you do it. You – and only you – have the power to choose how you will act in every situation.

POINTS TO PONDER

Does what you think and do every minute of every day create what your life will be like – or does that depend on something else?

How do you set priorities and make good decisions about your actions and time?

EXERCISES

Use your daily meditation/quiet times to think about how you create a life for yourself that truly reflects your beliefs and values.

Choose one thing that you frequently react to that you would like to change – something that 'makes' you do things in a way that you know is not best – and practise acting rather than reacting for one whole week. Write about the effects of this in your journal, including how your self-esteem is affected.

VIEWPOINT

When you exercise your physical muscles, they get stronger. When you exercise your spiritual muscles through the choices you make, they get stronger too. This does not happen automatically. We have to make it happen, just like we have to train our muscles if we want to grow strong. You can use any experience in life to build your spiritual muscles. Life is a spiritual workout and awareness that it's all about gaining strength can make the tests more stimulating.

7

Know Your*self* *Your*self

Becoming a spiritual being means getting to know your true self, both your material/lower self and your spiritual/higher self. Learning about yourself is a lifelong process.

READING

> Far, far from Thy glory be what mortal man can affirm of Thee, or attribute unto Thee, or the praise with which he can glorify Thee! Whatever duty Thou hast prescribed unto Thy servants of extolling to the utmost Thy majesty and glory is but a token of Thy grace unto them, that they may be enabled to ascend unto the station conferred upon their own inmost being, the station of the knowledge of their own selves.
>
> Bahá'u'lláh, *Gleanings*, pp. 4–5

VIEWPOINT

How can we find out about our own selves?

The most important thing to remember when you're learning about yourself and your motives is to be truthful. It's always important to be truthful, but it can be more difficult when you're looking at your own actions and motives than it is at other times. As 'Abdu'l-Bahá tells us:

Truthfulness is the foundation of all human virtues. Without truthfulness progress and success, in all the worlds of God, are impossible for any soul. When this holy attribute is established in man, all the divine qualities will also be acquired.

'Abdu'l-Bahá, in *Compilation*, vol. 2, p. 338

POINTS TO PONDER

If you aren't truthful, can you be dealing with reality?

Does a lack of truthfulness mean you are building your life on a shaky foundation that could crumble with the first big test?

If you can't trust your foundation, can you feel safe and secure?

Since it's *your* foundation, it's totally up to you how well it's built – no one else can decide whether you'll be truthful or untruthful, can they?

READING

How can we come to know our own selves? Bahá'u'lláh gives us many ways, including, as we have seen, prayer and meditation. Here He tells us of another way:

> Bring thyself to account each day ere thou art summoned to a reckoning; for death, unheralded, shall come upon thee and thou shalt be called to give account for thy deeds.
>
> Bahá'u'lláh, *Hidden Words*, Arabic no. 31

VIEWPOINT

If this sounds grim and conjures up visions of going over and over endless faults and failures, it's probably a culturally induced reaction! In fact, if you account for something, you're going over credits and debits and getting an objective overview of your spiritual assets – and these spiritual assets are your true self. Bahá'u'lláh and 'Abdu'l-Bahá encourage everyone to keep their eyes on the strengths and perfections that they desire. This is not to say that a sincere and truthful assessment of areas that need your conscious focus is not required. It is. Daily.

READING

The first Ṭaráz and the first effulgence which hath dawned from the horizon of the Mother Book is that man should know his own self and recognize that which leadeth unto loftiness or lowliness, glory or abasement, wealth or poverty.

Bahá'u'lláh, *Tablets of Bahá'u'lláh*, pp. 34–5

Absolute repose does not exist in nature. All things either make progress or lose ground. Everything moves forward or backward, nothing is without motion.

'Abdu'l-Bahá, *Paris Talks*, p. 88

VIEWPOINT

When we come to know ourselves, we discover that we have a choice: to stay as we are (which, as 'Abdu'l-Bahá says, is the same as going backwards) or develop our spiritual/higher selves – that is, sacrificing our material/lower-nature so that we can focus on our higher self.

If you choose to sacrifice your material/lower-nature qualities and reactions and to replace them with the attributes of God, here are some hints about how to go about it:

- Check out the contents of your mind: start watching for times when you react in a negative or hostile way to something or someone; reactions and resistances are manifestations of your lower self. Your reaction is showing you that there is a lesson for your higher self to deal with.

- If you become aware that you are reacting rather than acting with love, take time to look at your reaction objectively. Be grateful for it, since it is bringing you a lesson to build your spiritual strength. Pray and meditate about it and discover the purpose of the reaction: your lower nature has a reason for reacting – and will make the reason look attractive in an attempt to convince your higher nature to leave it alone. Just putting the light of awareness on your reactions is helpful.

• By asking yourself some questions, you can choose to sacrifice the reaction or negative feeling and to replace it with a higher choice – or you can choose to keep it. At least you will be aware of it and why it's in your life.

POINTS TO PONDER

Here are some questions to ask yourself – be sure to add your own to the list:

What *exactly* are my feelings?

Have I felt this way before (is there a recognizable pattern)?

What is the purpose of this reaction or feeling? (How is it useful to me?)

What is it maintaining in my life? (For example, it makes me feel like I'm a better person than she is and I really like feeling good about myself this way.)

What is the outcome of this feeling or reaction?

How does it affect me? others? the spirit of unity? (i.e. if I allow my feelings to be hurt, how does it affect community unity?)

Does it reflect my highest choices and beliefs?

Does this feeling or reaction show forth my true convictions? (For example, does it help bring peace and unity to the world? Could I be perpetuating estrangement and lack of harmony by not dealing honestly with it?)

How can I best deal with it? (i.e. consultation, transmutation?)

What resources do I have to draw on for clarification/support

(i.e. prayer, the writings, family, friends, Assembly, etc.)

Does it make me a person I like and admire? Would I *really* admire this if someone else was acting this way?

How can I use this reaction to help me become the person I choose to be?

Would I do this if I realized I was in the presence of 'Abdu'l-Bahá?

If I choose to release (sacrifice) this reaction or feeling, what do I choose to replace it with? (If you don't choose a strength to replace a weakness, you will not have a loving action ready to use when another test arises – and *it will*, because your ego nature wants things to stay as they are. In any case, your higher nature can use every opportunity to become strong!)

VIEWPOINT

Knowing and becoming our true spiritual selves requires hard work, patience and love. Indeed, in this task we all need encouragement – which comes from *coeur*, the heart. Encourage yourself and others frequently and consciously. Living from the heart brings with it the courage that is required to do it!

Section VI

The Word of God — Pass It On

I

The Word of God

READINGS

It is written, Man shall not live by bread alone, but by every word that proceedeth out of the mouth of God.

Matt. 4:4

Man is like unto a tree. If he be adorned with fruit, he hath been and will ever be worthy of praise and commendation . . . The Water for these trees is the living water of the sacred Words uttered by the Beloved of the world.

Bahá'u'lláh, Tablets of Bahá'u'lláh, p. 257

Peace of mind is gained by the centering of the spiritual consciousness on the Prophet of God; therefore you should study the spiritual Teachings, and receive the Water of Life from the Holy Utterances. Then by translating these high ideals into action, your entire character will be changed, and your mind will not only find peace, but your entire being will find joy and enthusiasm.

Letter written on behalf of Shoghi Effendi, in Lights of Guidance, p. 112

POINTS TO PONDER

How can you gain peace of mind?

So, what should you do if you desire to gain peace of mind?

If you do study and receive, then what is the next step towards finding joy and enthusiasm?

Through the power of the words He hath uttered the whole of the human race can be illumined with the light of unity, and the remembrance of his Name is able to set on fire the hearts of all men, and burn away the veils that intervene between them and His glory.

Bahá'u'lláh, *Gleanings*, pp. 286–7

Every word that proceedeth out of the mouth of God is endowed with such potency as can instil new life into every human frame, if ye be of them that comprehend this truth. All the wondrous works ye behold in this world have been manifested through the operation of His supreme and most exalted Will, His wondrous and inflexible purpose.

Bahá'u'lláh, *Gleanings*, p. 141

VIEWPOINT

The Words of the Manifestations are referred to as 'the Creative Word'. 'They are endowed with such potency that they penetrate into the hearts and move the people to obey them. Indeed, the greatest mission of every Manifestation of God during His own Dispensation has been to release such spiritual forces into the world as to revitalize all those who turn to Him' (Taherzadeh, *Revelation of Bahá'u'lláh*, vol. 3, p. 130).

EXERCISE

In your own words, write in your journal your thoughts about why the Words of God brought by the Manifestations are called 'the Creative Word'.

READING

Ponder the advances in transportation and communication that have come about since 1844, when the Revelation of the unity of mankind began: does this give you some insight into the power of the Word of God?

The vitality of men's belief in God is dying out in every land; nothing short of His wholesome medicine can ever restore it. The corrosion of ungodliness is eating into the vitals of human society; what else but the Elixir of His potent Revelation can cleanse and revive it? Is it within human power . . . to effect in the constituent elements of any of the minute and indivisible particles of matter so complete a transformation as to transmute it into purest gold? Perplexing and difficult as this may appear, the still greater task of converting satanic strength into heavenly power is one that We have been empowered to accomplish. The Force capable of such a transformation transcendeth the potency of the Elixir itself. The Word of God, alone, can claim the distinction of being endowed with the capacity required for so great and far-reaching a change.

Bahá'u'lláh, *Gleanings*, p. 200

VIEWPOINT

The Words of the Manifestations are like an ocean – vast and complex, teeming with life and energy, with many, many things to discover. The Words of the Manifestations have many levels of meaning, which will unfold to you as you apply them in your life, study them and discuss them with others. Don't just wade in the shallows; dive deeply!

READINGS

Divine things are too deep to be expressed by common words. The heavenly teachings are expressed in parable in order to be understood and preserved for ages to come. When the spiritually minded dive deeply into the ocean of their meaning they bring to the surface the pearls of their inner significance. There is no greater pleasure than to study God's Word with a spiritual mind.

'Abdu'l-Bahá, in *Compilation*, vol. 1, p. 203

O My servants! My holy, My divinely ordained Revelation may be likened unto an ocean in whose depths are concealed innumerable pearls of great price, of surpassing lustre. It is the duty of every seeker to bestir himself and strive to attain the shores of this ocean, so that he may, in proportion to the eagerness of his search and the efforts he hath exerted, partake of such benefits as have been pre-ordained in God's irrevocable and hidden Tablets.

Bahá'u'lláh, *Gleanings*, p. 326

We speak one word and by it we intend one and seventy meanings . . .

Bahá'u'lláh, Kitáb-i-Íqán, p. 255

MEMORIZE

The understanding of His words and the comprehension of the utterances of the Birds of Heaven are in no wise dependent upon human learning. They depend solely upon purity of heart, chastity of soul, and freedom of spirit.

Bahá'u'lláh, Kitáb-i-Íqán, p. 211

POINTS TO PONDER

Does one have to be well-educated, or even literate, to understand and comprehend the words of God brought by the Manifestations?

What are some things you think your spirit should be free of in order to understand and comprehend the meanings of the Words of God?

How do you attain purity of heart and chastity of soul? Does this mean that you have to be perfect or could it mean that your understanding will grow and develop as you grow and develop spiritually?

2

They're Only Words

All words that you think and speak influence your reality to a great extent, even though you may not be aware that this is so. It's a good idea to be careful with the words you say and think and to search behind the words for the knowledge, volition and action they engender and support.

READINGS

Glorified be God! Man's treasure is his utterance . . .
Bahá'u'lláh, Tablets of Bahá'u'lláh, p. 62

No man of wisdom can demonstrate his knowledge save by means of words . . . Moreover words and utterances should be both impressive and penetrating. However, no word will be infused with these two qualities unless it be uttered wholly for the sake of God and with due regard unto the exigencies of the occasion and the people . . . Every word is endowed with a spirit, therefore the speaker or expounder should carefully deliver his words at the appropriate time and place, for the impression which each word maketh is clearly evident and perceptible . . . One word may be likened unto fire, another unto light, and the influence which both exert is manifest in the world . . . Therefore an enlightened man of wisdom should primarily speak with words as mild as milk, that the children of men may be nurtured and edified thereby and may attain the ultimate goal of human existence which is the station of true understanding and nobility . . . One word is like unto springtime causing the tender saplings of the rose-garden of knowledge to become verdant and

By the wise is meant men whose knowledge is not confined to mere words and whose lives have been fruitful and have produced enduring results.
Bahá'u'lláh, *Tablets*, p. 62

flourishing, while another word is even as a deadly poison. It behoveth a prudent man of wisdom to speak with utmost leniency and forbearance so that the sweetness of his words may induce everyone to attain that which befitteth man's station.

Bahá'u'lláh, *Tablets of Bahá'u'lláh*, pp. 172–3

Some material things have a spiritual effect. The spoken words cause a vibration which produces an effect on the ear. This is material, but the effect is spiritual – that is the spirit of man feels the effect – either of gladness or sadness.

'Abdu'l-Bahá, quoted in Goodall and Cooper,
Daily Lessons Received at 'Akká, p. 13

POINTS TO PONDER

Think of some words that have burned you. Think of some that have enlightened you. What influence did each of these have on your actions and your relationships in the world?

Are you aware of the effect of your words on others?

3

Words & Speech – What They're For

The heart is like a box, and language is the key.
'Abdu'l-Bahá, *Promulgation of Universal Peace*, p. 60

It behoveth every man to blot out the trace of every idle word from the tablet of his heart, and to gaze, with an open and unbiased mind, on the signs of His Revelation, the proofs of His Mission, and the tokens of His glory.
Bahá'u'lláh, *Gleanings*, p. 11

idle not engaged in any action; futile, trivial, worthless

tablet a small slab for writing on; a slab bearing an inscription

POINTS TO PONDER

What are some insights you receive when you meditate on the meaning of the words 'tablet of [your] heart'?

What are heart words?

What are the *idle* words in your heart?

How could idle words affect the quality of your thoughts, your perceptions and your life?

What can you use to blot them out?

READING

Bahá'u'lláh gives us this warning:

Material fire consumeth the body, whereas the fire of the

☺ The children's rhyme 'Sticks and stones may

215

tongue devoureth both heart and soul. The force of the former lasteth but for a time, whilst the effects of the latter endureth a century.

Bahá'u'lláh, Gleanings, p. 265

POINTS TO PONDER

Have you ever been burned by someone's words – even if that person didn't necessarily *intend* to hurt you?

Ponder how the effects of backbiting could endure a century and consume heart and soul.

EXERCISES

Spend some time every day being conscious of how you're talking to yourself (and others, too, of course, but usually we're more careful about what we say to others than we are about what we say and think about ourselves).

Practise rephrasing things to support your strengths and highest choices. If what you're saying to yourself doesn't attract and lead you to positive action, rephrase and re-visualize with a consciousness of attraction and love.

MEMORIZE

O companion of My throne! Hear no evil, and see no evil, abase not thyself, neither sigh and weep. Speak no evil, that thou mayest not hear it spoken unto thee, and magnify not the faults of others that thine own faults may not appear great . . .

Bahá'u'lláh, Hidden Words, Persian no. 44

POINTS TO PONDER

Why were we given the power of speech? This is a uniquely human gift: meditate on what a treasure it is.

break my bones, but words will never hurt me!' is just so much bravado – empty words, in fact! Maybe it should be phrased: 'Sticks and stones may break my bones, but words do some *real* damage!'

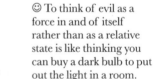

☺ To think of evil as a force in and of itself rather than as a relative state is like thinking you can buy a dark bulb to put out the light in a room. There is no doubt, though, that lovelessness exerts influence, just as darkness does.

What would it be like if there were no power of speech?

What do you think 'evil' speaking might be?

Does hearing and seeing evil – lovelessly – apply to your treatment of yourself as much as it applies to your treatment of others?

Does this make you re-assess your outlook on the meaning of true humility and servitude?

READING

> . . . backbiting quencheth the light of the heart, and extinguisheth the life of the soul.
>
> Bahá'u'lláh, *Gleanings*, p. 265

STORY

This story is about Mírzá Abu'l-Faḍl, the great Bahá'í scholar:

> Mírzá never encouraged any talk which might lead to inharmony. Once, a friend came to him and said that another believer was doing harm to the Faith. Mírzá listened carefully. Then he told me to translate his answer word for word:
>
> 'Do you believe that Bahá'u'lláh is the promised Lord of Hosts?'
>
> 'Yes.'
>
> 'Well, if He is that Lord, these are the Hosts. What right have we to speak ill of the Hosts?'
>
> Taherzadeh, *Revelation of Bahá'u'lláh*, vol. 4, p. 266

4

Pass It On

What Does 'Teach the Faith' Mean?

INTRODUCTION

A very good use of words is teaching the Faith. When we teach
we not only use our words, we use the Word of God.
We're living in the day that humankind has waited and prayed
for since before recorded history – the coming of age of the
human race, the fulfilment of the prophecies of all the religions
of the past, the inception of the 'Kingdom of God on earth'.
And you are invited to participate fully and consciously in the
dawning of this realization. Do you appreciate the Day in which
you live?

A mystic poet says:

Life is so short,
we must live it very slowly.

READING

Henri-Frédéric Amiel's lovely verse reminds us:

> Life is short and we have
> not too much time for gladdening
> the hearts of those
> who are travelling the dark way
> with us.
> O, be swift to love!
> Make haste to be kind.

VIEWPOINT

One of the six requisites of spiritual growth is teaching the

Cause of God. The fact that this is a requirement for everyone means that it is not only possible for each of us to do it, it is essential for *our own* spiritual progress that we do.

For many of us, the word 'teaching' conjures up the dry or forceful presentation of facts and information that we have been subjected to in our schools and churches. However, for Bahá'ís, teaching is essentially an act of worship and depends on purity of motive and attraction. There are many Bahá'í writings and the example of 'Abdu'l-Bahá to guide and inspire us as we learn what teaching the Faith means.

READINGS

> Consort with all men, O people of Bahá, in a spirit of friendliness and fellowship. If ye be aware of a certain truth, if ye possess a jewel, of which others are deprived, share it with them in a language of utmost kindliness and good-will. If it be accepted, if it fulfil its purpose, your object is attained. If any one should refuse it, leave him unto himself, and beseech God to guide him. Beware lest ye deal unkindly with him. A kindly tongue is the lodestone of the hearts of men. It is the bread of the spirit, it clotheth the words with meaning, it is the fountain of the light of wisdom and understanding.
>
> Bahá'u'lláh, *Gleanings*, p. 188

> Utterance must needs possess penetrating power. For if bereft of this quality it would fail to exert influence. And this penetrating influence dependeth on the spirit being pure and the heart stainless. Likewise it needeth moderation, without which the hearer would be unable to bear it, rather he would manifest opposition from the very outset. And moderation will be obtained by blending utterance with the tokens of divine wisdom which are recorded in the sacred Books and Tablets. Thus when the essence of one's utterance is endowed with these two requisites it will prove highly effective and will be the prime factor in transforming the souls of men. This is the station of supreme victory and celestial dominion. Whoso attaineth thereto is invested with the power to teach the Cause of God and to prevail over the hearts and minds of men.
>
> Bahá'u'lláh, *Tablets of Bahá'u'lláh*, pp. 198–9

The wise are they that speak not unless they obtain a hearing, even as the cup-bearer, who proffereth not his cup till he findeth a seeker, and the lover who crieth not out from the depths of his heart until he gazeth upon the beauty of his beloved. Wherefore sow the seeds of wisdom and knowledge in the pure soil of the heart, and keep them hidden, till the hyacinths of divine wisdom spring from the heart and not from mire and clay.

Bahá'u'lláh, *Hidden Words*, Persian no. 36

Surely the ideal way of teaching is to prove our points by constant reference to the actual words of Bahá'u'lláh and the Master. This will save the Cause from being misinterpreted by individuals. It is what these divine Lights say that is truth and therefore they should be the authorities of our statements. This, however, does not mean that our freedom of expression is limited. We can always find new ways of approach to that truth or explain how they influence our life and condition. The more deep our studies the more we can understand the significance of the teachings.

In the Cause we cannot divorce the letter from the spirit of the words. As Bahá'u'lláh says we should take the outward significance and superimpose upon it the inner. Either without the other is wrong and defective.

Letter written on behalf of Shoghi Effendi, in *Compilation*, vol. 1, p. 215

EXERCISE

Discuss or write about examples from your own experience that demonstrate the wisdom of using moderation in our speech when teaching.

POINT TO PONDER

Would forcing your views, even the most enlightened and loving views, on another prove that you weren't living by the very precepts you were trying to force on another? Remember, sovereignty is an attribute of God. The development of personal sovereignty requires that every individual use his or her God-given right and responsibility to make choices for himself or herself. Responding to the Word of God from anything but inner conviction and personal attraction offers no true foundation for the development of faith and certitude.

However, teaching is not only about *words*; it's about the energy they carry and the intention behind them.

STORIES

In 1914 the Master wrote to the friends in Denver concerning how to convey the message of Bahá'u'lláh: 'The three conditions of teaching the Cause of God are the science of sociability, purity of deeds and sweetness of speech. I hope each one of you may become confirmed with these attributes.'

Earlier in New York City, He had spoken to His friends about their going to Green Acre, the Bahá'í summer school in Maine: 'You must give the message through action and deed, not alone by word. Word must be conjoined with deed . . . May everyone point to you and ask 'Why are these people so happy?' I want you to be happy . . . to laugh, smile and rejoice in order that others may be made happy by you.'

On the same subject He wrote: 'Caution and prudence, however, must be observed even as recorded in the Book. The veil must in no wise be suddenly rent asunder.'

The teacher should also be concerned about the listener's physical needs. This practical approach was apparent in 'Abdu'l-Bahá's words: 'Never talk about God to a man with an empty stomach. Feed him first.'

Honnold, *Vignettes*, pp. 119–20

Howard Colby Ives learned this about public speaking from 'Abdu'l-Bahá:

I think it was in connection with the plans for His approaching visit to the Brotherhood Church that He said to me one day: that He had noticed that many ministers and public speakers prepare their addresses in advance, often committing them to memory and speaking the same words to many different audiences. He paused and looked at me a little humorously, a little sadly, and added: that He wondered how they can be sure of what God wants them to say until they look into the faces of their people.

Ives, *Portals to Freedom*, pp. 72–3

By referring to sociability as a *science*, is 'Abdu'l-Bahá pointing out that there is a structure to it that can be learned – that it's not simply a thing of personality or temperament?

READING

In teaching the Cause, much depends on the personality of the teacher and on the method he chooses for presenting the message. Different personalities and different classes and types of individuals need different methods of approach. And it is the sign of an able teacher to know how to best adapt his methods to various types of people whom he happens to meet. There is no one method one can follow all through. But there should be as many ways of approach as there are types of individual seekers. Flexibility and variety of method is, therefore, an essential prerequisite for the success of every teaching activity.

Letter written on behalf of Shoghi Effendi, in *Compilation*, vol. 2, p. 308

VIEWPOINT

Teaching the Faith is no different from anything else you want to accomplish: it requires knowledge, volition and action – and, especially with teaching, the knowledge, volition and action are all love. Putting your efforts into becoming attracted and loving is enormously more effective – and satisfying for all concerned! – than studying teaching strategies and methods. Bahá'u'lláh has the same method for every one of us: He *loves* us.

It's not what you say that's important, it's that *you* don't block the flow of His love with agendas or ego-issues. Being a self-conscious teacher of the Bahá'í Faith is an oxymoron: if you're self-conscious, you're not teaching about Bahá'u'lláh – you're talking – or you're possibly *informing*, but not *teaching*. Follow the oath that physicians are to follow: First, do no harm. Anything that impedes the flow of love is harmful.

oxymoron putting together apparently contradictory ideas or terms

READING

Bahá'u'lláh, speaking of His regard for 'Abdu'l-Bahá (here

referred to as the Most Great Branch) describes the perfect 'method' for teaching:

> A pleasing, kindly disposition and a display of tolerance towards the people are requisites of teaching the Cause. Whatever a person says, hollow and product of vain imaginings and a parrot-like repetition of somebody else's views though it be, one ought to let it pass. One should not engage in disputation leading to and ending with obstinate refusal and hostility, because the other person would consider himself worsted and defeated. Consequently further veils intervene between him and the Cause, and he becomes more negligent of it. One ought to say: right, admitted, but look at the matter in this other way, and judge for yourself whether it is true or false; of course it should be said with courtesy, with kindliness, with consideration. Then the other person will listen, will not seek to answer back and to marshal proofs in repudiation. He will agree, because he comes to realize that the purpose has not been to engage in verbal battle and to gain mastery over him. He sees that the purpose has been to impart the word of truth, to show humanity, to bring forth heavenly qualities. His eyes and his ears are opened, his heart responds, his true nature unfolds, and by the grace of God, he becomes a new creation. The Most Great Branch gives a willing ear to any manner of senseless talk, to such an extent that the other person says to himself: He is trying to learn from me. Then, gradually, by such means as the other person cannot perceive, He gives him insight and understanding.
>
> Bahá'u'lláh, quoted in Balyuzi, *'Abdu'l-Bahá*, p. 27

STORY

An incident from the biography of Hand of the Cause Corinne True:

> For Corinne it was another lesson that one of the major aims of life is to learn to rely on Divine protection in all aspects of life. She knew the Master did. She also knew that whatever He did was for the benefit of those with Him. A great concern of hers was whether she would be able to acquire just a fraction of the kind of faith the Master always displayed.

Her faith would soon be tested by 'Abdu'l-Bahá. It took place on the railroad station platform on the last day of His Chicago visit. While waiting for His train to St Paul, Minnesota, the Master turned to Corinne and said, 'Mrs True, I want you to speak in public. I want you to tell the people about the Faith.'

Stunned, she replied, 'But Master, I can't do it; I have no training, no experience . . . I'm too frank.' Corinne had always been reserved. Public speaking wasn't her forte. There were so many gifted orators among the Bahá'ís, especially the men. She was in a dilemma, because the Master had made this request. She wouldn't know how to begin to become an able speaker; but she knew she had to make a beginning. And 'Abdu'l-Bahá, as if reading her mind, provided her with guidelines to follow. 'Forget what you can't do,' He said. 'Stand up and turn your heart wholly toward me. Look over the heads of the audience and I'll never fail you.'

Though the prospect of having to give a public talk frightened her, her fear of failing to heed the Master's appeal drove her to speak as He urged her to do. From then on she was able to speak easily and fluently to all audiences.

Rutstein, *Corinne True*, pp. 107–8

Could use of the terms 'Bahá'í' and 'non-Bahá'í' highlight a subtle prejudice – a way of seeing difference or distinction? Did 'Abdu'l-Bahá ever refer to anyone as a 'non-Bahá'í'?

Isn't it the case that we're *all* learning about the Faith and becoming Bahá'ís (or not) with every thought and action?

'Abdu'l-Bahá says that He hopes we 'will all become the well-wishers of the world of mankind' (*Selections*, p. 29). Does concentrating your efforts on 'becoming a well-wisher of the world of mankind' help clarify what 'teaching the Faith' means?

VIEWPOINT

The closer we can come to uniting our heart to another's, the larger the doorway for Bahá'u'lláh to enter becomes. We are simply a channel, not the water. Stay clear! And don't go hosing down people who'd rather stay dry – appreciate their dryness and let them wade into the ocean of His love as they choose. Our job is to have the ocean available to them, to point it out and let them get a feel for it. As they become attracted, we will be there to invite them in for a swim.

> The aim of the Bahá'í teacher is that the Message of God may be glorified and that the individual may be enabled to embrace His Cause, celebrate His praise, and draw nearer to Him. The act of teaching, more than anything else, evokes the good-pleasure of God.
>
> Taherzadeh, *Revelation of Bahá'u'lláh*, vol. 2, p. 94

5

Deeds, Not Words

Beware, O people of Bahá, lest ye walk in the ways of them whose words differ from their deeds. Strive that ye may be enabled to manifest to the peoples of the earth the signs of God, and to mirror forth His commandments. Let your acts be a guide unto all mankind, for the professions of most men, be they high or low, differ from their conduct. It is through your deeds that ye can distinguish yourselves from others. Through them the brightness of your light can be shed upon the whole earth. Happy is the man that heedeth My counsel, and keepeth the precepts prescribed by Him Who is the All-Knowing, the All-Wise.

professions open declarations

Bahá'u'lláh, *Gleanings*, p. 305

Love manifests its reality in deeds, not only in words – these alone are without effect.

'Abdu'l-Bahá, *Paris Talks*, p. 35

People have grown weary and impatient of rhetoric and discourse, of preaching and sermonizing. In this day, the one thing that can deliver the world from its travail and attract the hearts of its peoples is deeds, not words; example, not precept; saintly virtues, not statements and charters issued by governments and nations on socio-political affairs. In all matters, great or small, word must be the complement of deed, and deed the companion of word: each must supplement, support and reinforce the other.

rhetoric the art of good speaking or writing; speech or writing too showy, often insincere or empty

discourse a speech, sermon, lecture; to converse formally

precept a rule to guide one's action; a commandment

Letter written on behalf of Shoghi Effendi, in *Compilation*, vol. 1, p. 62

complement that which completes

The essence of faith is fewness of words and abundance of deeds; he whose words exceed his deeds, know verily his death is better than his life.

Bahá'u'lláh, *Tablets of Bahá'u'lláh*, p. 156

POINTS TO PONDER

What does 'the essence of faith' mean?

Does 'his death is better than his life' tell us anything about hypocrisy?

Section VII

Being Happy
Laws, Intentions, Faith, Tests

I

Laws = Love Applied

INTRODUCTION

The laws brought to humanity by the Manifestations of God are the source of vision and knowledge – the vision of who we are and the knowledge that forms the basis of self-respect and morality. Responding to these spiritual laws creates, develops and enhances genuine morality and self-respect, thus ensuring personal well-being and enthusiasm for actively participating in the realization of an ever-advancing civilization. This self-respect and morality are synonymous with 'the fear of God'.

Read about the Fear of God in Section IX.

Discipline and training are indispensable in all aspects of life. It is obvious that if a child is left entirely undisciplined and untrained, it will not be fit to be in human society – the capacity and potential in its life will be tragically wasted and misspent. The three kinds of education mentioned below are each essential for the progress of humanity, individually and collectively.

discipline please note that the root of this word is the same as for disciple – an active adherent of a movement or philosophy

READING

When we consider existence, we see that the mineral, vegetable, animal and human worlds are all in need of an educator . . . If there were no educator, there would be no such things as comforts, civilization or humanity. If a man be left alone in a wilderness where he sees none of his own kind, he will undoubtedly become a mere brute; it is then clear that an educator is needed.

But education is of three kinds: material, human and spiritual. Material education is concerned with the progress and development of the body, through gaining its sustenance, its material comfort and ease . . . Human education signifies civilization and progress . . . Divine education is that of the Kingdom of God: it consists in acquiring divine perfections, and this is true education . . .

'Abdu'l-Bahá, *Some Answered Questions*, pp. 7–8

VIEWPOINT

Education – all education – requires submission to discipline and sacrifice: we must be willing to give up our ignorance in order to learn anything and to sacrifice our lesser motives and qualities in order to grow and develop socially and spiritually.

MEMORIZE

The Great Being saith: The structure of world stability and order hath been reared upon, and will continue to be sustained by, the twin pillars of reward and punishment.

Bahá'u'lláh, *Gleanings*, p. 219

POINTS TO PONDER

What sustains the structure of world stability?

Is this true of the spiritual as well as the physical laws?

Are you 'punished' – do you suffer – if you don't obey a physical law, even if you didn't *know* the law?

Is the same true of spiritual laws?

Would it be a good idea, for your own protection, to know the laws?

READINGS

The primary purpose, the basic objective, in laying down powerful laws and setting up great principles and institutions dealing with every aspect of civilization, is human happiness; and human happiness consists only in drawing

closer to the Threshold of Almighty God, and in securing
the peace and well-being of every individual member, high
and low alike, of the human race; and the supreme agencies
for accomplishing these two objectives are the excellent
qualities with which humanity has been endowed . . . For
results which would . . . secure the peace and well-being of
man, could never be fully achieved in a merely external
civilization.

'Abdu'l-Bahá, *The Secret of Divine Civilization*, pp. 60–1

What is the purpose of obeying these laws?

The purpose is the result which is accomplished – love and
unity among mankind. For the world is dark with discord
and selfishness, hearts are negligent, souls are bereft of God
and His heavenly bestowals. Man is submerged in the affairs
of this world. His aims, objects and attainments are mortal,
whereas God desires for him immortal accomplishments. In
his heart there is no thought of God. He has sacrificed his
portion and birthright of divine spirituality.
   . . . The bliss of man is the acquiring of heavenly
bestowals, which descend upon him in the outflow of the
bounty of God. The happiness of man is in the fragrance of
the love of God. This is the highest pinnacle of attainment
in the human world.

'Abdu'l-Bahá, *Promulgation of Universal Peace*, p. 185

When reality envelops the soul of man, love is possible. The
divine purpose in religion is pure love and agreement.

'Abdu'l-Bahá, *Promulgation of Universal Peace*, p. 234

MEMORIZE

When the love of God is established, everything else will be
realized.

'Abdu'l-Bahá, *Promulgation of Universal Peace*, p. 239

VIEWPOINT

There are physical laws, such as gravity, that make it possible to
enjoy living on the earth. These laws have two sides to them: you
could say that all laws have rewards and punishments built into

them. Gravity – which literally makes it possible for you to remain on earth – will pull you to the ground, and fire – with all its wonderful uses – will burn you if you touch it. Would it make sense to walk off the edge of a roof or stick your hand in a fire and expect to be unhurt? The pain is 'punishment' or 'retribution' for breaking a natural law. The punishment is for your training and guidance: in the future, you probably won't walk off a roof (☺ at least not that very same roof!) or stick your hand in the fire.

On the other hand, if you break a spiritual law, you will be 'punished' by being far from God, distant from your source of consciousness and love. The unhappiness in the world is caused by breaking spiritual laws, which hurts more than just yourself. Society suffers when laws are broken, whether they be civil or spiritual. Our higher nature fears causing this kind of damage and confusion. This 'fear', like the fear of putting your hand in a fire, is a powerful reminder to pay attention to the law – helpful for our overall well-being and a sign of the mercy and grace of God.

On all levels – physical, civil and spiritual – there are consequences to breaking laws. Breaking the law results in these consequences, which are not dependent upon knowledge of the law. Learning what the laws are and obeying them preserves us from unnecessary tests and helps us avoid unnecessary suffering.

> Laws restrict freedom in order to safeguard, enhance and develop personal and social well-being – thereby providing more freedom than we would have without them.

READINGS

... the fundamental purpose of all religions – including our own – is to bring man nearer to God, and to change his character, which is of the utmost importance. Too much emphasis is often laid on the social and economic aspects of the Teachings; but the moral aspect cannot be overemphasized.
Letter written on behalf of Shoghi Effendi, in *Lights of Guidance*, 3rd ed., p. 506

The inestimable value of religion is that when a man is vitally connected with it, through a real and living belief in it and in the Prophet Who brought it, he receives a strength greater than his own which helps him to develop his good characteristics and overcome his bad ones. The whole purpose of religion is to change not only our thoughts but our acts; when we believe in God and His Prophet and His

Teachings, we find we are growing even though we perhaps thought ourselves incapable of growth and change!

Letter written on behalf of Shoghi Effendi, in *Lights of Guidance*, 3rd ed., p. 508

It is the challenging task of the Bahá'ís to obey the law of God in their own lives, and gradually to win the rest of mankind to its acceptance.

In considering the effect of obedience to the laws on individual lives, one must remember that the purpose of this life is to prepare the soul for the next. Here one must learn to control and direct one's animal impulses, not to be a slave to them. Life in this world is a succession of tests and achievements, of falling short and of making new spiritual advances. Sometimes the course may seem very hard, but one can witness, again and again, that the soul who steadfastly obeys the law of Bahá'u'lláh, however hard it may seem, grows spiritually, while the one who compromises with the law for the sake of his own apparent happiness is seen to have been following a chimera: he does not attain the happiness he sought, he retards his spiritual advance and often brings new problems upon himself.

Shoghi Effendi, in *Compilation*, vol. 1, pp. 63–4

VIEWPOINT

As you deepen and apply the daily requisites for spiritual growth to your life, you will become aware that Bahá'u'lláh's laws, ordinances and exhortations cover every facet of life and are accessible throughout the writings, prayers and Tablets. Many of Bahá'u'lláh's laws can be found in the Kitáb-i-Aqdas, the Book of Laws, the Most Holy Book.

MEMORIZE

. . . order your lives in accordance with the first principle of the divine teaching, which is love.

'Abdu'l-Bahá, *Promulgation of Universal Peace*, p. 8

Everything must be done in order that humanity may live under the shadow of God in the utmost security, enjoying happiness in its highest degree.

'Abdu'l-Bahá, *Promulgation of Universal Peace*, p. 270

It's *not* up to you to enforce these laws in anyone else's life.

chimera a creation of the imagination; a foolish fancy

. . . for the will and law of God is love, and love is the bond between human hearts.
'Abdu'l-Bahá, *Promulgation of Universal Peace*, p. 287

Believe in order that you may understand; unless you shall believe, you shall not understand.
St Augustine

Have you ever noticed that 'It's the principle of the thing' becomes a justification for righteous indignation and estrangement? Well, the 'principle of the thing' – anything and all things! – is love, so it is not possible to justify indignation or estrangement on matters of principle any more.

235

2

Intentions

There is another aspect to spiritual laws: intention. It is not enough merely to know the laws and not break them; to develop our spirituality, we must form the intention of actively carrying out the spirit of the law. If I do or say something thoughtless and it makes you sad, I can say I didn't intend to hurt you. However, you *were* hurt because I wasn't consciously intending to love you or loving you wasn't *really* my priority. We are always forming intentions; we are rarely conscious of them. For example, my intention to watch the television might overcome my higher, but forgotten, choice of being courteous and loving to a visitor who drops by or a family member who wants to talk.

If I had remembered my intention to be actively conscious of the spirit of the laws (to be kind and loving), I would have been less likely to hurt you thoughtlessly or to be rude to my visitor. Bahá'u'lláh's laws about daily prayer and meditation are to help us remain conscious of our true intentions, as are the 'Six Requisites for Spiritual Growth' we studied previously in this User's Guide.

STORY

One morning in 'Akká 'Abdu'l-Bahá spoke to a pilgrim who was leaving:

> You must always do your best to behave spiritually, not physically, so that everyone who meets you will know that your intention is to do good to mankind and your aim to serve the world of humanity. Whatever you do, let the people

know you are doing it for good, not only to earn your own living. By doing thus you will be able to serve every city to which you go. Now associate with good people. You must try to associate with those who will do you good and who will be the cause of your being more awakened, and not with those who will make you negligent of God . . . In short, I mean that you will try to be with those who are purified and sanctified souls. Man must always associate with those from whom he can get light, or be with those to whom he can give light. He must either receive or give instructions. Otherwise, being with people without these two intentions, he is spending his time for nothing, and, by so doing, he is neither gaining nor causing others to gain.

'Abdu'l-Bahá, quoted in *The Diary of Juliet Thompson*, pp. 49–50

MEMORIZE

Intention brings attainment.

'Abdu'l-Bahá, quoted in Grundy, *Ten Days in the Light of 'Akká*, p. 31

'Abdu'l-Bahá reminds us to prioritize our intentions:

Nothing is too much trouble when one loves and there is always time.

'Abdu'l-Bahá, quoted in Ives, *Portals to Freedom*, p. 52

VIEWPOINT

Notice that 'Abdu'l-Bahá uses the qualification 'when one loves'. Unless loving action is your conscious intention, a whole bunch of things are too much trouble and there generally isn't time! Don't you usually find time for the things you really love?

EXERCISE

Review your priorities daily in light of 'Abdu'l-Bahá's statement (a major part of bringing yourself to account, isn't it?) and, when necessary, set new priorities that better serve your ideals.

Don't try – intend!

If you boarded an airplane and, just as you were about to fasten your seat belt, the captain announced, 'We're going to *try* to take this plane to New York today', would you feel confident about staying on the plane? Learning to speak and think and act with *intention* brings attainment.

You can find out what you *really* love and support in your life by looking at how you spend your resources – the three ts: time, talent, treasure.

This story about 'Abdu'l-Bahá demonstrates the reality that
when one loves, nothing is too much trouble and there is always
time:

The last morning came. The secretaries and several friends
were ready to start for the train.

'Abdu'l-Bahá sat calmly writing. We reminded Him that
the hour to leave for the train was at hand. He looked up,
saying: 'There are things of more importance than trains,'
and He continued to write.

Suddenly in breathless haste a man came in, carrying in
his hand a beautiful garland of fragrant white flowers.
Bowing low before the Master, he said: 'In the name of the
disciples of Zoroaster, The Pure One, I hail Thee as the
"Promised Sháh Bahrám"!'

Then the man, for a sign, garlanded 'Abdu'l-Bahá, and
proceeded to anoint each and all of the amazed friends who
were present with precious oil, which had the odour of fresh
roses.

This brief but impressive ceremony concluded, 'Abdu'l-
Bahá, having carefully divested Himself of the garland,
departed for the train.

We had witnessed a solemn act in the Mysterious Sacred
Drama of the World.

Blomfield, *The Chosen Highway*, pp. 173–4

3

What is 'Faith'?

The question was asked, 'What is real Faith?' 'Abdu'l-Bahá answered:

Faith outwardly means to believe the Message a Manifestation brings to the world and accept the fulfilment in Him of that which the Prophets have announced. But, in reality, Faith embodies three degrees: – To confess with the tongue; to believe in the heart; to give evidence in our actions. These three things are essential in true Faith. The important requirement is the Love of God in the heart. For instance, we say a lamp gives light. In reality, the oil which burns produces the illumination, but the lamp and the chimney are necessary before the light can express itself. The Love of God is the light. The tongue is the chimney or the medium by which that Love finds expression. It also protects the Light. Likewise, the members of the body reflect the inner Light by their actions. So the tongue confesses in speech, and the parts of the body confess in their actions the Love of God within the soul of a true believer . . . Many claim to possess the true Faith, but it is rare and when it exists it cannot be destroyed. 'Many are called but few are chosen.' Many believe themselves to be courageous, but the battlefield of tests and trials will prove whether they have the real strength to stand firm.

'Abdu'l-Bahá, quoted in Grundy, *Ten Days in the Light of 'Akká*, pp. 59–60

There is always an important difference between friends and tested friends. No matter how precious the first type may be, the future of the Cause rests upon the latter.

Letter written on behalf of Shoghi Effendi, in *Compilation*, vol. 1, p. 165

MEMORIZE

The first sign of Faith is love.

'Abdu'l-Bahá, *Promulgation of Universal Peace*, p. 337

POINTS TO PONDER

What does this mean?

How can we tell if we have faith?

VIEWPOINT

We are each of us, alone, responsible for the development of the spirit of faith within us. No one else can be blamed if we fail to recognize and respond.

READINGS

. . . every man hath been, and will continue to be, able of himself to appreciate the Beauty of God, the Glorified. Had he not been endowed with such a capacity, how could he be called to account for his failure? . . . For the faith of no man can be conditioned by any one except himself.

Bahá'u'lláh, *Gleanings*, p. 143

. . . the core of religious faith is that mystic feeling that unites man with God. This state of spiritual communion can be brought about and maintained by means of meditation and prayer . . .

The believers, particularly the young ones, should therefore fully realize the necessity of praying. For prayer is absolutely indispensable to their inner spiritual development, and this, already stated, is the very foundation and purpose of the Religion of God.

Letter written on behalf of Shoghi Effendi, *Compilation*, vol. 2, p. 238

I know God is with me, because I know I am with God.

Bob Stevens

240

By faith is meant, first, conscious knowledge, and second, the
practice of good deeds.

'Abdu'l-Bahá, *Bahá'í World Faith*, p. 383

VIEWPOINT

The very word 'faith', as 'Abdu'l-Bahá defines it, includes the
three essentials for achieving anything: knowledge, volition and
action. With 'conscious knowledge' we are connected to the
source of all love and enthusiasm, making the practice of good
deeds almost inevitable!

POINTS TO PONDER

What do you think 'Abdu'l-Bahá means by 'conscious
knowledge'?

If you truly have conscious knowledge of the love surrounding
all creation, is it possible to sit still or to be apathetic?

Is faith something you just have or is it something that must be
consciously developed?

How can you know what 'good deeds' are?

VIEWPOINT

By now you may be asking yourself, how can I acquire faith?
Where does it come from?
   Remember attraction? In order to develop faith, develop
attraction. Think of ways to use all of your powers – physical
and spiritual – to develop attraction, to develop the spirit of faith
in yourself.

READINGS

The flame of the fire of love, in this world of earth and

water, comes through the power of attraction and not by
effort and striving.

'Abdu'l-Bahá, *Some Answered Questions*, p. 130

Beg everything thou desirest from Bahá'u'lláh. If thou art
asking faith, ask of Him. If thou art yearning after
knowledge, He will grant it unto Thee. If thou art longing
for the love of God, He will bestow it upon thee. He will
descend upon thee all His blessings.

'Abdu'l-Bahá, quoted in *Star of the West*, vol. 9, no. 9, p. 104

Begging itself requires
knowledge – that you
want something; volition
– willingness to ask for it;
and action – sincerely and
urgently asking for it.

VIEWPOINT

Above we read that 'Abdu'l-Bahá described 'faith' as 'first,
conscious knowledge, and second, the practice of good deeds'
('Abdu'l-Bahá, *Bahá'í World Faith*, p. 383). However, the Báb tells
us that 'deeds are secondary to faith in Him [Bahá'u'lláh] and
certitude in His Reality' (The Báb, *Selections from the Writings of the
Báb*, p. 133).

POINTS TO PONDER

Can these two statements be reconciled?

Is 'conscious knowledge' the same as faith in Bahá'u'lláh?

Why do you think that deeds are secondary to faith in
Bahá'u'lláh?

If you are doing good deeds but are not making choices from
your higher self, are you developing spiritual strength?

If you are doing what's 'right' but have no idea why or are only
doing it because of what others might think, is your heart
brought closer to God?

READING

. . . attaining the presence of God . . . this is the object of our
creation and the sole purpose underlying every virtuous

deed we may perform . . . Know thou, that thou wilt succeed
in doing so if thou believest with undoubting faith.

The Báb, *Selections from the Writings of the Báb*, p. 110

Is it selfish to want to attain the presence of God or arrogant to
think that you can? Ponder this. What is the source of
selflessness and genuine humility?

Do you believe with undoubting faith that you can attain the
presence of God at will? If not, review the quotation of the Báb
above: do you believe that the Manifestation of God is
misleading you or somehow left you out?

READINGS

Lo, I am with you always means when you look for God,
God is in the look of your eyes,
in the thought of looking, nearer to you than your self,
or things that have happened to you
There's no need to go outside.

Rúmí

I desire communion with thee,
but thou wouldst put no trust in Me.
The sword of thy rebellion hath felled the tree of thy hope.
At all times I am near unto thee,
but thou art ever far from Me.
Imperishable glory I have chosen for thee,
yet boundless shame thou hast chosen for thyself.
While there is yet time, return,
and lose not thy chance.

Bahá'u'lláh, *Hidden Words*, Persian no. 21

MEMORIZE

Do you recall this passage from the chapter 'Deeds, Not Words'?

The essence of faith is fewness of words and abundance of

deeds; he whose words exceed his deeds, know verily that his death is better than his life.

Bahá'u'lláh, *Tablets of Bahá'u'lláh*, p. 156

Faith is not so much what we believe as what we carry out.

'Abdu'l-Bahá quoted in Grundy, *Ten Days in the Light of 'Akká*, p. 13

POINTS TO PONDER

If I tell you that I have faith in the power of unity and then I talk behind your back or I am thoughtless or cruel to you, do I really have faith in the power of unity? Does my belief in unity do us any good?

How does the quotation that begins 'The essence of faith' apply to your personal commitment to transformation?

Does the motive behind the deed or thought determine whether we are being faithful or not?

If I don't follow the teachings because I want to be comfortable, what do I *really* believe in: the teachings or the need to be comfortable?

READINGS

Our Actions reveal what we are, no matter what the tongue speaks.

'Abdu'l-Bahá, quoted in Grundy, *Ten Days in the Light of 'Akká*, p. 5

Is not faith but another word for implicit obedience, whole-hearted allegiance, uncompromising adherence to that which we believe is the revealed and express will of God, however perplexing it might first appear, however at variance with the shadowy views, the impotent doctrines, the crude theories, the idle imaginings, the fashionable conceptions of a transient and troublous age? If we are to falter or hesitate, if our love for Him should fail to direct us and keep us within His path, if we desert Divine and emphatic principles, what hope can we any more cherish for healing the ills and sicknesses of this world?

Shoghi Effendi, *Bahá'í Administration*, pp. 62–3

☺ A story about faith and belief:

You're walking down a city street. You see a tightrope walker set up his high wire between two buildings several floors above the street. He walks back and forth on the wire, pushing a wheelbarrow. He stops and shouts to you, 'Do you believe I can walk across this wire again?' Having witnessed his skill several times, you say, 'Yes.' Then he calls down, 'Do you have faith that I can do this again?' Your answer is again 'Yes'. The tightrope walker immediately says, 'O.K.! Get in the wheelbarrow!'

implicit understood, meant though not actually said; unquestioning

Can you tell what your true goals are by what you do and how you act?

What is the 'revealed and express will of God'?

Is it beneficial to be obedient to God's laws brought by Bahá'u'lláh even if you don't yet understand the reason for the law?

Whether or not you *believe* in the spiritual laws, are they as binding upon you as physical laws such as gravity? Do you have to understand the reason for gravity in order to be obedient to its demands?

Are there consequences to not obeying God's laws?

Does becoming a Bahá'í mean that you are consciously committed to making daily efforts to live in the spirit of Bahá'u'lláh's Teachings?

4

Faith in Disguise

Expectations and Balance

z

READINGS

. . . whatsoever ye shall ask in prayer, believing, ye shall receive.

Matt. 21:22

According to your faith be it unto you.

Matt. 9:29

Ask, and it shall be given you; seek, and ye shall find; knock, and it shall be opened unto you.

Matt. 7:7

What things soever ye desire, when ye pray, believe that ye receive them, and ye shall have them.

Mark 11:24

INTRODUCTION

Expectation and faith are related concepts. If we expect something to happen, we generally have faith that it will – and we plan and live our lives in anticipation of it. For example, if I have a dreaded and very important test tomorrow – one that I'm sure I'll do badly in – I'm not likely to be sparkling and happy now. On the other hand, knowing that I'll be with good friends tomorrow and that we'll have time to enjoy each other makes me happy today.

We were created to love and if we don't protect, develop and apply this essential aspect of ourselves appropriately, instead of

246

bringing us closer to God, it will distract and destroy us. This is also true of the power of expectation, the capacity for faith. Misapplied, it can be disastrous; if left undeveloped and under the rule of the ego, we have 'blind faith'. True faith is *never* blind – in fact, it is the essence and source of clarity and vision.

The saying 'What you see is what you get' is often true in matters large and small. Our focus creates our perception of our experiences, influencing ourselves and others; so it is important to check on our thoughts and expectations and to learn to keep them in line with our true priorities. For instance, what are we really expecting – putting our faith in – when we are worrying about something or looking for faults in ourselves or others?

An awareness of the value of each day – and the importance of remaining conscious and grateful for whatever opportunities come along – enlivens each moment with powers and possibilities. How can we anticipate anything but success and joy – especially in sharing the Faith with others – if we really believe what Bahá'u'lláh tells us?

Here's Rúmí on the subject of perceptions:

You're like the child that has turned round and round
and now you think
the house is turning.

MEMORIZE

'Abdu'l-Bahá tells us that we can expect to receive powers and blessings if we have faith:

> And now I give you a commandment which shall be for a covenant between you and Me – that ye have faith; that your faith be steadfast as a rock that no storms can move, that nothing can disturb, and that it endure through all things even to the end . . . be not shaken in your faith; for I am with you to the end. As ye have faith so shall your powers and blessings be. This is the balance – this is the balance – this is the balance.
>
> 'Abdu'l-Bahá, quoted in Balyuzi, *'Abdu'l-Bahá*, p. 73

Remember, a covenant is a promise between at least two parties – you promise to do something in return for something else.

VIEWPOINT

The point of balance is the point where any number of forces and objects and outlooks come together in unity and harmony. Our powers and blessings absolutely depend on our faith in the covenant: our faith in the unifying power of love must outweigh our ego's faith in power struggles and all sorts of defensive

247

manoeuvres. If we don't want to lose our balance and fall on our faces, it's vitally important that we remember to stand on the point of equilibrium, loving one another as 'Abdu'l-Bahá loves us.

☺ The point of balance is the Point of Balance! The point is not in the things or viewpoints or forces being balanced; the focal point is the balance itself, the Centre of the Covenant, 'Abdu'l-Bahá. Our mutual attraction to this point is what allows us to experience true unity, which would be impossible otherwise.

EXERCISE

The emphasis 'Abdu'l-Bahá puts on the concept of balance and its relationship with faith and the covenant makes a wonderful focus for meditation.

POINTS TO PONDER

How can you be sure that 'Abdu'l-Bahá is with you?

When He says 'I am with you always' in the quotation above, do you believe it really means *you?*

Does this mean that as your faith (conscious knowledge and the practice of good deeds) grows, your powers and blessings will, too?

If you are feeling that your powers and blessings aren't very good, can you remedy that by having more faith?

What does having more faith mean? Does it mean creating something blindly with your imagination and trying to convince yourself it's true, or is it a matter of focus on and attraction to the will of God?

If you believe that things will go badly or that you can't do something, does that mean that you have a sort of negative faith?

Could negative expectations cause things to work out badly as you expect them to?

Is the power of expectation like the power of faith: does it change things and affect our perceptions?

What is the will of God for this age?

How can you develop more genuine faith that will develop your strength and assurance in a positive way?

EXERCISES

Why does 'Abdu'l-Bahá say 'This is the balance'? What does 'balance' mean in this quotation? How does it relate to our expectations of life? What happens if you're out of balance – or unbalanced – physically? Spiritually? Think about this and discuss it in your group or write about it in your journal.

Here's another quotation about balance. Discuss or write in your journal what it means and its relationship to 'Abdu'l-Bahá's quotation above.

> Set before thine eyes God's unerring Balance and, as one standing in His Presence, weigh in that Balance thine actions every day, every moment of thy life.
>
> Bahá'u'lláh, *Gleanings*, p. 236

- It may be helpful to remind yourself that you're one of very few on earth right now who are consciously and intentionally participating actively in the building of 'the Kingdom of God on earth'. Remember, standing in His Presence is standing in the Presence of love – how do your actions measure up to the standard of love and unity?

- Is it important to note your progress as well as areas that need to be worked on in your life – to remember it's a process? Why?

- When setting your priorities after reflecting on this passage, remember to include actively participating in the plans set by the Universal House of Justice.

VIEWPOINT

If you really want something, the fastest way to *get* it is to *become*

it. Want the world to change into paradise? Change your heart into paradise. Suppose you want a friend. What are all the things you'd want in a friend? Be specific. Now, attract those attributes into your heart and daily actions. You will *never* be without a friend again. Want gifts? Be generous.

This use of desires will never let you down or lead you astray, because your higher nature is working with your material nature and both will find it joyful and fulfilling. This is the balance to which 'Abdu'l-Bahá refers. This brings the integration of the material (ego) nature and the higher, spiritual nature and results in true integrity.

5

Tests = Opportunities
Winning the 'Battle of Life'

INTRODUCTION

Equipment is tested from time to time to see if it works as well as it should. We are constantly testing ourselves too – at work, in sports, at school and at games – to see how we are performing.

If you're in school and have been keeping up with your school work and you know the material, you probably look forward to tests because they give you an opportunity to find out how well you're doing. It's only if you haven't been keeping up or you don't understand the material that you dread tests. Then tests show where your weaknesses are – and your ego self is *not* fond of finding its weaknesses!

READINGS

Do men think when they say 'We believe' they shall be let alone and not put to proof?

Qur'án 71:26

Were it not for tests, the courageous could not be separated from the cowardly. Were it not for tests, the people of faithfulness could not be known from the disloyal. Were it not for tests, the intellectuals and the faculties of the scholars in great colleges would not develop. Were it not for tests, sparkling gems could not be known from worthless pebbles. Were it not for tests, nothing would progress in this contingent world.

'Abdu'l-Bahá, quoted in *Contentment*, p. 17

EXERCISE

Discuss your understanding of the meaning of this quotation or write about it in your journal.

VIEWPOINT

Ever tried to walk or drive on ice? Without friction (tests?), progress is very difficult! Without tests you'd never be able to apply your free will or develop your ability to make choices. Remember, though, that your struggle is within yourself, not with others. As you strengthen your spiritual responses, you will find your self-respect growing. If you don't live up to your own ideals, you will never win your own self-respect – so it won't help much if you are popular with others, will it? Spiritual challenges bring spiritual strength.

MEMORIZE

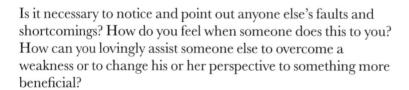

Each one of us is responsible for one life only, and that is our own.

Letter written on behalf of Shoghi Effendi, *Lights of Guidance*, p. 91

POINTS TO PONDER

Can anyone (even your parents) change or improve you? Isn't it always your choice, even if someone else is showing you how to do something or trying to force you to change?

Is it necessary to notice and point out anyone else's faults and shortcomings? How do you feel when someone does this to you? How can you lovingly assist someone else to overcome a weakness or to change his or her perspective to something more beneficial?

VIEWPOINT

Shoghi Effendi says, 'Ultimately all the battle of life is within the individual' (*Compilation*, vol. 2, p. 12).

This is good news and bad news! The good news is that we don't have to battle with anyone else: in fact, if we *are* battling with someone else, it's a sign that we're losing the real battle! The bad news is that there *will* be a battle – and that it will be between yourself and yourSELF.

Do you think that following the teachings of Bahá'u'lláh is difficult? Since most of your friends probably don't know the value (and difficulty) of spiritual development, and it is not, at present, greatly valued – in fact it is generally scorned – it is easy to feel that your spiritual efforts are undermined daily. Developing a spiritual outlook and discipline is not very popular in the world today.

'Abdu'l-Bahá faced difficulty all of His life. His father was put in prison and tortured when 'Abdu'l-Bahá was a small boy. The family was exiled, their home and property taken, and they were harassed and threatened most of the time. Friends and loved ones were killed in the streets. There are many stories of how 'Abdu'l-Bahá dealt with these sufferings. When we're faced with trials – and we will be, from inside and out – we can remember what He did and how He acted towards those who were hateful to Him. Remember, we're each of us changing the world by changing ourselves. Every hateful or fearful thought we replace with a thought of love makes the world a better place.

Tests are painful so that we will notice and remember to turn back to God, to review our priorities and recommit ourselves to act on our higher choices. It is also important to remember that when we commit to sacrificing a habit or quality, tests will keep coming so that we can remind ourselves of our highest choice, until the weakness has been replaced by a strength.

For example, if you decide to be more patient, all day things will happen to test your decision and to give you a chance to strengthen your commitment. The tests are almost always your ego (lower nature) and your higher, spiritual self battling over change – the ego doesn't usually like change at all. Everything that's between you and your goal of patience will get in your way so that you can choose to remove it and replace it with your higher choice. This is a blessing and a sign of the love of God. If you don't know this about tests, you might begin to think it's too hard to change – or that you're being punished for trying to change.

READING

For everything there is a sign. The sign of love is fortitude
under My decree and patience under My trials.

Bahá'u'lláh, Hidden Words, Arabic no. 48

POINTS TO PONDER

What does 'fortitude' mean?

Recall a time when you needed fortitude. How did you respond?

What is God's decree?

To what trials could He be referring?

MEMORIZE

O Son of Man! If adversity befall thee not in My path, how
canst thou walk in the ways of them that are content with
My pleasure? If trials afflict thee not in thy longing to meet
Me, how wilt thou attain the light in thy love for My beauty?

Bahá'u'lláh, Hidden Words, Arabic no. 50

EXERCISE

In your own words, write in your journal why tests are a sign of
love. Note in your journal a specific test from your own
experience that has helped you review your priorities and made
you stronger.

READING

The same test comes again in greater degree, until it is
shown that a former weakness has become a strength, and
the power to overcome evil has been established.

'Abdu'l-Bahá, quoted in Star of the West, vol. 6, no. 6, p. 45

6

Suffering?

As change is inevitable in life, no matter what choices we make, suffering is also inevitable: the ego/material nature, in its desire to protect and control, grieves over changes and throws up a lot of pain and anger in an attempt to keep things 'safe' and stable. This is a natural process and only becomes 'negative' or damaging if we get stuck in the ego's perception and grieve over what we're 'losing'.

READING

The more you beat upon the steel, the sharper is your sword. The longer you leave the gold in red-hot fire, the purer will it be.

Even among the people of the world, busy with their material pursuits, tests and trials play the same part. The more a man struggles, the more trials he bears in learning a profession or craft, the more skilful and adept he becomes. One whose days are leisurely and inactive never becomes proficient in anything.

'Abdu'l-Bahá, quoted in Gail, *Summon Up Remembrance*, pp. 255–6

VIEWPOINT

Is it worth suffering to grow and develop spiritually and to assist in the building of the 'Kingdom of God on earth'? To provide a valid answer to this question, better ask: 'Will I have to suffer *more* if I don't do this?' There is struggle and suffering involved in all things: hobbies, friendships, study, building, looking good, drawing, writing, learning *anything*. The more we are attracted, the more we are likely to use different words for this struggle and suffering: training, studying, figuring it out, talking it over, practising, caring, and working out. Notice how differently it affects your spirit when you use a word like 'learning' instead of a word like 'suffering'. It's *all* perception, isn't it?

The Heat of Midnight Tears

Listen, my friend, this road is the heart opening,
kissing His feet, resistance broken, tears all night.

If we could reach the Lord through immersion in water,
I would have asked to be born a fish in this life.
If we could reach Him through nothing but berries and wild
    nuts
Then surely the saints would have been monkeys when they
    came from the womb!
If we could reach Him by munching lettuce and dry leaves
Then the goats would surely get to the Holy One before us!

If the worship of stone statues could bring us all the way,
I would have adored a granite mountain years ago.

Mirabai says: The heat of midnight tears will bring you to
    God.

Mirabai

VIEWPOINT

By consciously choosing the spiritual path and using all of life's experiences to draw us closer to God – to develop our spiritual nature – we can never be victimized. 'Abdu'l-Bahá was the victim of oppression and persecution all of His life but He never allowed Himself to react negatively or with self-pity, nor did any of His difficulties affect His self-esteem or degrade Him. Every trial that came His way was used to prove the powers and possibilities available to all of us and to demonstrate the nobility of humankind under any and all conditions. The very recognition that anything can be used to draw us to our goal and to perfect our spirit enables us to meet all our experiences with the expectation of bounty and strength. 'Unless one accepts dire vicissitudes, not with dull resignation, but with radiant acquiescence, one cannot attain this freedom' ('Abdu'l-Bahá, quoted in Honnold, *Vignettes*, p. 10).

We gain power *through* our experiences, not *over* them. Life is a mystery to be lived, not a problem to be solved. This plane of existence is theatre and fable and myth – reflections of reality for the lessons involved.

STORY

On October 10 [1912] in San Francisco 'Abdu'l-Bahá went to visit Charles Tinsley, a black Bahá'í who had been laid up for a long time with a broken leg. 'I am impatient,' said Mr Tinsley, 'to be up and out to work for the Cause.'

The Master told him:

'You must not be sad. This affliction will make you spiritually stronger . . . you are dear to me. I will tell you a story:

'A certain ruler wished to appoint one of his subjects to a high office; so, in order to train him, the ruler cast him into prison and caused him to suffer much. The man was surprised at this, for he expected great favours. The ruler had him taken from prison and beaten with sticks. This greatly astonished the man, for he thought the ruler loved him. After this he was hanged on the gallows until he was nearly dead. After he recovered he asked the ruler, "If you love me, why did you do these things?" The ruler replied: "I wish to make you prime minister. By having gone through these ordeals you are better fitted for that office. I wish you to know how it is yourself. When you are obliged to punish, you will know how it feels to endure these things. I love you so I wish you to become perfect."'

'Abdu'l-Bahá then said to Charles:

'Even so with you. After this ordeal you will reach maturity. God sometimes causes us to suffer much and to have many misfortunes that we may become strong in His Cause.'

Brown, *Memories of 'Abdu'l-Bahá*, pp. 46–7

7

Don't Worry, Be Happy!

O God! Refresh and gladden my spirit. Purify my heart.
Illumine my powers. I lay all my affairs in Thy hand. Thou
art my Guide and my Refuge. I will no longer be sorrowful
and grieved; I will be a happy and joyful being. O God! I will
no longer be full of anxiety, nor will I let trouble harass me. I
will not dwell on the unpleasant things of life.

   O God! Thou art more friend to me than I am to myself. I
dedicate myself to Thee, O Lord!

'Abdu'l-Bahá, Bahá'í Prayers, p. 152

Know ye not that the Hand of God
   is over your hands,
      that His irrevocable Decree transcendeth all your devices,
      that He is supreme over His servants,
      that He is equal to His Purpose,
      that He doth what He wisheth,
      that He shall not be asked of whatever He willeth,
      that He ordaineth what He pleaseth,
      that He is the Most Powerful, the Almighty?
If ye believe this to be the truth,
      wherefore, then, will ye not cease from troubling
      and be at peace with yourselves?

Bahá'u'lláh, Gleanings, p. 224

Sorrow not if, in these days and on this earthly plane, things
contrary to your wishes have been ordained and manifested
by God, for days of blissful joy, of heavenly delight, are
assuredly in store for you. Worlds, holy and spiritually
glorious, will be unveiled to your eyes. You are destined by
Him, in this world and hereafter, to partake of their benefits,

to share in their joys, and to obtain a portion of their
sustaining grace. To each and every one of them you will, no
doubt, attain.

Bahá'u'lláh, Gleanings, p. 329

POINTS TO PONDER

Do you believe this? Really?

When you are able to keep this in your consciousness, how does
it affect your life?

MEMORIZE

> The troubles of this world pass, and what we have left is what
> we have made of our souls; so it is to this we must look – to
> becoming more spiritual, drawing nearer to God, no matter
> what our human minds and bodies go through.
>
> Letter written on behalf of Shoghi Effendi, Compilation, vol. 2, p. 20

POINTS TO PONDER

What will we have left after our bodies die? So what are our
highest priorities?

VIEWPOINT

Bahá'u'lláh suggests that if we learn to 'see the end in the
beginning' we can begin to 'see peace in war and friendliness in
anger' (*Seven Valleys*, p. 15). That would pretty well change our
viewpoint on 'suffering', wouldn't it? It's a good practice to keep
the drama of suffering to a minimum if you want to be happy.
Expectations create attraction.

☺ If you don't believe
that your beliefs create
your perception of reality,
you're proving yourself
wrong!

STORY

One might easily imagine the daily life of a family of
prisoners – even a Holy Family – as sad and depressing to the

visitor but, strange to say, in the 'Most Great Prison' quite the reverse is the case. Although absolute regularity of living is not possible – nearly every domestic event being subject to the rise of unexpected circumstances – the calm serenity of those beautiful people is never broken. They pursue their daily tasks, render their sweet service, make their little sacrifices, teach their children – and play with them, too – in short, carry on, under the most extraordinary circumstances, a perfect ideal of human family life. One never hears complaint of hard conditions, only a calm acceptance of God's Will and Wisdom in every little happening, and a sure understanding of the future blessings which will be the fruit of their present patience, blessings for all the people of the world.

Although each individual, from the youngest servant to the Greatest Holy leaf, is constantly on guard, no parade is made of their watchfulness. Not even the creak of a distant door or a strange footfall escapes their attentive ears, yet the visitor is never reminded that he is the cause of anxiety. When it becomes necessary to move the whole supper table suddenly into another room to escape the observation of the Turkish callers, it is done with a quiet smile and no hint of inconvenience. How obvious and easy it would be to impress the sensitive pilgrim with their daily martyrdom and the constant strain of their precarious position. That they do just the contrary is another lesson to us!

Were is not for the close proximity of the barracks and its guards, one would never realize that he was visiting a Turkish prison.

Another delight to the visitor is the discovery of their spontaneous and charming humour. They make merry over every little jest, extracting all the laughter possible from it, and encourage one another to see the bright side of all things, thus distracting their minds from the tragic side of their existence. 'Abdu'l-Bahá Himself seemed to come so close to us in His playful moods. With a merry twinkle in His eye, He would ask Miss Jack how she liked being on the roll of the prisoners (she is to remain there a year to teach English). When she answered that she would like to be written down as 'the woman who had just found her freedom', He laughed with the rest, and was highly pleased that she responded to Him in the same tone. Never have we heard more joyous laughter than in that Household.

Every day 'Abdu'l-Bahá came to our door and called us to

His table, which was bountifully spread with material and spiritual food, saying in English, 'Come here, come here, sit down, sit down. How are you – very well?' and when we answered, 'We are very well,' He said in Persian, 'Very good, very good; it makes me happy to sit at table with you because you are the servants of Bahá'u'lláh.' We replied that *He* made us happy. He said, 'Very good, I am glad you are here. It makes Me rejoice when I see you, for I love you very much.'

'Abdu'l-Bahá's perfectly natural manner indicates the entire absence of self-consciousness, and throughout the Household there is absolute simplicity, a constant service, and all the members take a common-sense view of all things.

When emotion is shown, 'Abdu'l-Bahá says, 'No, no, not that, not that; be happy, be happy,' and when one shows enthusiasm and happiness, it seems to lighten His burdens.

The pressure of life there is very great, and sometimes 'Abdu'l-Bahá is very weary, but a quick response to His greeting, or incidents related that show the activity and steadfastness of the believers, will cause His eyes to shine instantly, and His step to become more buoyant. He listens intently to every word, no matter how trifling.

Goodall and Cooper, *Daily Lessons Received at 'Akká*, pp. 9–11

VIEWPOINT

Although all aspects of life will involve struggle at times, it's not struggling or the lack of it that is the point. Your life has an ecology just as the earth does. Pain and struggle are only a part of the landscape, part of your spiritual ecology. If you try to get rid of or avoid them, you will meet them somewhere else because the balance must be maintained. But you don't have to remove *or* stand in your spiritual swamps any more than you have to drain or stand in the earth's physical ones: in fact, it can cause great problems to do so. Allow the swamps to be there and build your house somewhere else! The struggle is not to get God to love us – He always does! – but to quiet our busy thoughts enough to receive His love. Struggling to get God to love us – struggling to be happy – can be compared to a fish in a pond struggling to find water. It's not about struggling, it's about swimming! Not allowing yourself to notice and consciously enjoy God's love is sort of like the fish not allowing itself to breathe and swim!

MEMORIZE

Man is, in reality, a spiritual being, and only when he lives in the spirit is he truly happy.

'Abdu'l-Bahá, *Paris Talks*, p. 72

POINTS TO PONDER

What does 'living in the spirit' mean to you?

How can you learn to do it? Give specific examples.

EXERCISE

List as many attributes of a spiritual being as you can (at least five).

POINTS TO PONDER

Are you happy? Right now?

If you hesitated or answered 'no', what is between you and the realization of happiness?

Who controls your perception of happiness or the lack of it?

What can you do to remove the perception that something is between you and the realization of happiness?

Is it the will of God that you be happy?

Can you strive and struggle and suffer and *still* be happy?

☺ Your condition is *always* conditional! Usually, unhappiness is pollution from the past or dire fortune-telling about the future; staying present and in the Presence is the secret to being happy *now*. Happiness is, obviously, a purely subjective experience and is not dependent upon external conditions – therefore, it's always an option, isn't it?

READINGS

I want you to be happy . . . to laugh, smile and rejoice in order that others may be made happy by you. I will pray for you.

'Abdu'l-Bahá, *Promulgation of Universal Peace*, p. 218

262

By thy life, O my beloved! if thou didst know what God had ordained for thee, thou wouldst fly with delight and thy happiness, gladness and joy would increase every hour.

'Abdu'l-Bahá, *Bahá'í World Faith*, p. 363

☺ Don't ever try to compare your insides to other people's outsides.

and while we're flying, here's a wonderful poem by Naomi Shihab Nye:

So Much Happiness

It is difficult to know what to do with so much happiness.
With sadness there is something to rub against,
a wound to tend with lotion and cloth.
When the world falls in around you, you have pieces to pick
up, something to hold in your hands, like ticket stubs or
change.

But happiness floats.
It doesn't need you to hold it down.
It doesn't need anything.
Happiness lands on the roof of the next house, singing,
and disappears when it wants to.
You are happy either way.
Even the fact that you once lived in a peaceful tree house
and now live over a quarry of noise and dust
cannot make you unhappy.
Everything has a life of its own,
it too could wake up filled with possibilities
of coffee cake and ripe peaches,
and love even the floor which needs to be swept,
the soiled linens and scratched records . . .

Since there is no place large enough
to contain so much happiness,
you shrug, you raise your hands, and it flows out of you
into everything you touch. You are not responsible.
You take no credit, as the night sky takes no credit
for the moon, but continues to hold it, and share it,
and in that way, be known.

Naomi Shihab Nye, *Words Under the Words*, p. 88

Section VIII

Unity

I

What You See Really is What You Get!

MEMORIZE

The earth is full of the signs of God; may your eyes be
illumined by perceiving them.

'Abdu'l-Bahá, quoted in Blomfield, *The Chosen Highway*, p. 176

POINTS TO PONDER

What are some of the signs of God?

What illumines your eyes: the fact that the earth is full of the
signs of God or the fact that you perceive them?

Which ones in particular illumine your eyes right now?

READING

Be in perfect unity. Never become angry with one
another . . . Love the creatures for the sake of God and not
for themselves. You will never become angry or impatient if
you love them for the sake of God. Humanity is not perfect.
There are imperfections in every human being, and you will
always become unhappy if you look toward the people
themselves. But if you look toward God you will love them
and be kind to them, for the world of God is the world of
perfection and complete mercy. Therefore, do not look at the
shortcomings of anybody; see with the sight of forgiveness.
The imperfect eye beholds imperfections. The eye that
covers faults looks toward the Creator of souls. He created
them, trains and provides for them, endows them with

capacity and life, sight and hearing; therefore, they are the
signs of His grandeur.

'Abdu'l-Bahá, *Promulgation of Universal Peace*, p. 93

Why are we called 'creatures' in the quotation? Is it because we
are all created and that which is created is a creature?

Do you find that you have to practise a lot to learn never to be
angry or impatient?

Would it help to imagine everyone as 'Abdu'l-Bahá in disguise?

How do you practise loving for 'the sake of God'? How do you
'look toward God'?

If you want to enjoy being in a world of perfection and
complete mercy, how can you get there?

Where is this world of perfection and complete mercy? Is it
somewhere you have to go to or is it a condition that you can
allow to develop within yourself?

If you are angry or impatient or focusing on imperfections (in
yourself or others), what does it tell you about your own 'eye'?

How can you perfect your eye – how do you develop an eye that
covers faults?

Does having an eye that covers faults mean that we're denying or
pretending that there are no faults in ourselves or others, or does
it mean that we know that imperfections and weaknesses exist
and we choose to concentrate our attention on the perfections
and strengths (to build on high ground rather than in the
swamp).

Does it imply that we should allow others to abuse us or treat us
in any way unjustly?

Would the effects of denial be entirely different from the effects

☺You could think of life
as a gym for spiritual
muscle-building – and
don't we all have
relationships that will
keep us in great shape if
we use them
appropriately? Every day
provides ample
opportunity for a
workout. Just don't forget
– your own training is
what it's all about, no one
else's. Your reactions and
resistances are your
personal trainers,
reminding you of areas in
you that need work. You
don't need to train
whatever it is you're
resisting any more than
you need to train the
weights you lift at the
gym.

of choosing to concentrate our attention on the perfections and strengths? In what way?

How will concentrating on the perfections and strengths of others create unity?

MEMORIZE

As the divine bounties are endless, so human perfections are endless.

'Abdu'l-Bahá, *Some Answered Questions*, p. 230

. . . human perfections are infinite.

'Abdu'l-Bahá, *Some Answered Questions*, p. 237

VIEWPOINT

Although we are on this earth to gain spiritual perfections, there will never come a time when we are absolutely perfect. All perfections are relative: this means that as we develop, we become more perfect than we were. 'Abdu'l-Bahá says that perfections are limitless, so we don't have to worry about getting bored. It's pretty clear that it's a waste of time and energy to be upset about our imperfections, which, after all, must be as limitless as our perfections, right?

READINGS

Blessed are they who are the means of making unity among the friends, and pity on those who *in the right or wrong* are the cause of discord . . . The friends must be prepared to efface themselves at all times. Seeking the approval of men is many times the cause of imperiling the approval of God.

'Abdu'l-Bahá, quoted in *Star of the West*, vol. 6, no. 6, p. 45

efface to keep from being noticed; conduct oneself inconspicuously or humbly

We must be patient with each other's shortcomings, and always strive to create love and unity among the believers, who, after all, are still immature in many ways and far from perfect.

Letter written on behalf of Shoghi Effendi, *Compilation*, vol. 1, p. 383

☺ Alas, I know if I ever became truly humble, I would be proud of it.
Benjamin Franklin

269

... the most hateful characteristic of man is fault-finding. One must expose the praiseworthy qualities of the souls and not their evil attributes. The friends must overlook their shortcomings and faults and speak only of their virtues and not their defects.

'Abdu'l-Bahá, in *Lights of Guidance*, p. 91

Thus is it incumbent upon us, when we direct our gaze toward other people, to see where they excel, not where they fail.

'Abdu'l-Bahá, *Selections from the Writings of 'Abdu'l-Bahá*, p. 169

incumbent rests on a person as a duty

VIEWPOINT

Creating unity implies overlooking not only our own imperfections but the imperfections of others. If we are looking for the 'signs of God' and concentrating on the strengths and perfections of those we meet, there won't be much time for fault-finding.

READING

'Abdu'l-Bahá tells us:

> To look always at the good and not at the bad. If a man has ten good qualities and one bad one, to look to the ten and forget the one; and if a man has ten bad qualities and one good one, to look at the one and forget the ten.
>
> 'Abdu'l-Bahá, quoted in Esslemont, *Bahá'u'lláh and the New Era* p. 80

☺ If this is giving you trouble, remember that *everyone* has at least the attribute of cohesion!

STORY

'Abdu'l-Bahá told this story:

> The disciples of Jesus, passing along the road and seeing a dead dog, remarked how offensive and disgusting a spectacle it was. Then Christ turning to them said, 'Yes, but see how white and beautiful are his teeth' – thus teaching that there is some good in everything.
>
> 'Abdu'l-Bahá, quoted in Grundy, *Ten Days in the Light of 'Akká*, p. 103

2

We are *the World*

In this Day of God, our unity is an article of faith, not just a nice idea. Unity in our love for God gives us the vision, strength and commitment to overcome our ego-centred inclinations and to forge unified communities, in turn building a unified world order. 'Abdu'l-Bahá pointed out that if we're not unified, we can't unify the world: the same is true of our dual nature; if we're not unified within our own s(S)elves, how can we live in unity with others? This self-unity is referred to as 'integrity' – the true integration of our higher and lower nature. The lower self can only be transcended or 'overcome' with – guess what? – love!

integrity wholeness; soundness

READING

Of Being Woven

The way is full of genuine sacrifice.

The thickets blocking the path are anything
that keeps you from that, any fear
that you may be broken to bits like a glass bottle.
This road demands courage and stamina,
yet it's full of footprints! Who *are*
these companions? They are rungs
in your ladder. Use them!
With company you quicken your ascent.

You may be happy enough going along,
but with others you'll get farther, and faster.

. . .
When ink joins with a pen, then the blank paper
can say something. Rushes and reeds must be *woven*
to be useful as a mat. If they weren't interlaced,
the wind would blow them away.
Like that, God paired up
creatures, and gave them friendship.
~
Stay together, friends.
Don't scatter and sleep.
Our friendship is made
of being awake.

Rúmí

VIEWPOINT

One place Bahá'ís begin to build world unity is within the Bahá'í community. There is no model for Bahá'í communities other than the writings and we usually bring a lot of 'old world' ideas and habits with us when we become Bahá'ís. These habits and ideas are so natural to us that we don't question them; however, they frequently cause resentment and estrangement in our communities. As the Universal House of Justice has offered Bahá'í communities as a model for society, perhaps we'd best learn what we're about!

There can be no transformation of community life without personal, individual transformation. The more we come to experience a compassionate community, the sooner we will be able to model what Bahá'í community *is* – which is what the Universal House of Justice expects of us. Commit to joy. Don't indulge your ego nature in relationships that tear you or anyone else down.

See *The Promise of World Peace*, paragraph 57, in which the Universal House of Justice offers the Bahá'í experience as a model for study.

We're like a flock of eagles (do eagles come in flocks?), raised on a chicken farm. No one told us we could fly or modelled it for us in our daily life and we've been suffering from a state of deep, but unnecessary, amnesia. We now *know* and the sooner we put 'eagleness' into practice, the better!

READING

Without the spirit of real love for Bahá'u'lláh, for His Faith and its Institutions, and the believers for each other, the Cause can never really bring in large numbers of people.

Letter written on behalf of Shoghi Effendi, *Compilation*, vol. 2, p. 315

This transformation of our communities – as with the world – is not only possible but inevitable: as an act of will (daily, daily) or through enormous pain and suffering. Until we *live* the unity we're calling the world to experience, there can be no entry by troops. This is our unique gift to the world. How can we give it if we keep forgetting we have it?

To foster community – the perception of unlimited, unlimiting possibilities in all relationships, which 'Abdu'l-Bahá modelled for us – is to become acquainted with our true selves and our highest choices and consciously to develop the ability to reach through each other's 'veils' (egos) to the reality of love that we are *all* created from and for – that, in fact, we all are. We can only begin to do this when we learn to recognize the veils – all veils of separateness – as our own. A Bahá'í community is a wonderful 'support group' for personal growth and development; recognizing and appreciating this allows us to experience it – if we don't, we won't!

Standing on the common ground of our faith, we develop our awareness of the oneness of humanity by experiencing it and appreciating the diversity of the expression of the love of Bahá'u'lláh. This is made possible and essential by the teachings. One can only become a Bahá'í in relationship and community. Unity always requires more than one.

☺ The veils of ego are *extremely flammable* and should never be used as clothing or personal coverings!

☺ Mark Twain said that the person holding the cat by the tail was gaining two or three times more information than the guy standing there watching. This is true of activity in the Bahá'í community too. If you want to gain lots of information about yourself, become active. Grab your ego cat by the tail and take part in the opportunities involved in creating community!

If we Bahá'ís cannot attain this cordial unity among ourselves, then we fail to realize the main purpose for which the Báb, Bahá'u'lláh, and the Beloved Master lived and suffered.

In order to achieve this cordial unity one of the first essentials insisted on by Bahá'u'lláh and 'Abdu'l-Bahá is that we resist the natural tendency to let our attention dwell on the faults and failings of others rather than on our own. Each of us is responsible for one life only, and that is our own. Each of us is immeasurably far from being 'perfect as our heavenly father is perfect' and the task of perfecting our own life and character is one that requires all our attention, our will-power and energy. If we allow our attention and energy to be taken up in efforts to keep others right and remedy their faults, we are wasting precious time . . .

On no subject are the Bahá'í teachings more emphatic than on the necessity to abstain from faultfinding and backbiting while being ever eager to discover and root out our own faults and overcome our own failings.

If we profess loyalty to Bahá'u'lláh, to our Beloved Master and our dear Guardian, then we must show our love by obedience to these explicit teachings. Deeds not words are what they demand, and no amount of fervour in the use of expressions of loyalty and adulation will compensate for failure to live in the spirit of the teachings.

Letter written on behalf of Shoghi Effendi, *Compilation*, vol. 2, pp. 3-4

All the spiritual laws are directed toward ourselves – *we* are the *only* ones we must change.

This is the age of unity and unity is not an individual thing! Even physics is coming to realize that there are no 'things'; 'things' exist only in relationships.

VIEWPOINT

Unity implies the coming together and harmonizing of different elements – a synthesis. This is not uniformity or sameness, which is a monotony of one thing. The difference between unity and uniformity is the difference between striking the same note over and over on several pianos and playing a lovely symphony with many notes and instruments. The symphony is one thing and is composed of many elements working in unity and harmony. The 'oneness of humanity' implies a comprehensiveness that permits and values every personality's right of development and differentiation and every race and culture's expression of its unique temperament – transforming what was previously experienced as limitation and separation into opportunity for the celebration of diversity.

READING

Whensoever holy souls, drawing on the powers of heaven, shall arise with such qualities of the spirit, and march in unison, rank on rank, every one of those souls will be even as one thousand, and the surging waves of that mighty ocean will be even as the battalions of the Concourse on high. What a blessing that will be – when all shall come together, even as once separate torrents, rivers and streams, running brooks and single drops, when collected together in one place will form a mighty sea. And to such a degree will the inherent unity of all prevail, that the traditions, rules, customs and distinctions in the fanciful life of these populations will be effaced and vanish away like isolated drops, once the great sea of oneness doth leap and surge and roll.

'Abdu'l-Bahá, *Selections from the Writings of 'Abdu'l-Bahá*, pp. 260-1

VIEWPOINT

The creation of a unified community that truly embraces all of humanity can never take place on the level of our personalities or temperaments: we must be united in our mutual love and service to Bahá'u'lláh. This is why, if there is no knowledge, volition or action, there is no real love, no real Bahá'í community. This kind of unity cannot be faked – either we're glowing or we're not. Anything less is miserable hypocrisy.

Remember Rúmí's lines:
The lamps of lovers connect,
not at their bases,
but in their lightedness.

READING

We must reach a spiritual plane where God comes first and great human passions are unable to turn us away from Him. All the time we see people who either through the force of hate or the passionate attachment they have to another person, sacrifice principle or bar themselves from the Path of God.

We must love God, and in this state, a general love for all men becomes possible. We cannot love each human being for himself, but our feeling towards humanity should be motivated by our love for the Father Who created all men.

Letter written on behalf of Shoghi Effendi, *Compilation*, vol. 2, p. 22

Remember, if you don't like what you're looking at, it's *your* eyes – and the remote's in your control: change the channel!

VIEWPOINT

The interpersonal problems we struggle with can't be solved from our lower natures. We can talk and talk and go round and round and promise and commit but until we integrate our lower nature's defences and reactions with our highest choices and get it clear which aspect of our nature is captain of the ship, we'll go in circles (at best – actually, we'll generally end up crashed on the rocks).

The principle of the oneness of humanity means that we are to create communities of unparalleled diversity *now*. All those who come into this Faith bring with them their own past, their culture, values, expectations, hopes, dreams, desires and wounds – even you! If we don't greet each other with the full authenticity of our love for Bahá'u'lláh and with a sense of wonder at what He is able to achieve through us, we will not ever enjoy the benefits of a true Bahá'í community. We can never do this from our egos. This is what 'second birth' is all about – breaking the chains of past and allowing the wounds to be healed, coming into a new life.

READING

'Abdu'l-Bahá's farewell address to the American Bahá'ís reminds us that the only way we can build unified communities is by transforming our own selves into spiritual beings:

> These are the days of my farewell to you . . . I must, therefore give you my instructions and exhortations today, and these are none other than the teachings of Bahá'u'lláh.

> You must manifest complete love and affection toward all mankind.

> Do not exalt yourselves above others, but consider all as your equals, recognizing them as the servants of one God.

> Know that God is compassionate toward all; therefore, love all from the depths of your hearts, prefer all religionists before yourselves, be filled with love for every race, and be kind toward the people of all nationalities.

> Never speak disparagingly of others, but praise without distinction.

> Pollute not your tongues by speaking evil of another.

> Recognize your enemies as friends, and consider those who wish you evil as the wishers of good.

> You must not see evil as evil and then compromise with your

opinion, for to treat in a smooth, kindly way one whom you consider evil or an enemy is hypocrisy, and this is not worthy or allowable. You must consider your enemies as your friends, look upon your evil-wishers as your well-wishers and treat them accordingly.

Act in such a way that your heart may be free from hatred.

Let not your heart be offended with anyone.

If some one commits an error and wrong toward you, you must instantly forgive him.

Do not complain of others.

Refrain from reprimanding them, and if you wish to give admonition or advice, let it be offered in such a way that it will not burden the bearer.

Turn all your thoughts toward bringing joy to hearts.

Beware! Beware! lest ye offend any heart.

Assist the world of humanity as much as possible.

Be the source of consolation to every sad one, assist every weak one, be helpful to every indigent one, care for every sick one, be the cause of glorification to every lowly one and shelter those who are overshadowed by fear.

In brief, let each one of you be as a lamp shining forth with the light of the virtues of the world of humanity.

Be trustworthy, sincere, affectionate and replete with chastity.

Be illumined, be spiritual, be divine, be glorious, be quickened of God, be a Bahá'í.

'Abdu'l-Bahá, *Promulgation of Universal Peace*, pp. 452-3

When our community is functioning properly and

harmoniously, we can rely on one another to call forth and strengthen our highest choices. We can anticipate a loving relationship of mutual support and helpfulness. Not only will it be more difficult for each of us to be ruled by ego, but we will consciously attract and inspire each other to fulfil our highest aspirations.

READING

> . . . the believers have not yet fully learned to draw on each other's love for strength and consolation in time of need. The Cause of God is endowed with tremendous powers, and the reason the believers do not gain more from it is because they have not learned to fully draw on these mighty forces of love and strength and harmony generated by the Faith.
>
> Letter written on behalf of Shoghi Effendi, *Compilation*, vol. 2, p. 9

POINTS TO PONDER

How should we go about ensuring that we draw fully on these mighty forces of love and strength and harmony?

Does our belief that these forces aren't to be found within the Bahá'í community create and perpetuate this reality?

Is the development of the Bahá'í community assisted by drawing on these forces?

How can drawing on these forces create unity within the community?

Section IX

Nearness to God

I

What is the 'Fear of God' (and Why Would I Want It?)

INTRODUCTION

You will probably be given lots of opportunities to strengthen your faith by asking Bahá'u'lláh to help you love Him more when things are hard and you're making efforts to overcome the extreme difficulties of choosing to live and experience unity in this fragmented age. We should not be afraid of these opportunities.

MEMORIZE

> Love is a light that never dwelleth in a heart possessed by fear.
>
> Bahá'u'lláh, *Four Valleys*, p. 58

VIEWPOINT

The fear that this quotation is referring to is a negative expectation – a belief that something will be painful or bad, a belief that avoiding this pain is more important than loving God. This sort of fear is like putting our faith in our lower/material nature rather than in our higher/spiritual one. It is very seductive and convincing. When we allow this kind of belief or fear to control us, we have chosen our negative expectation over our belief in the power and love of God. The light of our loving capacity is darkened by fear.

Fear is always useful as a warning or a signal. If what we fear is not a real, recognizable danger that we need to deal with but is rather in our minds and hearts, it is probably coming from our lower nature. It's still a warning or signal – it's just not warning us of what we might at first think the danger is. This kind of fear or anxiety is warning us that we have put our faith in the material world instead of in God. It is there to alert us that we are in a dangerous situation because we have turned away from love. It reminds us to return to love. As soon as we do, there is nothing more to fear because there *is* nothing to fear in the spiritual realm. The ego doesn't recognize what the spirit knows: the fact that we have personal power not over events, but in moving through them.

POINTS TO PONDER

What is fear? How can you use it in your spiritual development?

What is its best application for your spirituality?

READING

> You have read in the text where *They love him*
> blends with *He loves them.*
> Those joining loves
> are both qualities of God. Fear is not.
>
> What characteristics do God and human beings
> have in common? What is the connection between
> what lives in time and what lives in eternity?
>
> If I kept talking about love,
> a hundred new combinings would happen,
> and still I would not say the mystery.
>
> The fearful ascetic runs of foot, along the surface.
> Lovers move like lightning and wind.
> No contest.
> Theologians mumble, rumble-dumble,
> necessity and free will,
> while lover and beloved
> pull themselves
> into each other.

Rúmí

VIEWPOINT

Our ego (lower nature) finds all sorts of things to fear. It fears change and 'loss' and all sorts of imagined separation and pain. Suppose you are so afraid of being different or strange that you just go along with the crowd and don't make decisions from your higher/spiritual nature. Isn't this because your heart is so full of fear (negative expectation – 'they won't like me if . . .') that you don't have room for the love of God and your spiritual self?

'Abdu'l-Bahá reminds us: 'Seeking the approval of men is many times the cause of imperiling the approval of God' (quoted in *Star of the West*, vol. 6, no. 6, p. 45).

It is natural to seek approval. Practise asking yourself whose approval or comfort is more important to you – that of your friends and acquaintances (or even your ego) or God's. By learning to make choices from your higher self and using these personal and social tests as spiritual weight-lifting exercises, you will gain spiritual strength every day. If you learn to respond with loving action rather than defensively or with anger or fear, you will have proved your strength. Every time you overcome an ego reaction with a loving action you have overcome evil – your weakness will have become a strength.

The ego fears the invincible power of love more than it fears its own weakness because love is the only power strong enough to overcome ego. This is why if you have no fear of God (that is, if you aren't totally grounded in love and faith to overcome the promptings of the ego), the ego will make you a mass of fears in its effort to 'keep you safe' and in control. There is no security in ego-centredness – it's the state of 'fearing all things'.

MEMORIZE

If he feareth not God, God will make him to fear all things . . .

Bahá'u'lláh, *Four Valleys*, p. 58

POINTS TO PONDER

If the first quotation says 'Love . . . never dwelleth in a heart possessed by fear', why does the second one tell us we should fear God?

Is the fear referred to in the second quotation a natural outcome of loving and recognizing the source of your happiness and strength?

Given that love is a light, should we fear having to live in spiritual darkness?

What does the 'fear of God' mean?

Could 'fearing God' mean fearing being far from God – knowing that being out of touch with your higher/spiritual self will be dangerous for you, spiritually and physically? As you develop your spiritual senses and realize that God's laws are for your own happiness and safety, you fear breaking the laws and losing your spiritual compass – you know you will be disoriented and are likely to suffer.

When you recognize that there are natural consequences to breaking the spiritual laws, just as there are for breaking the physical laws (☺ remember gravity?), wouldn't you respect the spiritual laws as much as you respect the edge of the roof of a high building?

Could the fear of God mean that you fear making your spiritual self miserable?

It's natural to fear punishment (in some places in the Bahá'í writings, it's referred to as 'retribution'). If you fear being left out or unpopular more than you fear breaking spiritual laws, what could happen to you? When you develop your spiritual qualities, you will begin to fear the pain of breaking spiritual laws more than the pain of being unpopular.

If you don't live from your higher/spiritual choices, is there *anything* that is secure – can you really trust and rely on anything that is based on the material world only? Could this be what 'God will make him to fear all things' means?

Here is a paradox. One quotation says 'Love is a light that never dwelleth in a heart possessed by fear' while the other says 'If he feareth not God, God will make him to fear all things.' The very love of God that is the source of our transformation and evolving spiritual invincibility and genuine fearlessness brings with it, of course, the 'fear of God'. The purpose is always to warn and prevent us from harmful motives and actions.

READINGS

The fear of God hath ever been the prime factor in the

education of His creatures. Well is it with them that have
attained thereunto!

Bahá'u'lláh, Epistle to the Son of the Wolf, p. 27

Fear ye God, and be not of them that have denied Him.
Withhold not yourselves from that which hath been revealed
through His grace.

Bahá'u'lláh, Epistle to the Son of the Wolf, p. 38

In several Tablets Bahá'u'lláh has described the fear of God
as the cause of nearness to Him. This statement may be
difficult for some to appreciate. For why should a loving God
be feared? Fear is engendered in man when he feels
inadequate to deal with a situation, and confidence is
generated when he finds himself completely in control. For
example, a man who has been given a responsibility but has
failed to fulfil his obligations will be filled with fear when he
meets his superiors, because he knows that they will deal
with him with justice. Man, in this life, fails to carry out the
commandments of God. He commits sin and violates the
laws of God. In such a case how can he feel at ease when he
knows that one day he will be called on to account for his
deeds? If man does not fear God, it is a sign either that he is
without shortcomings or that he has no faith in the next life
when he will have to answer for his wrongdoings. In *The
Hidden Words* Bahá'u'lláh counsels His servants in these
words:

> *O Son of Being!*
> Bring thyself to account each day ere thou art summoned
> to a reckoning; for death, unheralded, shall come upon
> thee and thou shalt be called to give account for thy deeds.

The closer one draws to God, the more he becomes
conscious of his wrong-doings and the more he will fear
God.

Taherzadeh, Revelation of Bahá'u'lláh, vol. 2, pp. 94-5

You ask him about the fear of God: perhaps the friends do
not realize that the majority of human beings need the
element of fear in order to discipline their conduct? Only a
relatively very highly evolved soul would always be
disciplined by love alone. Fear of punishment, fear of the
anger of God if we do evil, are needed to keep people's feet

on the right path. Of course we should love God – but we must fear Him in the sense of a child fearing the righteous anger and chastisement of a parent; not cringe before Him as before a tyrant, but know His mercy exceeds His justice!

Letter written on behalf of Shoghi Effendi, *Compilation*, vol. 1, p. 306

POINTS TO PONDER

Authentic and invincible courage and power come only as a result of the fear of God:

Strive as much as ye can to turn wholly toward the Kingdom, that ye may acquire innate courage and ideal power.

'Abdu'l-Bahá, *Selections from the Writings of 'Abdu'l-Bahá*, p. 206

innate inborn; natural

ideal answering to one's highest conception; perfect or supremely excellent

How can we *acquire* innate courage and ideal power?

READINGS

And we have known and believed the love that God hath to us. God is love; and he that dwelleth in love dwelleth in God, and God in him . . . There is no fear in love: but perfect love casteth out fear: because fear hath torment. He that feareth is not made perfect in love. We love Him, because He first loved us.

John 4:16-19

I sought the Lord, and He heard me, and delivered me from all my fears.

Psalm 34:4

Be not idle, but active, and fear not.

'Abdu'l-Bahá, *Bahá'í World Faith*, p. 362

2

Becoming an Angel

What are angels? Paintings show them with wings and white gowns, so many people don't really believe they exist. However, both Bahá'u'lláh and 'Abdu'l-Bahá affirm that there are angels.

READINGS

. . . inasmuch as these holy beings have sanctified themselves from every human limitation, have become endowed with the attributes of the spiritual, and have been adorned with the noble traits of the blessed, they therefore have been designated as 'angels'.

Bahá'u'lláh, Kitáb-i-Íqán, pp. 79-80

Here's what 'Abdu'l-Bahá says about angels (and you!):

Ye are the angels, if your feet be firm, your spirits rejoiced, your secret thoughts pure, your eyes consoled, your ears opened, your breast dilated with joy, and your souls gladdened . . .

'Abdu'l-Bahá, Bahá'í World Faith, p. 360

POINTS TO PONDER

Does being in the attitude of prayer make you an angel?

What does 'if your feet be firm' mean? Could it refer to steadfastness?

What can you practise doing to keep 'your secret thoughts pure'?

What do you do to make 'your spirit rejoice'?

. . . to 'console your eyes'?

Is 'Abdu'l-Bahá referring to physical eyes or spiritual eyes? or both?

Could having your ears opened mean that you're able to hear 'the language of the spirit'?

Do you sometimes feel, when you're very, very happy, as though your heart will burst through your chest? That's a breast 'dilated with joy'! Why does this happen?

Could the artists who paint angels with wings and beautiful gowns be using symbolism to represent transcendent beauty? How would wings and gowns show that?

transcendent above and independent of the material world, spiritual

READINGS

'Abdu'l-Bahá describes the soul as having 'wings':

> Regarding the 'two wings' of the soul: These signify wings of ascent. One is the wing of knowledge, the other of faith, as this is the means of the ascent of the human soul to the lofty station of divine perfections.
>
> 'Abdu'l-Bahá, *Bahá'í World Faith*, p. 382

He also says:

> By 'angel' is meant the power of the confirmations of God . . .
>
> 'Abdu'l-Bahá, *Selections from the Writings of 'Abdu'l-Bahá*, p. 166

confirmations things or events that show that something is true or correct

> Render continual thanks unto God so that the confirmations of God may encircle you . . .
>
> 'Abdu'l-Bahá, *Promulgation of Universal Peace*, p. 189

When you're feeling very thankful to God, you can be sure that angels are encircling you – wonder if they have wings and beautiful gowns?

288

Are the good feelings in your heart confirmations of God?

Rendering continual thanks to God will cause confirmations to encircle you. Think of several reasons why this would be true.

MEMORIZE

. . . for man can receive no greater gift than this, that he rejoice another's heart. I beg of God, that ye will be bringers of joy, even as are the angels in Heaven.

'Abdu'l-Bahá, *Selections from the Writings of 'Abdu'l-Bahá*, pp. 203-4

VIEWPOINT

May you always have angels in your heart! And know that you are an angel. Please don't go around in disguise!

READING

The blessed Person of the Promised One is interpreted in the Holy Book as the Lord of Hosts – the heavenly armies. By heavenly armies those souls are intended who are entirely freed from the human world, transformed into celestial spirits and have become divine angels. Such souls are the rays of the Sun of Reality who will illumine all the continents. Each one is holding in his hand a trumpet, blowing the breath of life over all the regions. They are delivered from human qualities and the defects of the world of nature, are characterized with the characteristics of God, and are attracted with the fragrances of the Merciful. Like unto the apostles of Christ, who were filled with Him, these souls also have become filled with His Holiness Bahá'u'lláh; that is, the love of Bahá'u'lláh has so mastered every organ, part and limb of their bodies, as to leave no effect from the promptings of the human world.

'Abdu'l-Bahá, *Tablets of the Divine Plan*, p. 49

3

Real Miracles

When we look around ourselves with the eyes of true perception, it becomes astonishingly and delightfully apparent that we are, truly, living in days of signs and wonders and miracles – and that most of the world is totally unconscious of this. Every time we transmute estrangement into love or fear into courage in our daily life it is a miracle. All of the incredible advances in worldwide technology and tools for the realization of the oneness of humanity are miraculous. Miracles large and small occur every moment of every day, in our own lives and in the world.

READING

Praise be to God! The springtime of God is at hand. This century is, verily, the spring season. The world of mind and kingdom of soul have become fresh and verdant by its bestowals. It has resuscitated the whole realm of existence. On one hand, the lights of reality are shining; on the other, the clouds of divine mercy are pouring down the fullness of heavenly bounty. Wonderful material progress is evident, and great spiritual discoveries are being made. Truly, this can be called the miracle of centuries, for it is replete with manifestations of the miraculous. The time has come when all mankind shall be united, when all races shall be loyal to one fatherland, all religions become one religion, and racial and religious bias pass away. It is a day in which the oneness of humankind shall uplift its standard and international peace, like the true morning, flood the world with its light.

'Abdu'l-Bahá, *Promulgation of Universal Peace*, p. 153

Want to experience a miracle? You can, at will, every time you choose from your higher self. A miracle is, in reality, a shift in thinking – from fear to love. It is a healing of perception, a breakthrough in conscious awareness. What could be more miraculous than to recognize that you are always in the presence of love and true, unlimited security? that you have available to you at all times the power to change estrangement to love and fear to invincible courage? that you can never be victimized or shamed from outside, no matter what others do to you. The miracles are revealed in living the lessons, healing the wounds – taking the base metal of our lower nature and transmuting it into the gold of spirituality. Miracles aren't 'things' – they are realizations and transformations: they are always returning to love. The Covenant is the source of all that is miraculous.

POINTS TO PONDER

Is it possible for you consciously to experience the miraculous right now?

What did you choose to recognize as your miracle?

What constitutes the most miraculous happening in your life? the most miraculous that you recognized *today*?

READINGS

Bahá'u'lláh reminds us that we are never to use stories of miraculous events and happenings as a proof of the validity of His mission:

> This Wronged One hath never had, nor hath He now any desire for leadership. Mine aim hath ever been, and still is, to suppress whatever is the cause of contention amidst the peoples of the earth, and of separation amongst the nations, so that all men may be sanctified from every earthly attachment, and be set free to occupy themselves with their own interests. We entreat Our loved ones not to besmirch the

hem of Our raiment with the dust of falsehood, neither to allow references to what they have regarded as miracles and prodigies to debase Our rank and station, or to mar the purity and sanctity of Our name.

Bahá'u'lláh, *Epistle to the Son of the Wolf,* p. 33

However, miracles do occur:

> One thing . . . he wishes again to bring to your attention, namely that miracles are always possible, even though they do not constitute a regular channel whereby God reveals His power to mankind. To reject miracles on the ground that they imply a breach of the laws of nature is a very shallow, well-nigh a stupid argument, inasmuch as God Who is the Author of the universe can, in His Wisdom and Omnipotence, bring any change, no matter how temporary, in the operation of the laws which He Himself has created.
>
> Letter written on behalf of Shoghi Effendi, *Lights of Guidance,* p. 489

You might like to read more about the miracles performed by the Manifestations of God in *Some Answered Questions,* pp. 36-9 and 100-5.

EXERCISE

Explain in your journal, in your own words, why we are not to use miracles as proof of Bahá'u'lláh's revelation.

READINGS

In the chapter on using the Word of God to teach the Faith, we studied this quotation from Bahá'u'lláh. Now let us think of it in the context of miracles – the power that the Word of God has to change everything:

> The vitality of men's belief in God is dying out in every land; nothing short of His wholesome medicine can ever restore it. The corrosion of ungodliness is eating into the vitals of human society; what else but the Elixir of His potent Revelation can cleanse and revive it? Is it within human power . . . to effect in the constituent elements of any of the minute and indivisible particles of matter so complete a transformation as to transmute it into purest gold? Perplexing and difficult as this may appear, the still greater task of converting satanic strength into heavenly power is one that We have been empowered to accomplish. The

Force capable of such a transformation transcendeth the potency of the Elixir itself. The Word of God, alone, can claim the distinction of being endowed with the capacity required for so great and far-reaching a change.

Bahá'u'lláh, *Gleanings*, p. 200

Every word that proceedeth out of the mouth of God is endowed with such potency as can instil new life into every human frame, if ye be of them that comprehend this truth. All the wondrous works ye behold in this world have been manifested through the operation of His supreme and most exalted Will, His wondrous and inflexible purpose.

Bahá'u'lláh, *Gleanings*, p. 141

EXERCISE

In your journal, explain what 'instilling new life into every human frame' means. Be sure to include what it has meant to you personally and how your new life differs from your previous one.

VIEWPOINT

Would you consider any of the following to be miraculous if they came about? Having the world at peace, humanity living in harmony and unity, personal creative expression valued, education and development of craftsmanship available to every child and adult.

Do you know that these things – the effects of humanity becoming spiritualized and free to express its higher inclinations – are not only possible but inevitable owing to the influence of Bahá'u'lláh? It is a good idea to focus on the outcome of this Revelation and its effects on daily human life so that it will become your reality. We are witnessing 'the inauguration of a world civilization such as no mortal eye hath ever beheld or human mind conceived'. As Shoghi Effendi asks, 'Who can measure the heights to which human intelligence, liberated from its shackles, will soar? Who can visualize the realms which the human spirit, vitalized by the outpouring light of Bahá'u'lláh, shining in the plenitude of its glory, will discover?' (Shoghi Effendi, *World Order of Bahá'u'lláh*, p. 206).

The world will be in great turmoil in the next few years and if we are not grounded in reality, we could lose our footing and slide away into a truly terrifying and ungodly abyss.

See *World Order of Bahá'u'lláh*, pp. 202-6, for a concise statement by Shoghi Effendi about what we can look forward to in the future.

READING

abyss a very steep gorge or deep crack in a mountain or on the earth; a yawning

In the estimation of historians this radiant century is equivalent to one hundred centuries of the past. If comparison be made with the sum total of all former human achievements, it will be found that the discoveries, scientific advancement and material civilization of this present century have equaled, yea far exceeded the progress and outcome of one hundred former centuries. The production of books and compilations of literature alone bears witness that the output of the human mind in this century has been greater and more enlightening than all the past centuries together. It is evident, therefore, that this century is of paramount importance. Reflect upon the miracles of accomplishment which have already characterized it: the discoveries in every realm of human research. Inventions, scientific knowledge, ethical reforms and regulations established for the welfare of humanity, mysteries of nature explored, invisible forces brought into visibility and subjection – a veritable wonder-world of new phenomena and conditions heretofore unknown to man now open to his uses and further investigation. The East and West can communicate instantly. A human being can soar in the skies or speed in submarine depths. The power of steam has linked the continents. Trains cross the deserts and pierce the barriers of mountains; ships find unerring pathways upon the trackless oceans. Day by day discoveries are increasing. What a wonderful century this is! It is an age of universal reformation.

'Abdu'l-Bahá, *Promulgation of Universal Peace*, pp. 143-4

This talk was given on 25 May 1912! Think what has happened since, especially in the fields of communication and travel.

4

Real Heaven, Real Hell

INTRODUCTION

'Abdu'l-Bahá tells us 'Nearness is likeness' ('Abdu'l-Bahá, *Promulgation of Universal Peace*, p. 148). 'Heaven' is nearness to God and 'hell' is being far from God. These are not places or conditions of the body but spiritual conditions. You don't have to 'die' to be in heaven or hell: you can do that at any time! When we choose nearness to God, the rest melts away. The form the darkness takes ceases to be relevant once the light's turned on.

READINGS

. . . the paradise and hell of existence are found in all the worlds of God, whether in this world or in the spiritual heavenly worlds.

'Abdu'l-Bahá, *Some Answered Questions*, p. 223

Heaven and hell are conditions within our own beings.

Letter written on behalf of Shoghi Effendi, in *High Endeavours*, p. 50

. . . the 'Heaven' of Christ is that invisible world which is beyond the sight and comprehension of mere man. It is the spiritual condition. Therefore, the 'Heaven' of Christ is the Will of God. The Sun of that Heaven will never set. In it the Moon and Stars are always shining. It is the limitless Kingdom of God. It is sanctified from all place. Christ is always there . . . It is sanctified from all comprehension.

'Abdu'l-Bahá, quoted in Grundy, *Ten Days in the Light of 'Akká*, p. 27

The opposite of heaven is hell, but how can all-encompassing love have an opposite? It's all in your perception: Love in your thoughts = love in your life = heaven; fear and lovelessness in your thoughts = fear and lovelessness in your life = hell. *You* have the remote control – change the channel!

☺ In reality we are all extra-terrestrials (over and above the earthly bodies, which are our tools in this life). At the deepest level, we all know we're living in exile while on earth.

To be near to God, to be in heaven, means to be like God. To be like God, we have to know what God is like. The Manifestations of God are sent to show us the qualities or attributes of God, and in this age Bahá'u'lláh provided us with 'Abdu'l-Bahá as an example of what 'nearness' looks like in daily life. Want to experience a heavenly life? Become like 'Abdu'l-Bahá!

MEMORIZE

Nearness is verily of the soul, not of the body; and the help that is sought, and the help that cometh, is not material but of the spirit . . .

'Abdu'l-Bahá, *Selections from the Writings of 'Abdu'l-Bahá*, p. 182

READING

. . . we learn that nearness to God is possible through devotion to Him, through entrance into the Kingdom and service to humanity; it is attained by unity with mankind and through loving-kindness to all; it is dependent upon investigation of truth, acquisition of praiseworthy virtues, service in the cause of universal peace and personal sanctification. In a word, nearness to God necessitates sacrifice of self, severance and the giving up of all to Him. Nearness is likeness.

'Abdu'l-Bahá, *Promulgation of Universal Peace*, p. 148

POINTS TO PONDER

How can we become 'like' God?

What sort of attributes, or virtues, would we have to acquire in order to be 'like' God and grow near to Him?

READING

To 'get to heaven' as you say is dependent on two things –

faith in the Manifestation of God in His Day, in other words in this Age in Bahá'u'lláh; and good deeds, in other words living to the best of our ability a noble life and doing unto others as we would be done by. But we must always remember that our existence and everything we have or ever will have is dependent upon the Mercy of God and His Bounty, and therefore He can accept into His heaven, which is really nearness to Him, even the lowliest if He pleases. We always have the hope of receiving His Mercy if we reach out for it.

Letter written on behalf of Shoghi Effendi, Lights of Guidance, p. 209

MEMORIZE

They say: 'Where is Paradise, and where is Hell?' Say: 'The one is reunion with Me; the other thine own self . . .'

Bahá'u'lláh, Tablets of Bahá'u'lláh, p. 118

POINTS TO PONDER

Where are heaven and hell?

Do you have to die to go to heaven or hell?

When you are very happy, do you feel like you're in heaven? and have you ever spent some miserable time in hell?

If God is love, do you think it would be true to say that hell is lovelessness?

Of hell 'Abdu'l-Bahá says, 'there is no fiercer hell, no more fiery abyss, than to possess a character that is evil and unsound; no more darksome pit nor loathsome torment than to show forth qualities which deserve to be condemned' (Selections from the Writings of 'Abdu'l-Bahá, p. 136).

Does this quotation indicate that your own character and qualities are hell if they aren't trained and developed properly?

What would a character that is evil and unsound be like? Give an example.

What are qualities that deserve to be condemned?

Section X

Coming Attractions: Life after Life

I

The Soul

INTRODUCTION

The soul is our spiritual being. Throughout this User's Guide we have been highlighting ways of developing the soul, bringing it closer to God. We've looked at the powers of the soul and how to enhance them and refine them through prayer and meditation, following the laws of Bahá'u'lláh and learning detachment – undertaking the process of becoming a spiritual being. Did you know that the process of becoming a spiritual being goes on forever? This is why we say the soul is immortal.

immortal living forever

READING

Some think that the body is the substance and exists by itself, and that the spirit is accidental and depends upon the substance of the body, although, on the contrary, the rational soul is the substance, and the body depends upon it. If the accident - that is to say, the body – be destroyed, the substance, the spirit, remains . . .

The rational soul – that is to say, the human spirit – has neither entered this body nor existed through it; so after the disintegration of the composition of the body, how should it be in need of a substance through which it may exist? On the contrary, the rational soul is the substance through which the body exists. The personality of the rational soul is from its beginning; it is not due to the instrumentality of the body, but the state and the personality of the rational soul may be strengthened in this world; it will make progress and will attain to the degrees of perfection, or it will remain in the lowest abyss of ignorance, veiled and deprived from beholding the signs of God.

rational able to reason

'Abdu'l-Bahá, Some Answered Questions, pp. 239-40

POINTS TO PONDER

Why does the soul need a body in this world?

Why does the soul not need a body in the next world?

What do you think the 'personality of the rational soul' is?

How can it be strengthened?

READINGS

The soul originates from the spiritual worlds of God. It is exalted above matter and the physical kingdom. The individual comes into being when the soul, emanating from these spiritual worlds, becomes associated with the embryo before birth. But this association is far above material relationship such as egress or regress, entry or exit, since the soul does not belong to the world of matter. The relationship is like that of light to a mirror. The light which appears in the mirror is not *inside* it. The radiance comes from a source outside. Similarly, the soul is not *within* the body. It has a special relationship to the body and together they form the human being. But this relationship lasts only for the duration of mortal life. When that ceases, each returns to its origin, the body to the world of dust and the soul to the spiritual worlds of God. Having emanated from the spiritual realms to become an individual being created in the image and likeness of God, and capable of acquiring divine qualities and heavenly attributes, the soul will, after its separation from the body, progress for all eternity.

emanating to flow, come out from

egress going out

regress going back

But the condition of the soul after death depends upon the extent to which it has acquired divine virtues in this life. If a child is born without a limb, he will never acquire it after birth and will remain handicapped as long as he lives. Similarly, the soul, if it does not turn to God in this life to become illumined with His guidance, will, though progressing, remain relatively deprived and in darkness.

The soul can take with it only good qualities to the next world. It cannot take bad ones. For bad is only the absence of good, as poverty is the absence of riches. Therefore, an evil person is a soul poor in divine virtues. He carries with him

only a small measure of heavenly qualities. But a man who
has led a virtuous life in this world carries a much greater
measure. Through the bounty of God, however, both these
souls will progress, but each on its own level.

Taherzadeh, The Revelation of Bahá'u'lláh, vol. 1, pp. 72-3

With regard to the soul of man. According to the Bahá'í
Teachings the human soul starts with the formation of the
human embryo, and continues to develop and pass through
stages of existence after its separation from the body. Its
progress is thus infinite.

infinite without end or
limit

Letter written on behalf of Shoghi Effendi, Lights of Guidance, p. 204

POINTS TO PONDER

If the soul is not *in* the body, how can what we do affect the soul?

What are the 'spiritual realms'?

What is the difference between the baby born without a limb
and a person who does not acquire divine virtues? Does it have
something to do with choice?

What are the implications for the development of the soul if its
progress is infinite? Can you imagine this?

2

Preparing for the Next Life

When you plan a vacation or trip, you need to decide what to take with you. Are you going to a sunny beach? You'll need something to swim in, a beach towel and some suntan lotion. Off to the mountains to ski? You'll need a warm coat and some gloves – you can probably leave the beach towel behind. What kind of a vacation would you have if you forgot to pack something you needed – or packed the wrong thing. Imagine turning up on the beach in a thick jacket rather than a swimsuit! Did you bring the jacket because you didn't know where you were going – or did you just not prepare yourself very well? Either way, your vacation is probably ruined.

Travelling to the next life is much like going away on a vacation – only this time it is for good. You can't come back to pick up things you left behind, so it's important to make plans before you leave. And sometimes you have to leave in a hurry! So it's a good idea to prepare well in advance.

> If you have nothing in your life worth dying for, you have nothing in your life worth living for.

READING

Therefore, in this world he must prepare himself for the life beyond. That which he needs in the world of the Kingdom must be obtained here. Just as he prepared himself in the world of the matrix by acquiring forces necessary in this sphere of existence, so, likewise, the indispensable forces of the divine existence must be potentially attained in this world.

What is he in need of in the Kingdom which transcends the life and limitation of this mortal sphere? That world beyond is a world of sanctity and radiance; therefore, it is necessary that in this world he should acquire these divine

matrix womb

sanctity holiness, sacredness

304

attributes. In that world there is need of spirituality, faith, assurance, the knowledge and love of God. These he must attain in this world so that after his ascension from the earthly to the heavenly Kingdom he shall find all that is needful in that eternal life ready for him.

That divine world is manifestly a world of lights; therefore, man has need of illumination here. That is a world of love; the love of God is essential. It is a world of perfections; virtues, or perfections, must be acquired. That world is vivified by the breaths of the Holy Spirit; in this world we must seek them. That is the Kingdom of everlasting life; it must be attained during this vanishing existence.

vivified made to come alive; made lively

By what means can man acquire these things? How shall he obtain these merciful gifts and powers? First, through the knowledge of God. Second, through the love of God. Third, through faith. Fourth, through philanthropic deeds. Fifth, through self-sacrifice. Sixth, through severance from this world. Seventh, through sanctity and holiness . . . Day and night you must strive that you may attain to the significances of the heavenly Kingdom, perceive the signs of Divinity, acquire certainty of knowledge and realize that this world has a Creator, a Vivifier, a Provider, an Architect – knowing this through proofs and evidences and not through susceptibilities, nay, rather, through decisive arguments and real vision – that is to say, visualizing it as clearly as the outer eye beholds the sun. In this way may you behold the presence of God and attain to the knowledge of the holy, divine Manifestations.

philanthropic doing good to others

susceptibility being easily moved by emotions

'Abdu'l-Bahá, *Promulgation of Universal Peace*, pp. 226-7

POINTS TO PONDER

What do we need to do here to prepare for the life to come?

Is not doing this equivalent to not growing arms and legs and developing eyes in the womb?

Do you understand how a lack of understanding of immortality is demeaning to humanity? In your journal, write what you understand about this and how an understanding of immortality affects your life daily.

demeaning debasing in dignity or stature; degrading

Once a friend asked the Master, 'How should one look forward to death?'

He replied, 'How does one look forward to the goal of any journey? With hope and with expectation. It is even so with the end of this earthly journey. In the next world, man will find himself freed from many of the disabilities under which he now suffers. Those who have passed on through death, have a sphere of their own. It is not removed from ours; their work, the work of the Kingdom, is ours . . . but it is sanctified from what we call "time and place". Time with us is measured by the sun. When there is no more sunrise, and no more sunset, that kind of time does not exist for man. Those who have ascended have different attributes from those who are still on earth, yet there is no real separation.

'In prayer there is a mingling of station, a mingling of condition. Pray for them as they pray for you!'

'Abdu'l-Bahá, quoted in Honnold, Vignettes, p. 150

Eternity is not the same as an endless amount of time. It's an experience outside of time, without the pressure and stresses – the pollution of past and future. It's perhaps like being in a creative 'flow', where you step entirely out of time and later realize that many hours have passed while you were unaware of it. Time is simply a measure of something that, once we're no longer dealing with a body, is irrelevant.

3

Saying Goodbye

INTRODUCTION

When someone you know and love dies, you are usually very sad and upset and you miss having the person around.

It's important to remember is that you're grieving over your own perceived separation and loss of companionship, not for the one who has died – he or she is in a far better state than before.

It's important not to get stuck in the process – grief is like a dark tunnel: keep moving through it and someday you'll come back out into the light. It's a journey – as is everything else on earth – and not a destination.

While we're grieving our own loss, we can also rejoice that the person who has died is making progress towards God.

For an exquisite demonstration of authentic grief, read 'Abdu'l-Bahá's eulogy to Thomas Breakwell in *Selections from the Writings of 'Abdu'l-Bahá*, pp. 187-9.

READINGS

These lovely passages are from the *Hidden Words* of Bahá'u'lláh:

O Son of the Supreme!
I have made death a messenger of joy to thee.
Wherefore dost thou grieve?
I made the light to shed on thee its splendour.
Why dost thou veil thyself therefrom?

Arabic no. 32

O Son of Spirit!
With the joyful tidings of light I hail thee:
     rejoice!

To the court of holiness I summon thee;
    abide therein
that thou mayest live in peace for evermore.

Arabic no. 33

VIEWPOINT

Dying is a transition, a change, from one state of being to the next. Our spiritual self leaves the body behind and enters the 'court of holiness'. This is not frightening – it's exhilarating! The bird is released from the cage.

READINGS

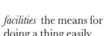

The honour with which the Hand of Mercy will invest the soul is such as no tongue can adequately reveal, nor any other earthly agency describe. Blessed is the soul which, at the hour of its separation from the body, is sanctified from the vain imaginings of the peoples of the world. Such a soul liveth and moveth in accordance with the Will of its Creator, and entereth the all-highest Paradise. The Maids of Heaven, inmates of the loftiest mansions, will circle around it, and the Prophets of God and His chosen ones will seek its companionship. With them that soul will freely converse, and will recount unto them that which it hath been made to endure in the path of God, the Lord of all worlds. If any man be told that which hath been ordained for such a soul in the worlds of God, the Lord of the throne on high and of earth below, his whole being will instantly blaze out in his great longing to attain that most exalted, that sanctified and resplendent station . . . The nature of the soul after death can never be described, nor is it meet and permissible to reveal its whole character to the eyes of men.

Bahá'u'lláh, Gleanings, p. 156

In His Tablets Bahá'u'lláh says that were we able to comprehend the facilities that await us in the world to come, death would lose its sting; nay rather we would welcome it as a gate-way to a realm immeasurably higher and nobler than this home of suffering we call our earth. You should therefore think of their blessings and comfort yourself for your momentary separation. In time all of us will join our

facilities the means for doing a thing easily

departed ones and share their joys.

Letter written on behalf of Shoghi Effendi, *Lights of Guidance*, p. 207

Bahá'u'lláh says that were we to have the proper vision to see the blessings of the other world we would not bear to endure one more hour of existence upon the earth. The reason why we are deprived of that vision is because otherwise no one would care to remain and the whole fabric of society will be destroyed.

Shoghi Effendi, *Lights of Guidance*, p. 207

Such earnest souls, when they pass out of this life, enter a state of being far nobler and more beautiful than this one. We fear it only because it is unknown to us and we have little faith in the words of the Prophets who bring a true message of certainty from that realm of the spirit. We should face death with joy especially if our life upon this plane of existence has been full of good deeds.

Letter written on behalf of Shoghi Effendi, *Lights of Guidance*, p. 208

POINTS TO PONDER

Are you afraid to die? If so, is this because the next life is unknown? or because your life is not yet 'full of good deeds'?

What can you do to lose your fear of dying?

EXERCISE

Write in your journal a convincing explanation of why you look forward to the next life.

4

What Happens Next?

You ask an explanation of what happens to us after we leave
this world: This is a question which none of the Prophets
have ever answered in detail, for the very simple reason that
you cannot convey to a person's mind something entirely
different from everything they have ever experienced.
'Abdu'l-Bahá gave the wonderful example of the relation of
this life to the next life being like the child in the womb; it
develops eyes, ears, hands, feet, a tongue, and yet it has
nothing to see or hear, it cannot walk or grasp things or
speak; all these faculties it is developing for this world. If you
tried to explain to an embryo what this world is like it could
never understand – but it understands when it is born, and
its faculties can be used. So we cannot picture our state in the
next world. All we know is that our consciousness, our
personality, endures in some new state, and that that world is
as much better than this one as this one is better than the
dark womb of our mother was . . .

See *Some Answered Questions*
and the Kitáb-i-Aqdas for
much more on this
subject, as well as for
Bahá'í burial laws. There
are also several excellent
compilations available.

Letter written on behalf of Shoghi Effendi, *Lights of Guidance*, pp. 208-9

POINTS TO PONDER

Why have the Prophets not given us much detail about the next life?

Can you think of some of the things we *do* know about it?

This present life is even as a swelling wave, or a mirage, or drifting shadows. Could ever a distorted image on the desert serve as refreshing waters? No, by the Lord of Lords! Never can reality and the mere semblance of reality be one, and wide is the difference between fancy and fact, between truth and the phantom thereof.

Know thou that the Kingdom is the real world, and this nether place is only its shadow stretching out. A shadow hath no life of its own; its existence is only a fantasy, and nothing more; it is but images reflected in water, and seeming as pictures to the eye.

phantom a ghost; a form without substance or reality

nether lower

'Abdu'l-Bahá, *Selections from the Writings of 'Abdu'l-Bahá*, pp. 177-8

POINTS TO PONDER

If this world is not the real world, why are we born into it?

What does this tell us about our true selves – who we really are?

5

Process and Progress in the Next Life

All through our life our spiritual selves are in the process of development. Nothing stands still. So too in the next life, which is really an extension of this one. There, our spiritual selves will continue to grow nearer and nearer to God. As we do so, we make progress. So it's still all about love and it's still all process. But no matter how far we progress in the next life, we can only ever be *human* spiritual beings.

READING

Know that nothing which exists remains in a state of repose – that is to say, all things are in motion. Everything is either growing or declining; all things are either coming from nonexistence into being, or going from existence into nonexistence. So this flower, this hyacinth, during a certain period of time was coming from the world of nonexistence into being, and now it is going from being into nonexistence. This state of motion is said to be essential – that is, natural; it cannot be separated from beings because it is their essential requirement, as it is the essential requirement of fire to burn.

Thus it is established that this movement is necessary to existence, which is either growing or declining. Now, as the spirit continues to exist after death, it necessarily progresses or declines; and in the other world to cease to progress is the same as to decline; but it never leaves its own condition, in which it continues to develop. For example, the reality of the spirit of Peter, however far it may progress, will not reach to the condition of the Reality of Christ; it progresses only in its own environment.

Look at this mineral. However far it may evolve, it only evolves in its own condition; you cannot bring the crystal to a state where it can attain to sight. This is impossible. So the moon which is in the heavens, however far it might evolve, could never become a luminous sun, but in its own condition it has apogee and perigee. However far the disciples might progress, they could never become Christ. It is true that coal could become a diamond, but both are in the mineral condition, and their component elements are the same.

'Abdu'l-Bahá, *Some Answered Questions*, pp. 233-4

apogee point in the orbit of the moon where it is furthest from the earth

perigee point in the orbit of the moon where it is nearest the earth

POINTS TO PONDER

What is the station of Bahá'u'lláh?

Will it be possible for us to reach the station of Bahá'u'lláh in the next world? Explain your answer.

READING

The progress of man's spirit in the divine world, after the severance of its connection with the body of dust, is through the bounty and grace of the Lord alone, or through the intercession and the sincere prayers of other human souls, or through the charities and important good works which are performed in its name.

'Abdu'l-Bahá, *Some Answered Questions*, p. 240

intercession the intervention of someone on behalf of another; one person asking God to help someone else

POINTS TO PONDER

What are the bounty and grace of God?

If our progress in the next life depends in part on the prayers of other people and their good works done in our name, what does this tell us about our relationships with others? with family? with friends?

MEMORIZE

The wealth of the other world is nearness to God.

'Abdu'l-Bahá, *Some Answered Questions*, p. 231

6

See You?

As to the question whether the souls will recognize each other in the spiritual world: This fact is certain; for the Kingdom is the world of vision where all the concealed realities will become disclosed. How much more the well-known souls will become manifest. The mysteries of which man is heedless in this earthly world, those he will discover in the heavenly world, and there will he be informed of the secret of truth; how much more will he recognize or discover persons with whom he hath been associated. Undoubtedly, the holy souls who find a pure eye and are favoured with insight will, in the kingdom of lights, be acquainted with all mysteries, and will seek the bounty of witnessing the reality of every great soul. Even they will manifestly behold the Beauty of God in that world. Likewise will they find all the friends of God, both those of the former and recent times, present in the heavenly assemblage.

'Abdu'l-Bahá, *Bahá'í World Faith*, p. 367

The possibility of securing union with his beloved in the next world is one which the Bahá'í Teachings are quite clear about. According to Bahá'u'lláh the soul retains its individuality and consciousness after death, and is able to commune with other souls. This communion, however, is purely spiritual in character, and is conditioned upon the disinterested and selfless love of the individuals for each other.

Letter written on behalf of Shoghi Effendi, *Lights of Guidance*, p. 207

An American friend who had enjoyed the privilege of more than one visit to 'Akká during the days of the exile of 'Abdu'l-Bahá, related an incident that took place at His table. With her sat persons of varied races, some of them traditional enemies who had now grown so to love one another that life and fortune would not have been too much to give, if called upon to do so. As the reality of their love gradually became plain to her, there was born a ray of the knowledge of the intimacy of the near ones in the world beyond. When the meal drew to a close, 'Abdu'l-Bahá spoke of the immortal worlds. As nearly as she could remember, the words He spoke were these: 'We have sat together many times before, and we shall sit together many times again in the Kingdom. We shall laugh together very much in those times, and we shall tell of the things that befell us in the Path of God. In every world of God a new Lord's Supper is set for the faithful!'

Honnold, *Vignettes*, p. 173

Ghosts and evil spirits? No such thing! 'There are no earthbound souls. When the souls that are not good die, they go entirely away from this earth and so cannot influence anyone. They are spiritually dead. Their thoughts can have influence only when they are alive on the earth … But the good souls are given eternal life and sometimes God permits their thoughts to reach the earth to help the people.

'Abdu'l-Bahá, quoted in Goodall and Cooper, *Daily Lessons Received at 'Akká*, pp. 35–6.

READINGS

O thou soul who art well assured,
Return to thy Lord,
well-pleased, and pleasing unto Him.
. . .
Enter thou among My servants,
And enter thou My paradise.

Qur'án 89:27–30

I came forth from God, and return unto
Him, detached from all save Him, holding fast to His
Name, the Merciful, the Compassionate.

Bahá'u'lláh, Kitáb-i-Aqdas, para. 129

Bibliography

'Abdu'l-Bahá. *Foundations of World Unity*. Wilmette, Ill.: Bahá'í Publishing Trust, 1945.
—— *Memorials of the Faithful*. Wilmette, Ill.: Bahá'í Publishing Trust, 1971.
—— *Paris Talks*. London: Bahá'í Publishing Trust, 1995.
—— *The Promulgation of Universal Peace*. Wilmette, Ill.: Bahá'í Publishing Trust, 1982.
—— *The Secret of Divine Civilization*. Wilmette, Ill.: Bahá'í Publishing Trust, 1990.
—— *Selections from the Writings of 'Abdu'l-Bahá*. Haifa; Bahá'í World Centre, 1978.
—— *Some Answered Questions*. Wilmette, Ill.: Bahá'í Publishing Trust, 1981.
—— *Tablets of the Divine Plan*. Wilmette, Ill.: Bahá'í Publishing Trust, 1980.

Báb, The. *Selections from the Writings of the Báb*. Haifa: Bahá'í World Centre, 1976.

Bahá'í World Faith. Wilmette, Ill.: Bahá'í Publishing Trust, 2nd edn. 1976.

Bahá'u'lláh. *Epistle to the Son of the Wolf*. Wilmette, Ill.: Bahá'í Publishing Trust, 1971.
—— *Gleanings from the Writings of Bahá'u'lláh*. Wilmette, Ill.: Bahá'í Publishing Trust, 1983.
—— *The Hidden Words*. Wilmette, Ill.: Bahá'í Publishing Trust, 1990.
—— *The Kitáb-i-Aqdas*, Haifa: Bahá'í World Centre, 1992.
—— *Kitáb-i-Íqán*. Wilmette, Ill.: Bahá'í Publishing Trust, 1989.
—— *The Seven Valleys and the Four Valleys*. Wilmette, Ill.: Bahá'í Publishing Trust, 1991.
—— *Tablets of Bahá'u'lláh revealed after the Kitáb-i-Adqas*. Haifa: Bahá'í World Centre, 1978.

Balyuzi, H. M. *'Abdu'l-Bahá*. Oxford: George Ronald, 1971.

Blomfield, Lady. *The Chosen Highway*. Wilmette, Ill.: Bahá'í Publishing Trust, 1975.

Brown, Ramona Allen. *Memories of 'Abdu'l-Bahá*. Wilmette, Ill.: Bahá'í Publishing Trust, 1980.

Compilation of Compilations, The. Prepared by the Universal House of Justice 1963-1990. 2 vols. [Sydney]: Bahá'í Publications Australia, 1991.

Contentment. London: Bahá'í Publishing Trust, 1995.

Diary of Juliet Thompson, The. Los Angeles: Kalimát Press, 1983.

Divine Art of Living, The: Selections from the Writings of Bahá'u'lláh and 'Abdu'l-Bahá. Compiled by Mabel Hyde Paine, revised by Anne Marie Scheffer. Wilmette, Ill.: Bahá'í Publishing Trust, 1986.

Esslemont, J. E. *Bahá'u'lláh and the New Era*. London: Bahá'í Publishing Trust, 1974.

Gail, Marzieh. *Summon Up Remembrance*. Oxford: George Ronald, 1987.

Goodall, Helen S. and Cooper, Ella Goodall. *Daily Lessons Received at 'Akká*. Wilmette, Ill.: Bahá'í Publishing Trust, 1979.

Grundy, Julia M. *Ten Days in the Light of 'Akká*. Wilmette, Ill.: Bahá'í Publishing Trust, 1979.

Ḥaydar-'Alí, Ḥájí Mírzá. *Delight of Hearts*. Los Angeles: Kalimát Press, 1980.

Honnold, Annamarie. *Vignettes from the Life of 'Abdu'l-Bahá*. Oxford: George Ronald, rev. edn. 1991.

Hornby, Helen, comp. *Lights of Guidance*. New Delhi: Bahá'í Publishing Trust, 1988.

Ives, Howard Colby. *Portals to Freedom*. London: George Ronald, 1967.

Living the Life. London: Bahá'í Publishing Trust, 1984.

Mathews, Loulie Albee. *Not Every Sea Hath Pearls*. Milford, N. H.: The Cabinet Press, 1951.

Moffett, Ruth. *Do'a on Wings of Prayer*. Des Moines, Iowa: Wallace Homestead Co., rev. edn. 1974.
—— *Du'á: On Wings of Prayer*. Happy Camp, Calif.: Naturegraph Publishers, rev. edn. 1984.

Principles of Bahá'í Administration. London: Bahá'í Publishing Trust, 1963.

The Reality of Man. Wilmette, Ill.: Bahá'í Publishing Trust.

Rutstein, Nathan. *Corinne True: Faithful Handmaid of 'Abdu'l-Bahá*. Oxford: George Ronald, 1987.
—— *He Loved and Served*. Oxford: George Ronald, 1982.

Shoghi Effendi. *The Advent of Divine Justice*. Wilmette, Ill.: Bahá'í Publishing Trust, 1990.
—— *Bahá'í Administration*. Wilmette, Ill.: Bahá'í Publishing Trust, 1968.
—— *Directives from the Guardian*. New Delhi: Bahá'í Publishing Trust, 1973.
—— *High Endeavours: Messages to Alaska*. [Anchorage]: National Spiritual Assembly of the Bahá'ís of Alaska, 1976.
—— *Messages to America*. Wilmette, Ill.: Bahá'í Publishing Trust, 1947.
—— *The Unfolding Destiny of the British Bahá'í Community*. London: Bahá'í Publishing Trust, 1981.
—— *The World Order of Bahá'u'lláh*. Wilmette, Ill.: Bahá'í Publishing Trust, 1991.

Star of the West. Rpt. Oxford: George Ronald, 1984.

Taherzadeh, Adib. *The Revelation of Bahá'u'lláh*, vol. 1. Oxford: George Ronald, 1974.
—— *The Revelation of Bahá'u'lláh*, vol. 2. Oxford: George Ronald, 1977.
—— *The Revelation of Bahá'u'lláh*, vol. 4. Oxford: George Ronald, 1987.

Ward, Allan L. *239 Days*. Wilmette, Ill.: Bahá'í Publishing Trust, 1979.